SO YOU WANT TO SING CCM (CONTEMPORARY COMMERCIAL MUSIC)

So You Want to Sing

Guides for Performers and Professionals

A Project of the National Association of

Teachers of Singing

So You Want to Sing: Guides for Performers and Professionals is a series of works devoted to providing a complete survey of what it means to sing within a particular genre. Each contribution functions as a touchstone work not only for professional singers but also for students and teachers of singing. Titles in the series offer a common set of topics so readers can navigate easily the various genres addressed in each volume. This series is produced under the direction of the National Association of Teachers of Singing, the leading professional organization devoted to the science and art of singing.

So You Want to Sing Music Theater: A Guide for Professionals, by Karen S. Hall, 2013

So You Want to Sing Rock 'n' Roll: A Guide for Professionals, by Matthew Edwards, 2014

So You Want to Sing Jazz: A Guide for Professionals, by Jan Shapiro, 2015

So You Want to Sing Country: A Guide for Performers, by Kelly K. Garner, 2016

So You Want to Sing Gospel: A Guide for Performers, by Trineice Robinson-Martin, 2016

So You Want to Sing Sacred Music: A Guide for Performers, edited by Matthew Hoch, 2017

So You Want to Sing Folk Music: A Guide for Performers, by Valerie Mindel, 2017

So You Want to Sing Barbershop: A Guide for Performers, by Diane M. Clark & Billy J. Biffle, 2017

So You Want to Sing A Cappella: A Guide for Performers, by Deke Sharon, 2017

So You Want to Sing Light Opera: A Guide for Performers, by Linda Lister, 2018

So You Want to Sing CCM (Contemporary Commercial Music): A Guide for Performers, edited by Matthew Hoch, 2018

SO YOU WANT TO SING CCM (CONTEMPORARY COMMERCIAL MUSIC)

A Guide for Performers

Edited by Matthew Hoch

Allen Henderson
Executive Editor, NATS

Matthew Hoch
Series Editor

A Project of the National Association of
Teachers of Singing

ROWMAN & LITTLEFIELD
Lanham • Boulder • New York • London

Published by Rowman & Littlefield
An imprint of The Rowman & Littlefield Publishing Group, Inc.
4501 Forbes Boulevard, Suite 200, Lanham, Maryland 20706
www.rowman.com

Unit A, Whitacre Mews, 26-34 Stannary Street, London SE11 4AB

Copyright © 2018 by The Rowman & Littlefield Publishing Group, Inc.

All rights reserved. No part of this book may be reproduced in any form or by any electronic or mechanical means, including information storage and retrieval systems, without written permission from the publisher, except by a reviewer who may quote passages in a review.

British Library Cataloguing in Publication Information Available

Library of Congress Cataloging-in-Publication Data

Names: Hoch, Matthew, 1975–
Title: So you want to sing CCM (contemporary commercial music) : a guide for performers / edited by Matthew Hoch.
Description: Lanham : Rowman & Littlefield, 2018. | Series: So you want to sing | "A Project of the National Association of Teachers of Singing." | Includes bibliographical references and index.
Identifiers: LCCN 2017049657 (print) | LCCN 2017050443 (ebook) | ISBN 9781538103623 (electronic) | ISBN 9781538113660 (cloth : alk. paper) | ISBN 9781538103616 (pbk. : alk. paper)
Subjects: LCSH: Singing—Instruction and study.
Classification: LCC MT820 (ebook) | LCC MT820 .S698 2018 (print) | DDC 783/.043—dc23
LC record available at https://lccn.loc.gov/2017049657

∞™ The paper used in this publication meets the minimum requirements of American National Standard for Information Sciences—Permanence of Paper for Printed Library Materials, ANSI/NISO Z39.48-1992.

Printed in the United States of America

CONTENTS

Foreword   vii
    Allen Henderson

Acknowledgments   ix

Introduction   xi
    Matthew Hoch

Online Supplement Note   xv

PART I   CONTEMPORARY COMMERCIAL MUSIC: AN INTRODUCTION

1   CCM Pedagogy: The Pioneering Generation   3
    Matthew Hoch

2   CCM versus Music Theater: A Comparison   15
    Matthew Edwards

3   Singing and Voice Science   33
    Scott McCoy

4   Vocal Health for the Contemporary Commercial Music (CCM) Singer   51
    Wendy LeBorgne

5	Using Audio Enhancement Technology *Matthew Edwards*	72

PART II PROFILES OF TWELVE CCM PEDAGOGUES

6	Katie Agresta, New York, New York	97
7	Irene Bartlett, Brisbane, Australia	110
8	Robert Edwin, Cinnaminson, New Jersey	124
9	Elisabeth Howard, Chicago, Illinois	134
10	Joan Lader, New York, New York	150
11	Jeannette LoVetri, New York, New York	159
12	Mark Meylan, London, United Kingdom	173
13	Lisa Popeil, Los Angeles, California	185
14	David Sabella, New York, New York	196
15	Cathrine Sadolin, Copenhagen, Denmark	211
16	Mary Saunders Barton, State College, Pennsylvania	222
17	Daniel Zangger Borch, Stockholm, Sweden	241

PART III CONTEMPORARY COMMERCIAL MUSIC: PAST, PRESENT, AND FUTURE

18	Effortless Singing: SLS™ and Its Influence *Darren Wicks*	251
19	Why It's Time to Add CCM to Your Studio *Matthew Edwards*	264
20	The Future of CCM Pedagogy *Matthew Hoch*	287

Glossary	291
Index	297
About the Editor and Contributors	317

FOREWORD

In *So You Want to Sing Contemporary Commercial Music*, the latest volume in the So You Want to Sing series, we bring together the diverse voices and perspectives of leaders in the field of contemporary commercial music (CCM) pedagogy from around the world and, for the first time, collect profiles on twelve leading pedagogues in the field to provide readers a unique insight into the development of specific pedagogies. Historically, the pedagogy of many of these styles was in most ways aural until recent times when researchers and voice teachers began to better understand the unique ways in which the complex instrument—the voice—functions when singing a variety of styles of music authentically. Some of the leaders profiled in this book were pioneers in the research and development of today's functional pedagogies that assist teachers and singers in developing flexible and adaptable singing voices. As music theater has been more recently influenced by pop/rock and other genres of contemporary music, the ability of singers and teachers to access a more codified set of techniques and better understand the complex interactions necessary to produce an authentic sound has never been more important.

Matthew Hoch and others who have contributed to this volume have provided an excellent resource for singers and teachers who wish to understand various CCM genres and how our knowledge about how they are authentically performed has evolved. This book is full of technical and practical wisdom from some of the world's leading CCM pedagogues.

This volume and others in the So You Want to Sing series offer the perspective that there are healthy and functional ways to explore and develop the many and varied sounds the voice can produce. Our hope is that—whether you sing these styles or teach them—you will always seek to be informed about the how the voice functions to sing in any style and to enjoy exploring your unique voice.

Allen Henderson
Executive Editor, So You Want to Sing Series
Executive Director, National Association of Teachers of Singing

ACKNOWLEDGMENTS

The editor would like to thank Natalie Mandziuk at Rowman & Littlefield, as well as Allen Henderson and the National Association of Teachers of Singing (NATS) for their support of this project. Thanks also to Matthew Edwards and Darren Wicks for their compelling supporting chapters to this volume. Their expertise very much completed this book. Most important, I am grateful to the twelve pedagogues who selflessly contributed their lifetime of wisdom to this publication. It was a great privilege and honor to interact with all of them over the course of the past eighteen months, and I am grateful to have had the opportunity to assist in some small way in preserving their legacies for future generations of singers and teachers.

NOTE ON TRADEMARKED METHODOLOGIES

Many of the methodologies discussed in this book, such as Somatic Voicework™, Speech Level Singing™, Voiceworks™, Vocal Power Method™, Complete Vocal Technique™, and the Estill Voice Model™ are trademarked entities, with terminology associated with each method trademarked as well. Rowman & Littlefield acknowledges and affirms these trademarks, but for a cleaner look and smoother reading experience—and to avoid excessive repetitions of the trademark symbol (™)—the symbol only will be used the first time the method appears in each chapter. The trademark symbol is also avoided in the book's glossary. The reader is trusted to understand which trademarked terms are appropriate for studio and professional use and which ones require certification by the governing body of each respective methodology. It should be emphasized that NATS does not endorse any particular method and respects the pedagogical and academic freedom of all pedagogues profiled in this publication.

INTRODUCTION

Matthew Hoch

Contemporary commercial music—or CCM, as many singing teachers and virtually all NATS members call it—has been a core theme running throughout the So You Want to Sing series since its conception. Most of the books conceived for the series focus on various nonclassical genres, all of which fall under the collective CCM umbrella: music theater, rock 'n' roll, jazz, gospel, country, folk, contemporary Christian music, and a cappella have all been profiled in previously published books, and other CCM genres, such as blues, cabaret, and many types of world music, will be featured in forthcoming books in the series. CCM, a more favorable alternative to the pejorative term "nonclassical," is the common label that binds these styles together, but what do these genres have in common, if anything? Also, how do singers and teachers of singing approach these genres, especially if they come from a traditional "classical" background that focused almost exclusively on opera and art song? Because music degree programs in the United States are still overwhelmingly classically oriented, this is a challenge that many twenty-first-century singing teachers confront.

In the summer of 2015, I was having a conversation with my mentor, colleague, and friend Jeannette LoVetri that wound up becoming the inspiration for this book. She remarked that no one had yet written a book comparing various CCM methodologies side by side. As the newly appointed editor of the So You Want to Sing series, I took this idea to Allen Henderson, executive director of NATS, and *So You Want to Sing CCM* was born. Our concept was to present an edited volume of pedagogical and technical advice from some of the greatest and most established luminaries in the field. The book that you are holding in your hands is the final result of this project, the culmination of more than two years of interaction with twelve of the most experienced voices in CCM pedagogy. It is also the first book of its kind to profile a variety of trademarked CCM methodologies, with discussions of Somatic Voicework™, Speech Level Singing™, Voiceworks™, Vocal Power Method™, Complete Vocal Technique™, and the Estill Voice Model™ published under a single cover for the first time.

The individuals featured in this book were chosen for many reasons, but most important, they represent a generation of pioneers: in the 1970s, 1980s, and 1990s, they founded a pedagogy where none existed. The National Association of Teachers of Singing, as Robert Edwin remarked in a seminal 1985 article, might as well have been called the "National Association of Teachers of *Classical* Singing."[1] Although the music theater and commercial music industries were thriving, very few singing teachers were out there teaching singers how to approach these styles in a healthy way.

There were, however, some names that began to emerge during this period, and these individuals began forming the pedagogical foundation that now allows for CCM pedagogy to stand proudly alongside classical pedagogy at national conferences and within professional organizations. Three of these individuals, Jeannette LoVetri, Robert Edwin, and Elisabeth Howard, have had long associations with NATS, and we are honored to feature them prominently in this volume. For many years, Edwin's "Bach to Rock" column in the *NATS Bulletin* and later the *Journal of Singing* formed an academic basis for CCM pedagogy as we know it today, and LoVetri and Howard both went on to found trademarked methods based on their pedagogical philosophy: Somatic Voicework and the Vocal Power Method.

Two other names from this era must also be mentioned. During the 1970s and 1980s, the pioneering work of Jo Estill cannot be understated. The Estill Voice Model, which forms the basis for the Estill Voice Train-

INTRODUCTION xiii

ing method, has made significant inroads not only in the United States but in England and Australia as well. Although Estill passed away in 2010, her legacy is represented here through Joan Lader, one of Jo's most famous students and a renowned CCM pedagogue in her own right. Another luminary from this era is Seth Riggs, the founder of Speech Level Singing. Riggs's legacy and influence is profiled in chapter 18, "Effortless Singing: SLS and Its Influence," in a superb tribute written by the Australian pedagogue Darren Wicks, a student and former colleague of Riggs.

Four other prominent American pedagogues are featured as well. Katie Agresta has sustained a reputation as one of New York's most prominent CCM pedagogues for more than four decades. In addition to her many Broadway clients, the rock and pop industry may know her best as the longtime teacher of Cyndi Lauper and Jon Bon Jovi, among others. Mary Saunders Barton also needs little introduction as one of the world's most famous teachers of music theater. The MFA in musical theatre pedagogy at Penn State University—a one-of-a-kind degree that she founded—speaks to her deep insight into the systematic pedagogy of CCM singing. David Sabella brings the wisdom of two careers—one in opera and one on Broadway—as a professional countertenor to his studio in New York City. As a two-term president of the New York Singing Teachers Association (NYSTA), he was also instrumental in the online delivery of NYSTA's professional development program, for which he taught the CCM pedagogy class on numerous occasions. Lisa Popeil represents the West Coast. She runs a thriving private studio in Los Angeles, is the founder of Voiceworks, and has written several books on CCM pedagogy.

The final four pedagogues chosen for this book hail from other parts of the world, each being a pioneer of CCM pedagogy in his or her respective country. Mark Meylan is widely regarded as the most prominent music theater pedagogue in London, actively working with many performers in the West End and CCM industry. Irene Bartlett, a jazz singer by trade who went on to forge an academic career at the Queensland Conservatorium at Griffith University, has done much to legitimize CCM pedagogy throughout Australia. Cathrine Sadolin, based in Copenhagen, is founder of Complete Vocal Institute, the largest singing institute for professional and semiprofessional singers and teachers in Europe. Finally, Daniel Zangger Borch represents Sweden. A professional rock singer and PhD student of Dr. Johan Sundberg, Zangger Borch is an important voice in CCM pedagogy, synthesizing science and practice in an insightful, unique, and engaging way.

My personal CCM journey began in 2007. As a recipient of that year's NATS Voice Pedagogy Award, I enrolled in Jeannette LoVetri's three levels of Somatic Voicework at Shenandoah University. My experience during those hot ten days in July opened my eyes to a whole new world and changed my teaching forever. As a classically trained pedagogue with a sincere interest in CCM pedagogy, working on this project was deeply fulfilling, and interacting with these twelve amazing individuals was one of the great privileges of my career. There were many moments when I was speaking with one of them, or editing something that they wrote, when I gasped aloud at a profound comment or felt deeply connected to a certain watershed or pivotal moment in the history of CCM pedagogy, grasping its significance for the first time. I keenly realized, on many occasions, that these individuals are living pioneers, primary sources whose stories cannot be forgotten.

In order to understand the present, and in order to chart a course for the future, we must first thoroughly understand our past. The legacies of these twelve CCM pioneers, their *stories*, *struggles*, and—most important—their *wisdom* should be digested, internalized, and never forgotten. Their chapters in this book are nothing less than essential core readings for the twenty-first-century voice pedagogue and CCM singer.

NOTE

1. Robert Edwin, "Are We the National Association of Teachers of Classical Singing?" *Journal of Singing* 41, no. 5 (1985): 40.

ONLINE SUPPLEMENT NOTE

So You Want to Sing CCM (Contemporary Commercial Music) features an online supplement courtesy of the National Association of Teachers of Singing. Visit the link below to discover additional exercises and examples, as well as links to recordings of the songs referenced in this book.

www.nats.org/So_You_Want_To_Sing_Book_Series.html

A musical note symbol (♪) in this book will mark every instance of corresponding online supplement material.

1

CONTEMPORARY COMMERCIAL MUSIC

An Introduction

1

CCM PEDAGOGY

The Pioneering Generation
Matthew Hoch

"In the beginning, everything was classical." This shameless biblical parody might well summarize the sentiments of virtually all the pedagogues who contributed to this volume when they describe the environment in which they lived and worked several decades ago. In the 1960s, 1970s, and even—to an extent—the 1980s, everything in the voice pedagogy world literally *was* classical. Belting, or singing any sort of amplified genre, was considered to be "less legitimate" than classical singing. Myths prevailed: "You'll ruin your voice if you perform *that* music," "Classical training is all you need to sing in any style," and (to women) "You'll develop nodules if you sing in your chest voice." The fact that so many professional singers and recording artists were already singing CCM styles in a healthy way and having long careers doing it seemed to do little to convince the pedagogical establishment of the legitimacy of the music and the need for qualified singing teachers in the field of CCM pedagogy.

Many of the teachers profiled in this book began their careers in this environment, founding a new pedagogy in a vacuum and attempting to convince the classical establishment—sometimes in vain—that it was indeed possible to sing these styles in a healthy way. Part of this attitude seems to have stemmed from a lack of respect for the music itself.

Throughout much of the twentieth century, any musical style that fell outside of the classical European canon was considered to be inferior. Jeannette LoVetri remarks that "our music—roots music—was never seen as being worthy of scholarly research or scientific study."[1] It was this same environment that inspired Robert Edwin to ask the question, "Are we the National Association of Teachers of Classical Singing?"[2]

Fortunately, thanks to pioneering voice pedagogues like LoVetri, Edwin, and others, a foundational CCM pedagogy did emerge during the latter part of the twentieth century, and it continues to evolve to this day. This opening chapter will introduce the reader to some of the most important and pivotal issues these pedagogues faced as they sought to establish a systematic pedagogy where none existed within a pedagogical community that was somewhat hostile to (what were at that time) radical ideas.

SEMINAL EVENTS

Perhaps it is not surprising that some of the earliest events in the history of CCM pedagogy occurred in and around New York City, which had long been established as the music theater capital of the world, as well as the home to a plethora of other CCM styles. Seminal figures in the New York voice teaching community during the 1970s and 1980s included several figures profiled in this book: Jeannette LoVetri, Katie Agresta, Elisabeth Howard, Mary Saunders Barton, and Robert Edwin, whose mother, Helena W. Monbo, was also a prominent teacher of "nonclassical" styles during this time. The first teacher to establish a method during this time was Jo Estill, whose work is represented in this book by Joan Lader, one of her most prominent disciples.

In 1983, the New York Singing Teachers Association (NYSTA) hosted an event entitled the "Music Theater and Popular Music Symposium," which featured several presenters, including Oren Brown and Jo Estill. The symposium proved to be controversial to the establishment because the concept of "legitimizing" these nonclassical styles was alarming to many of the classical voice teachers who served on NYSTA's board of directors. According to LoVetri, immediately after the symposium "the

NYSTA board of directors met, and half of them resigned in protest because people were 'dragging the organization down' by promoting 'that' music, which was really just noise."[3] While there was obviously still much work to do, the first steps toward establishing CCM pedagogy as a bona fide discipline had been made. ♪

Seventeen years would pass before the National Association of Teachers of Singing (NATS) would follow in NYSTA's footsteps. In 2000, NATS sponsored its first-ever "belting workshop" at the University of Miami. Norman Spivey and David Ward were the organizers, and presenters included Liz Caplan and Neil Semer, who were both teachers who lived and worked in New York. The success of this workshop led to a second one a year later, in 2001. This time, it was held in New York City. Neil Semer returned, along with Jo Estill, Jeannette LoVetri, and Mary Saunders Barton. By this time, the seeds of a new pedagogy were planted. With NATS finally supportive of exploring "nonclassical" styles, the road was paved for more progress to be made. ♪

It cannot be overstated that Robert Edwin was an extremely important figure—perhaps the most pivotal one—in convincing NATS to support other styles beyond classical singing. This was primarily due to his regular "Bach to Rock" column, which appeared in the *NATS Bulletin* and the *Journal of Singing* from 1985 through 2002. Edwin writes:

> In the early 1980s, Richard Miller was editor-in-chief of the *NATS Bulletin*, and he asked me to develop the first regular column dedicated to "nonclassical" voice pedagogy and repertoire. The "Bach to Rock Connection" debuted in the last issue of the *NATS Bulletin* in June of 1985 and continued to appear regularly for seventeen years in the *NATS Journal* from 1985 to 1995 and then in the *Journal of Singing* from 1995 to 2002. In 2002, I became an associate editor of the *Journal of Singing* and the column was retitled "Popular Song and Music Theater." That column continues to this day and—thanks to my colleague and friend Jeannette LoVetri—we now have a legitimate name for our work: contemporary commercial music (CCM) voice pedagogy rather than the vague and somewhat demeaning "nonclassical."[4]

As Edwin mentions, Jeannette LoVetri's coining of the term "contemporary commercial music" represents another pivotal moment in the history of CCM pedagogy. According to LoVetri, she first began using this term around the year 2000.[5] The term first appeared in print in a 2003 research paper by Jeannette LoVetri and Edrie Means Weekly.[6] In the early 2000s, several NATS chapters began offering annual music theater auditions alongside their classical ones, and eventually the national organization followed suit, encouraging these auditions. It is now unusual to find a NATS chapter that doesn't offer a music theater category at their student auditions. In 2014, with the inauguration of the National Student Auditions, national guidelines were established for both classical and music theater singers.

A PROLIFERATION OF METHODOLOGIES

Also essential to the establishment of CCM pedagogy during these early years was the proliferation of a variety of specific methodologies, all of which were founded by a single pedagogue and (later) trademarked. A list of the most famous methodologies—all of which are discussed in this volume—follows.

Estill

The first of these methods was developed by Josephine "Jo" Estill (1921–2010) in 1988. The Estill Voice Model™ (EVM) is a pedagogical method that includes thirteen "figures" that are combined into six voice "qualities." Estill also established a certification program for teachers built around the EVM known as Estill Voice Training™ (EVT). EVT is based on four operating principles: (a) knowledge is power—understanding how the voice works is a good thing; (b) voice production begins before the voice is heard—muscle effort makes it happen; (c) the breath must be allowed to respond to what it meets on the way out; and (d) voice training is optimized when separated in three disciplines: craft, artistry, and performance magic. A certification program continues to exist for teachers wishing to be trained in the Estill method. For more information on Jo Estill and her method, please see chapter 10, written by Joan Lader. ♪

Speech Level Singing

Speech Level Singing™ (SLS) is a vocal technique created by Seth Riggs (b. 1930) that dovetails traditional *bel canto* concepts with contemporary industry terms and CCM styles. While many early CCM pedagogues were based in New York, Riggs spent the majority of his career in Los Angeles, where he had significant impact on the commercial music industry. Speech Level Singing (SLS) is a trademarked term, and only certified teachers are licensed to use it or claim that they are SLS teachers. For a thorough discussion of Riggs and the SLS method, please refer to chapter 18, "Effortless Singing: SLS™ and Its Influence," by Darren Wicks, a longtime associate of Riggs. ♪

Somatic Voicework

Somatic Voicework™ (SVW) was created by the American pedagogue Jeannette LoVetri (b. 1949). Also known as the "LoVetri Method," SVW is a body-based method of training based on voice science, classical voice training, speech training, acting, movement, and various bodywork methods. The three levels of SVW certification are offered through periodic workshops, including an annual summer institute that was founded at Shenandoah Conservatory in Winchester, Virginia, in the early 2000s and now takes place at Baldwin Wallace Conservatory in Berea, Ohio. For more information about SVW, please see chapter 11, written by Jeannette LoVetri. ♪

Voiceworks

Voiceworks™ is a system of vocal technique developed by American pedagogue Lisa Popeil (b. 1956). Based in Los Angeles, Popeil disseminates her method through a series of "Total Singer" workshops and several books, including *The Total Singer* (1996) and *Sing Anything* (2012). For more information about SVW, please see chapter 13, written by Lisa Popeil. ♪

Complete Vocal Technique

Complete Vocal Technique™ (CVT) was developed by Danish pedagogue Cathrine Sadolin (b. 1958). The primary philosophy behind Complete Vocal Technique is that singing is not as difficult as many people think it is and that the most important aspect of the technique is expression, which allows singers to convey their individual artistic choices through the music they choose to sing. The method idiosyncratically uses four basic technical "modes" of singing: neutral, curbing, overdrive, and edge. CVT is immensely popular in Europe, with 390 authorized teachers in twenty-four countries as of 2017. For more information about CVT, please see chapter 15, written by Cathrine Sadolin. ♪

Vocal Power Method

The Vocal Power Method™ is a system of vocal technique developed by American pedagogue Elisabeth Howard (b. 1932). Howard has had a long career that began in New York and later relocated to Los Angeles. She now resides in Chicago and disseminates her method through a series of "Vocal Power Academy" workshops and several books, including *Sing!* (1980) and *The ABCs of Vocal Harmony* (2006). For more information about the Vocal Power Method, please see chapter 9, written by Elisabeth Howard. ♪

TECHNIQUE VERSUS STYLE

As one reads the chapters in this volume, a strong "theme" emerges. Virtually all of the pedagogues mention that—when they began their careers—there was a prevailing notion that classical training was all one needed, regardless of which style the singer was interested in performing. Robert Edwin writes about the absurdity of this notion:

> As late as the 1980s, the mantra for most voice teachers was, "If you learn to sing classically, you can sing anything." I heard this from many well-known pedagogues who truly believed that classical technique would serve all styles and genres of singing because, to them, there was only one voice technique. Our dance colleagues, however, knew differently.

They knew that a ballet dancer wanting to tap would have to learn the technique of tapping in order to succeed in that style. Technique always preceded repertoire. Specific genre training always preceded genre performance.[7]

Even today, the concept of having "one technique" to sing multiple styles still seems to persist in some circles. But an important distinction should be made between *technique* and *style*. Edwin clarifies this matter by elaborating further:

Technique serves style (genre). It is the foundation that enables the style (genre) to exist. Technique is "how" you do something. Style is "what" you do with that technique. For example, if I want to play golf, I will explore and develop golf technique with a golf coach. I will not go to a basketball coach to learn to play golf. If I want to dance ballet, I will seek out a ballet teacher, not a hip-hop teacher.[8]

Daniel Zangger Borch offers a startlingly similar analogy:

An important element in my teaching is grounding my exercises in the style that the singer is trying to sing. Using classical exercises to try to sing rock is worthless because the transition from one style to another is too vast and too difficult. You can't practice ping pong exclusively if you want to become a future tennis player. They both use a racket, but they're not the same game. The foundation of my whole teaching approach is the development of specific exercises that are directly connected to the styles I sing and teach.[9]

Indeed, to achieve stylistic accuracy at times requires a very different technique. Although this was denied in most classical pedagogy circles for decades, a major turning point occurred at the end of the twentieth century, when voice science began to show singing teachers that something very different was occurring acoustically and physiologically during CCM singing:

For the singing teacher community, the breakthrough came when the emerging field of voice science proved that different physiological things were happening when singers sang stylistically correct CCM repertoire. The pharynx narrowed, the larynx raised, the mouth spread in a lateral position, the soft palate lowered, and the *chiaro* dominated the *oscuro*—completely opposite of what a classically trained singer would be expected to do. Only then did "nonclassical" voice pedagogy, as it was called then, start to gain legitimacy and credibility.[10]

Matthew Edwards, in chapter 19 of this book, reinforces this point by citing published scientific data. In response to "it is all the same technique—the only difference is style," Edwards writes:

> Scientific research shows that this statement is not accurate. Differences in technique begin at the vocal-fold level. Christopher Barlow, Jeannette LoVetri, and David Howard investigated CQ (closed quotient) ratios in adolescent females singing in both classical and CCM styles. The investigators found that in 76 percent of the singers, CQ was greater in mix than in head voice. The findings also suggest that the closed quotients are indeed different between the two styles. An analysis of distorted singing in a single subject found that there were vibrations in both the glottis and the supraglottal mucosa, which was vibrating at one-third of the fundamental frequency. Subharmonic frequencies were present in the spectrographic readings, and subglottic pressure was measured at 20–45 cm compared to 4–36 cm found in classical singers. Vibration of the supraglottal mucosa is rarely if ever advocated in classical pedagogies, yet the quality is essential in many commercial styles.[11]

This twenty-first-century understanding of vocal function has perhaps done more to legitimize the field of CCM pedagogy than any other single factor. In the era of fact-based voice pedagogy, it is virtually impossible to argue that the "one size fits all approach" (i.e., classical singing is all one needs) would be effective in training the CCM singer.

MUSIC THEATER VERSUS CCM

Another theme that emerged as a result of this project was the changing nature of how music theater, which was until quite recently regarded as a CCM genre, is now often regarded as something very different indeed. While there are certainly a lot of CCM styles in music theater—since *Hair* in 1967, shows that require "legit" singing have gotten increasingly scarce—pedagogues have also begun to specialize in one or the other, acknowledging that CCM singers and music theater singers are a part of two very different industries. Chapter 2, written by Matthew Edwards, is devoted to untangling this emerging trend, articulating some of the differences between music theater and CCM. This task is not clear cut and can be very messy indeed.

This book is devoted to profiling the pioneering generation of CCM teachers, who began their careers in a time before the term "CCM" was even invented, in an era in which both music theater and CCM were considered to be in the same category (i.e., "nonclassical"). It is not surprising that, as time moved on, some teachers gained greater reputations within one industry as opposed to the other. Mary Saunders Barton, Joan Lader, and Mark Meylan, for instance, are primarily known today as music theater teachers, whereas Daniel Zangger Borch, Robert Edwin, Cathrine Sadolin, and Seth Riggs are better known as CCM specialists. Regardless, the overarching theme of this book is the establishment of a systematic CCM pedagogy worthy of standing alongside the classical establishment. In this sense, all of these pedagogues were on the same page, forging a way forward for future generations of "nonclassical" singers and teachers.

OTHER THEMES AND FACTORS

Registration and "Gender Bending"

One of the primary differences between classical and CCM singing is the singer's use of registration. In classical singing, the "correct" use of registration has been historically closely tied to the gender of the singer, although countertenors have challenged this tradition in recent decades. In classical singing, male singers sing primarily in chest voice with some mix on top, largely avoiding the "pure" head register (or falsetto), whereas most female singers ignore the chest register, spending virtually all their time in a head-mix and head voice. The "rules" of how to use one's registers in classical singing are clear cut and defined by one's gender, the repertoire, and tradition.

Registration use in CCM pedagogy, however, is completely different. Encouraging the healthy use of *all* registers—regardless of gender—is an essential element of CCM pedagogy. In CCM singing, there is comparatively little opportunity for the female singer to use head register. Unlike classical singing, the vast majority of the repertoire is sung in a chest or chest-mix. In turn, male singers are welcome to access their falsetto if the song and style require it. This "gender bending"—which is discussed at length by both Katie Agresta and David Sabella—suggests that CCM pedagogy is less binary than classical singing. CCM pedagogues need to train the *singer* as opposed to the *male singer* or *female singer*. Having fluent ability to sing comfortably in all registers is a must for the successful CCM singer.

Authenticity

One of the hallmarks of great CCM singing mentioned by virtually every contributor to this book is the importance of the singer cultivating his or her own idiosyncratic style, one that expresses something unique and sincere about the singer's personality. Expressive CCM singing is *authentic* singing. While it can be argued that some of the great opera singers also have a unique or idiosyncratic voice, the desire for "perfect technique" in the classical singing world perhaps regulates the authenticity or "uniqueness" factor to a lower tier than in the CCM world. While CCM teachers should always advocate for efficient vocal production, they should be careful to never discourage the unique vocal qualities or stylistic idiosyncrasies that make the CCM artist who he or she is.

A Changing Industry

With subscriptions to symphony orchestra seasons and opera houses rapidly declining and the commercial music industry thriving more with every passing year, there is no question that the dynamics of the industry are changing in a way that will only increase the demand for competent CCM pedagogues to train singers for the commercial music industry. In chapter 19, Matthew Edwards elaborates on some of the raw facts of the CCM industry, and these figures have important implications for voice pedagogues.

Respect

In the end, each of the pedagogues profiled in this book desired one thing perhaps above everything else: respect—respect for their art form, respect for their repertoire, respect for their industry, and respect for the styles in which they sang. Thanks to their pioneering efforts, CCM pedagogy finally has earned the stature worthy of standing alongside classical pedagogy. Just two decades ago, this twenty-first-century reality would have astonished many of the contributors to this volume.

FINAL THOUGHTS

This chapter has provided an overview of the basic themes for this book, the heart of which is the twelve profiles that constitute part II. The remainder of part I will provide additional primer material with chapters by Matthew Edwards, Scott McCoy, and Wendy LeBorgne. Part III—entitled "Contemporary Commercial Music: Past, Present, and Future"—will provide a profile of Seth Riggs's impact on CCM, with additional chapters by Matthew Edwards and the editor that summarize the volume and speculate on the future of CCM pedagogy.

NOTES

1. Personal correspondence with Jeannette LoVetri, May 15, 2017.
2. Robert Edwin, "Are We the National Association of Teachers of Classical Singing?" *Journal of Singing* 41, no. 5 (1985): 40.
3. Personal correspondence with Jeannette LoVetri, May 15, 2017. LoVetri also concedes, however, that many officers who threatened to resign also returned after their tempers quelled. (What drama!)
4. Personal correspondence with Robert Edwin, May 26, 2017. See also chapter 8.
5. Personal correspondence with Jeannette LoVetri, May 15, 2017.
6. Jeannette LoVetri and Edrie Means Weekly, "Contemporary Commercial Music (CCM) Survey: Who's Teaching What in Non-Classical Music," *Journal of Voice* 17, no. 2 (2003): 207–15.
7. Personal correspondence with Robert Edwin, May 26, 2017. See also chapter 8.

8. Ibid.

9. See chapter 17, written by Daniel Zangger Borch.

10. Personal correspondence with Robert Edwin, May 26, 2017. See also chapter 8.

11. See chapter 19, written by Matthew Edwards.

2

CCM VERSUS MUSIC THEATER

A Comparison
Matthew Edwards

At the turn of the twenty-first century, music theater pedagogy was often considered synonymous with CCM pedagogy. It was clear that the vocal requirements of many of the newer Broadway shows were "nonclassical" in nature and that classical voice lessons alone were insufficient to prepare aspiring music theater performers. However, as time moves forward, it is becoming increasingly clear that the "nonclassical" nature of music theater is perhaps one of the *only* things that the genre has in common with other CCM genres. As we near the end of the second decade of the twenty-first century, separate pedagogies are emerging that distinguish important differences in the training of commercial and music theater performers. This chapter attempts to delineate some of the defining characteristics of the two genres.

CCM: THE TERM AND ITS ORIGINS

The term "contemporary commercial music" (CCM) first appeared in print in a 2003 research paper by Jeannette LoVetri and Edrie Means

Weekly.[1] LoVetri clarified questions surrounding the term in a 2008 article in the *Journal of Voice*; she writes:

> Contemporary commercial music (CCM) is the new term for what we used to call non-classical music. This is a generic term created to cover everything including music theater, pop, rock, gospel, R&B, soul, hip-hop, rap, country, folk, experimental music, and all other styles that are not considered classical.[2]

The term is widely accepted in the voice pedagogy community, yet it has not caught on outside of our industry. For example, in music education, terms such as "commercial" and "popular" are more widely used. At the university level, you will find performance, practical, and musicology degrees that include such diverse offerings as songwriting, hip-hop studies, jazz, professional music, artist development, creative music performance, contemporary music, and urban music, but only one degree with CCM in the title.[3] In the recording industry, genres are called by their exact name, and there are many obscure subgenres with titles such as glitch pop, future garage, chillstep, dirty South, and psychedelic soul, among others.[4] In music theater, nontraditional genres are either identified by their exact category—country, gospel, disco, and so on—or generically called "pop/rock."

Part of the barrier to widespread acceptance of the acronym beyond our profession is that CCM has other associations. For example, it also refers to "contemporary Christian music" and is used by more than 150 organizations, most notably Cincinnati Conservatory of Music and Canada Cycle & Motor (the famous hockey equipment manufacturer).[5] LoVetri acknowledges this difficulty in her article, stating, "Perhaps in time a better term will emerge, but for the moment, CCM seems to be doing a good job in helping to eliminate the use of the pejorative term 'non-classical.'"[6] To that I wholeheartedly agree, as does the National Association of Teachers of Singing (NATS), American Academy of Teachers of Singing (AATS), New York Singing Teachers Association (NYSTA), and the Voice Foundation (TVF). Before we had the term CCM, all of the styles above were typically called "nonclassical." While accurate, it is rarely acceptable in other parts of society to call something by what it is not. As LoVetri frequently states, we don't call cats "non-dogs." So, while there are barriers toward widespread acceptance of the acronym, for pedagogical purposes, it has been a great benefit to have a word that describes what we teach instead of what we do not teach.

CONTROVERSY SURROUNDING THE WORD "COMMERCIAL"

Some pedagogues object to the word "commercial" being part of the acronym and have written letters to the editor of the *Journal of Singing* detailing why it is offensive.[7] However, "commercial" is an important part of the term and warrants further discussion. Let's begin with a few definitions according to Merriam-Webster:

1. occupied with or engaged in commerce or work intended for commerce;
2. viewed with regard to profit;
3. designed for a large market.[8]

To clarify, "commerce" is defined as "the exchange or buying and selling of commodities on a large scale."[9] In our context, commercial denotes consumer spending patterns as they relate to vocal music. The word "commercial" does not deny that one is an artist; it simply delineates the way the art is funded. For corporate labels such as Universal Music Group, Sony Music Entertainment, and Warner Music Group, artists are funded by record sales to the general public. In 2016, those sales totaled $7.7 billion with another $7.3 billion in revenue coming from live concerts.[10] With so much money at stake, profitability is a key factor in decisions related to artist development. A hit song can cost upward of one million dollars to write, record, and release.[11] If the label does not believe they can recoup their money, they are not going to support the artist and their songs.

For classical musicians in the United States, funding comes primarily through wealthy donors and grant organizations. For instance, Opera America reports that only 27 percent of the industry's $1.1 billion income comes from box office sales. The other $803 million of their operating expenses are funded by donations, grants, and returns on investments.[12] The performances produced by these companies are not being sustained by individual audience demand, but rather through benefactors who believe in the art form and are willing to donate money to keep it alive. In comparison, Broadway shows earned $1.37 billion in box office sales during the 2016–2017 season.[13] Like the music recording industry, Broadway shows are for-profit ventures. Without box office income from the general public, Broadway shows go out of business. Yes, it is true that Broadway shows are funded by investors, but those individuals are seeking a return on their investment.[14] If investors do not see potential to at least break even, they will not provide funding to get a project off the ground.

Clearly there is a massive difference in consumer spending among these diverse groups.[15] If opera had to live by the same financial structure as for-profit businesses without donors to underwrite production costs, it would likely cease to exist. As stated before, the term "commercial" does not define the quality of the music; it simply denotes how the art is funded. Classical music in the United States is donor funded, whereas "nonclassical" music is audience funded; thus, we call it "commercial."

THE NEED FOR INDIVIDUALIZED ATTENTION

In her article, LoVetri was clear that "each CCM style needs to be taken seriously on its own terms."[16] However, at the time of the publication of this book, anecdotal evidence suggests voice teachers and researchers are often clumping all "nonclassical" styles together under the blanket term "contemporary commercial music" without delineating the different qualities that make each style unique. In the early years of establishing the new term, this was understandable as research was sparse and only a few published texts and workshops were available to offer continuing education. However, times have changed. We now have an ever-expanding body of research, numerous doctoral dissertations, and a growing number of continuing education workshops available for the various styles under this umbrella. Lumping all CCM styles together as a singular group is now beginning to hold us back from taking our training of these artists to the next level. This chapter will look at some of the differences that need to be considered when teaching commercial and music theater performers and why we should consider them two separate but equal groups.

THE INTRICACIES OF MUSIC THEATER

Music theater spans more than 150 years, from *The Black Crook* (1866) to the present day.[17] While there are not as many subgenres of music theater as there are in contemporary commercial music, there are still significant differences that performers encounter when navigating traditional (musical drama and musical comedy), contemporary (concept and book musicals), and pop/rock musicals (jukebox and original works written for the stage by commercial artists). These subgenres require in-depth study to attain mastery, study that goes beyond the technical distinctions between legit, belt, and mix.

Traditional shows often contain multiple styles. "Legit" songs developed out of the operetta tradition and require the singer to integrate elements of classical technique. Think of show stoppers such as "Soliloquy" from *Carousel*, "Glitter and Be Gay" from *Candide*, and "Tonight" from *West Side Story*. These songs require seamless transition between registers, a clean legato line, and tasteful use of vibrato. In the case of shows such as *Guys and Dolls*, much of the music resembles Tin Pan Alley–era genres, which were musically influenced by ragtime and jazz. The speechlike, rhythmic delivery needed for a song like "I Cain't Say No" from *Oklahoma* is quite different than the long legato lines needed for "Vanilla Ice Cream" from *She Loves Me*. Similarly, a duet such as "If I Loved You" from *Carousel* requires performers to navigate sections of dialogue as well as speechlike and legit singing all within the same piece of music. To successfully perform in a traditional musical, the students must not only have the functional knowledge to navigate the technical challenges, but they must also understand how to bring out the intricacies of each musical style within the show.

Contemporary musicals, on the other hand, are driven more by story than their traditional predecessors. Acting was of course important in traditional-era music dramas, but beautiful singing would often take precedence. In contemporary shows, acting is often considered to be of greater importance than the singing. This sometimes results in casting choices that place a great actor who sings on the stage over a great singer who acts. Contemporary shows require many different technical abilities than their traditional counterparts, and in many cases, the singer must be able to sustain their belt or mix through long, high phrases. Whereas the highest belt notes in traditional musicals were usually B4 and C5 (with an occasional D5), contemporary musicals often push the belt voice to F♯5 and higher. Examples include "Defying Gravity" from *Wicked*, "Once upon a Time" from *BKLYN*, and "I'm Here" from *The Color Purple*.

Contemporary shows take advantage of the intimacy that can be conveyed with the use of microphones. Songs such as "Still Hurting" from *The Last Five Years* and "With You" from *Ghost* would be impossible to present on stage in the pre-microphone era. Many composers of contemporary pop shows take the use of audio technology to the next level by exploiting the power of recording studio technology in the creative process. *Jesus Christ Superstar* was released as a concept album in 1970 and made its Broadway debut a year later in 1971. However, in previous decades, the cast recordings were usually not recorded until after the show had opened. This shift in the distribution of recordings had a huge impact on audience expectations. When the audience has the opportunity to listen to the recording before seeing a show on stage, it changes their expectations of the live performance. Modern audiences want to hear a consistent performance; they expect that the singing on Broadway, on the West End, or on tour will closely resemble what they have been listening to on their devices. In essence, musicals became franchises, especially those that were part of the British Invasion, such as *Cats*, *The Phantom of the Opera*, *Les Misérables*, and *Miss Saigon*.[18]

The success of *Jesus Christ Superstar* not only influenced what audiences expected to hear in the theater, but it also helped fuel the contemporary pop movement in music theater. In this style, theater composers began copying popular music idioms and combining them with music theater traditions and conventions. Beginning in the 1970s, a series of revues created around the music of commercial artists—including *The Night That Made America Famous*, *Beatlemania*, and *Ain't Misbehavin'*—led to an explosion of shows called "jukebox musicals." There are also numerous original shows written by pop/rock artists for the stage, such as *Promises, Promises*; *Spring Awakening*; *American Idiot*;

and *Spider-Man: Turn Off the Dark*. Both jukebox and original pop/rock musicals require performers to journey beyond the vocal and physical skills that are commonly taught in university music theater training programs. These shows require rhythmic singing, vocal fry, growls, riffing, and a wide range of other stylistic tools that must be adapted for the storytelling needs of music theater. Because of all these differences, today's music theater voice teachers need an in-depth knowledge of music theater history and style—including pop/rock and classical—to help their students succeed in the business.

AMPLIFIED VERSUS UNAMPLIFIED SINGING

Commercial artists often view the microphone as an extension of their instrument. The advent of the electric microphone around 1925 made it possible for artists to convey a more intimate and conversational tone than was possible in the earlier days of acoustic recordings. While acoustic power had been a vital component of success in previous centuries, the microphone could amplify every little nuance of the voice, thus eliminating the need for a singer's formant. Radio and jazz-band singers quickly adopted the new technology and exploited the possibilities. By using microphones, they were able to create an artificial sense of intimacy with their audiences on the other side of the radio and allowed listeners to feel as if they were in the same room as the performer.[18] In the early days of microphone use, this breathy style of singing was called "crooning" and was received harshly by critics:

> Let us pause for a moment to examine this word "crooning." It is a horrible expression . . . associated with all the unpleasant, smeary, wobbling vocalisms that one ever heard. . . . Their efforts vary between "a low moaning sound, as of animals in pain" to "the soft singing of a mother to her child." (Al Bowlly, *Modern Style Singing* ["Crooning"], 1934)[20]

However, female audience members were much more receptive:

> Dear Rudy—you saved the day! The long tedious day—you whose heart was bared that we all might be uplifted. . . . There is a haunting tenderness of touch in your voice so like your music—it is astounding how closely al-

lied your voice is to your music—it thrills and soothes. (from a fan letter to Rudy Vallee, Manhasset, Long Island, 1928)[21]

As author Paula Lockheart states, the microphone gave the voice "sex."[22] Vocal qualities that were usually reserved for lovers in intimate moments were now being streamed over the airwaves into wooden boxes sitting in the owner's living room and providing a new and provocative experience for listeners. The controversy no doubt influenced voice teachers' opinions of the techniques necessary to sing this way, a bias that continues to exist today in some circles, although probably for different reasons than those expressed by Lockheart.

Audio technology considerations are more complex in music theater. While all modern Broadway shows are heavily amplified, it was not always that way; from *The Black Crook* to the late 1930s, microphones were not used at all. Shows such as *Porgy and Bess*, *Show Boat*, *Oklahoma*, and *Carousel* had operatic qualities that required singers to project acoustically with a strong singer's formant in order to be heard over the orchestra. In Tin Pan Alley–style shows, the singing was speechlike but required a trumpet-like timbre to carry to the back of the theater. Around 1939, producers began sporadically using floor microphones to boost the voices of performers on stage.[23] By the 1960s, hanging, shotgun, and wireless microphones were being utilized. It was not until *Hair* in 1968 that microphones were purposely used to create a rock concert atmosphere that pushed sound pressure levels beyond what singers could create acoustically.[24] In 1981, *Cats* became the first musical in which every cast member was wearing a wireless microphone.[25] In sum, there is approximately a one-hundred-year period—1866 until the late 1960s—during which musicals were written to be performed without amplification. Productions since 1981 have been written with amplification in mind. That leaves a hole in the middle—from 1968 to 1981—when the industry was in transition. Yet all musicals since *The Black Crook* technically fall under the umbrella term "contemporary commercial music," at least as the term is currently being used today.

If you take all of the above into consideration, the argument could be made that what we are really discussing when comparing traditional music theater, contemporary music theater, commercial music, and classical music is a difference between amplified and unamplified singing. Renowned voice scientist Ingo Titze has suggested that perhaps we would be better categorizing singing styles as acoustic and amplified rather than classical and CCM when it comes to voice science and functional training.[26] This argument has considerable merit.

COMMERCIAL GENRES ON THE RADIO VERSUS COMMERCIAL GENRES IN MUSICALS

While music theater is increasingly integrating commercial genres, the resulting performances are still uniquely theatrical. *Hamilton* solidified rap music's place in the music theater canon, but the style of Lin-Manuel's writing is quite different than that of Kanye, Snoop Dogg, Jay-Z, or any of the other platinum selling hip-hop artists that account for 18.2 percent of the music listened to by Americans.[27] Shows such as *Spring Awakening*, *Waitress*, and *Diner* are written by famous commercial artists, but the final product resembles "music theater" more than "Top 40." It is hard to imagine "Mama Who Bore Me" from *Spring Awakening* playing alongside "Bad Day" by Daniel Powter on Top 40 radio, even though both songs are written by chart-topping artists. Yet it is also startling for some to hear "Pinball Wizard" juxtaposed next to "If I Loved You" or even a contemporary piece such as "Here I Am" from *The Drowsy Chaperone*. While all the songs listed above come from musicals, they could not be more different.

Because performers in pop/rock musicals must also act and dance, most come from formal training programs and therefore carry over traditional vocal qualities—including "ring" and vibrato. While some commercial artists also have these traits, they are less common than what you will hear on the Broadway stage. For example, listen to the original recording of Green Day's *American Idiot* and then listen to the Broadway cast recording, or compare the cast recording of *Rock of Ages* to the recordings of the original artists. While pop/rock musicals have proliferated on Broadway in the past decade, these shows live in their own category; they are neither traditional music theater nor mainstream commercial music. They require a unique skill set that merges elements of both CCM and music theater styles and technique.

TECHNIQUE CONSIDERATIONS

What are the implications for singing teachers when training music theater as opposed to commercial performers? The following paragraphs outline several technical categories for consideration.

Tonal Goals

There are many tonal goal considerations that come to mind when discussing the differences among CCM styles. Tonal goals for music theater are pretty clear, thanks to decades of cast recordings that have archived the aesthetics of various creative teams. As you listen to cast recordings, you will find that it is standard for Adelaide from *Guys and Dolls* to sing with nasality and Eponine from *Les Misérables* to possess a strong chest-mix belt. If a performer enters an audition room and sings "Adelaide's Lament" with Italianate vowels or "On My Own" in head-mix, they have no chance of booking the show. Casting directors do want to hear unique takes on decades-old songs, but within limits. For instance, they do not want to hear "Maria" from *West Side Story* performed with vocal fry and riffing. They do, however, want to hear a nice legato line with appropriate registration, timbre, and judicious use of vibrato that will appeal to modern taste. When a casting director says they want a performer to "make a song their own," they are talking about a unique take on the character and acting choices that convey that unique point of view.

In pop/rock musicals, it is sometimes desirable to hire a singer that can mimic another performer. Think, for instance, of productions such as *Beautiful*, *Million Dollar Quartet*, and *Jersey Boys*. All of these shows need performers who can imitate the vocal quality of the original artists. To do so usually requires some form of vocal tract manipulation. While manipulation of the vocal tract is frequently looked upon with disdain by functional pedagogues, it is often necessary when working on jukebox and biographical productions.

In contrast, outside of cover bands, karaoke contestants, and Elvis impersonators, we rarely encounter professional solo artists in commercial styles who want to imitate someone else. The voice teachers who work with solo artists must focus on the tastes and desires of the performer in front of them. They must find functional pathways to protecting vocal health while maintaining the artist's unique timbre, all while making sure any adjustments are acceptable to the creative team. With solo artists, there are no limits—creating new and unusual sounds can often be the ticket to success.

Storytelling

Even though both music theater and commercial artists are in the business of telling stories, there are vast differences in the tools they use to craft a performance. When working with a commercial artist, the teacher can help bring the words and notes of the composer, who is often also the artist, to life. Most solo artists are part of the songwriting process to some extent and are either singing directly about their own life experience or relating it to something that is deeply personal to them.

Music theater performers are rarely part of the creative process and must therefore develop techniques that enable them to personalize the life experience they are conveying. In most instances, music theater performers try to see the piece through the eyes of the character they are portraying and use that lens to bring the work to life. They spend years studying the acting techniques of teachers such as Stanislavsky, Chekhov, Meisner, Hagen, Adler, Strasberg, and others to give them the tools necessary to live truthfully under imaginary circumstances.

The voice teachers working with these diverse groups must understand these differences and develop their toolbox to help their clients be successful in each situation. Not every voice teacher will function as an acting/performance coach for his or her clients. However, they must at least understand the industry expectations to make sure that what they are asking for vocally will complement performance practice and not inhibit the singer's ability to communicate effectively.

Performance Demands

Performance demands also have an impact on how we train CCM and music theater singers. The Broadway performer who must perform eight shows a week has a different set of challenges than the praise

Table 2.1. Comparisons between Classical, Music Theater, and CCM Styles

	Classical	Music Theater	CCM
Training Required	Most performers have at least an undergraduate degree in music, the most common being vocal performance. Many performers also hold a master's degree, artist diploma, and/or doctoral degree. Many singers spend several years in young artist programs before embarking on a full-time singing career.	Training is primarily at the undergraduate level. These degrees may be housed in the theater, music, or dance department. There are only a handful of graduate degrees in music theater, so for most students, the BFA/BA/BM will be their only academic training.	There are approximately twenty-three degree programs in the United States for commercial singers. With so few options, it is very common to encounter working performers who have not come up through the traditional pathways of their classical and music theater counterparts. Many of these artists learn on the job.
Venue	Traditionally opera houses were large venues constructed specifically for acoustic performances. The Metropolitan Opera in NYC is the largest opera house in the United States, seating 3,800 patrons. Modern opera companies often have to share space with other performing arts organizations, which sometimes requires them to perform in spaces that are less than ideal acoustically.	The largest Broadway theater is the Al Hirschfeld, which seats 1,437. All current Broadway theaters are designed for amplified performances. Regional theaters are often smaller and may or may not have built-in amplification systems. Touring productions perform in a wide range of venues from universities to performing arts centers and even athletic centers.	Commercial venues vary widely from small coffee shops to stadiums that can hold close to 100,000 people. Outdoor concerts can attract even greater numbers. In 2015, the Austin City Limits music festival welcomed 450,000 people.
Amplified versus Unamplified	Classical singers almost never perform with amplification. They take pride in their ability to project acoustically and consider it a hallmark of their art form.	The vast majority of venues are amplified; some local theaters with small houses may not use microphones. When opera companies perform musicals as part of their season, they are usually unamplified.	Venues are always amplified.

Vocal Demands	Opera singers at high-level companies will often have one or more nights off in between performances. It is uncommon to find a leading soloist singing more than two to three performances per week in the United States. A single opera can last as long as five hours and therefore requires great physical, emotional, and vocal stamina.	Broadway actors give eight performances a week. Those on national tours will usually have slightly less demanding schedules but will also be traveling in tour buses several times a month. The number of performances per week at regional theaters around the United States varies depending on the size of the community.	Emerging commercial artists will often be asked to perform multi-hour sets. In order to build a fan base, they must also work the merchandise table, talk with fans, and give interviews on morning radio shows. Established performers have many of the same demands but also contend with rigorous travel schedules.
Language/Text	Must learn to sing in Italian, French, German, and English. Some performers will also sing in Spanish, Czech, and Russian. Vowels and consonants are adjusted as needed to maintain beauty of tone.	Primarily sung in English in the United States. Performers who can speak foreign languages may be able to find work overseas singing translations of American shows. Intelligibility of the words is of prime importance.	Songs are written in the language(s) the performer speaks. Clarity of diction varies greatly.
Acting and Dance	Many operas were written before what is known as the Russian Revolution in acting. Until the 1930s, acting was gesture based and performers avoided feeling true emotions. Some modern stagings of operas try to integrate contemporary acting techniques, but most singers place beauty of tone above emotional truth. Dance numbers in opera are usually performed by a dance troupe. In some instances, singers may be asked to partner dance.	Music theater artists are trained in Stanislavsky acting technique or one of its offshoots (Meisner, Chekhov, Strasberg, etc.). These techniques train actors to live truthfully through imaginary circumstances. Many directors expect performers in music theater to put primary focus on acting and secondary focus on their voice. Performers are often expected to be able to dance; common styles include ballet, jazz, tap, and hip-hop.	Most performers do not have formal acting or performance training. Pop artists will often dance, although the training varies greatly.

(continued)

Table 2.1. (continued)

	Classical	Music Theater	CCM
Persona and Storytelling	In opera, art song, and oratorio, classical singers inhabit dramatic situations and embody specific characters and personalities.	In music theater, singing actors inhabit dramatic situations and embody specific characters and personalities.	Singers are themselves on stage, often telling a personal story.
Other Skills Required	Helpful to have experience in stage combat, makeup, audio and recording technology, video and photo editing, social media management, and basic financial skills necessary to manage daily business operations.	Performers who can play an instrument, especially guitar, enhance their chances of finding work. Many of these performers also read for television and film roles. If an actor is pursuing those opportunities, any additional skills they can develop from martial arts to home improvement to scuba diving can make them more marketable.	Should have working knowledge of audio and recording technology, video and photo editing, social media management, and basic financial skills necessary to manage daily business operations.
Representative Universities and Training Programs	Juilliard, Curtis, Indiana University, Florida State University, University of Cincinnati, New England Conservatory, Manhattan School of Music, Eastman School of Music, University of Michigan, San Francisco Conservatory	University of Michigan, Carnegie Mellon University, University of Cincinnati, Penn State University, Boston Conservatory, Ithaca College, Brigham Young University, Elon, Pace University, Montclair State University, Point Park University	Berklee, Belmont, University of Colorado–Denver, Brigham Young University, University of Southern California, Arizona Christian University, Missouri Baptist University

and worship leader who primarily performs on Sundays. The Billboard chart-topping solo artist who travels to ten states in the course of a single month has different challenges than the studio singer in Los Angeles. Those with day jobs who perform locally in the evenings have still another set of challenges. Gigging singers need to learn how to work with sound equipment, talk to sound board operators, conserve their voice at the merchandise table, and stay vocally healthy while traveling across country. If clients are playing multi-hour sets, they must learn to craft a playlist that will help them avoid fatigue.

Music theater performers must learn how to sing pop/rock, traditional, and contemporary pop shows back to back in the course of an eight-week summer stock season without getting fatigued. They must also learn how to sing with good technique while dancing, which is no small challenge. The pedagogue who works with these diverse populations must be able to help the performers develop coping strategies. Although performers in both scenarios are performing CCM styles, the skill set needed to overcome the specific challenges encountered in each situation is unique.

BEYOND THE STAGE AND RECORDING STUDIO

If we look beyond music theater performers and solo artists, we quickly find a plethora of other groups in desperate need of our help that are often lacking professional training by specialized pedagogues. Music therapists are being asked to perform a wider range of styles than ever before, most of which are commercial. However, in most university programs, they are not being trained to sing anything other than classical, a style they will likely never sing in a clinical setting. There are also a cappella pop groups at nearly every university that require performers to use a different technical approach than they are usually learning in their degree programs. Middle and high school show choirs are using commercial styles in their performances as well as music theater repertoire. Most directors of these groups have graduated from the traditional (classical) university structure and lack pedagogical tools to help their students unless they have spent their own time and money on continuing education. Until commercial and music theater pedagogy courses are offered in higher education as part of the curriculum, we cannot expect that this status quo situation will improve.

Unfortunately, most graduates of MM and DMA voice programs in the United States have not been formally prepared to teach anything other than classical. When they enter higher education as faculty members, they do not have the training to help students who will find themselves in the situations mentioned above. In order to move our profession forward, we must solve this problem and begin to offer university students the type of training they need for the music they will be performing and teaching upon graduation.

FINAL THOUGHTS

The acceptance of the term "contemporary commercial music" was a major step toward breaking through nonclassical singing barriers that had existed for decades. However, as the dust continues to settle, it is becoming clearer and clearer that we cannot think of CCM styles as requiring only one singular skill set. Fact-based pedagogy, which is quickly becoming the gold standard in our profession, enables teachers to dissect technical issues and provide appropriate corrections. However, as I have discussed in the previous pages, we have a lot of work to do in becoming proficient at understanding and addressing all of the intricacies of individual CCM genres.

The increasing complexities in the ever-expanding worlds of CCM and music theater have important implications for voice pedagogues, and specialists are emerging for each respective genre. While many singing teachers still have "a foot in each pond," it is becoming increasingly common for teachers to specialize in one or the other. In 2013, the International Congress of Voice Teachers (ICVT) in Brisbane, Queensland, Australia, acknowledged the distinction between music theater and CCM when they established three conference "tracks" and a keynote speaker for each: Håkan Hagegård (classical), Mary Saunders-Barton (music theater), and Daniel Zangger Borch (CCM). The establishment of the Musical Theater Educators Alliance (MTEA) in 1999 and Association for Popular Music Education (APME) in 2010 also highlights the distinct and emerging needs of each community. ♪

The profiles in this book will introduce the reader to a wide range of perspectives, some of which may seem contradictory. However, I encourage you to view each chapter through the lens each teacher uses to see the world around him or her. A teacher in Los Angeles will serve a very different clientele than a teacher in New York City, and he or she will have developed unique techniques and strategies to fill the needs of his or her clients. All of these teachers have had great success with their students, so clearly something is working. You may not agree with everything you read, but if you try to see it through their eyes, you are more likely to take something useful away from each chapter.

While the term "contemporary commercial music" has been crucial to the advancement of our profession, we must take into account that it was created as an umbrella term. One CCM voice pedagogy workshop is not enough to make you an expert in all of these styles—it is only a starting place on your own personal voyage. It is time we turn our focus to illuminating the internal differences among CCM styles rather than dwelling on the external differences (i.e., classical versus CCM). If we do this, I believe we can have an even greater impact on generations of singers to come.

NOTES

1. Jeannette LoVetri and Edrie Means Weekly, "Contemporary Commercial Music (CCM) Survey: Who's Teaching What in Non-Classical Music," *Journal of Voice* 17, no. 2 (2003): 207–15.

2. Jeannette LoVetri, "Editorial: Contemporary Commercial Music," *Journal of Voice* 22, no. 3 (2008): 260.

3. "Commercial Voice Degrees, Diplomas, and Certificates," Contemporary Voice Resources, accessed June 15, 2017, www.commercialvoiceresources.com/commercial-voice-programs-us.

4. "Genres of Music," Music Genre List, last accessed June 10, 2017, www.musicgenreslist.com.

5. "CCM," The Free Dictionary, last accessed June 12, 2017, acronyms.thefreedictionary.com/CCM.

6. LoVetri, "Editorial," 260.

7. "Letters to the Editor," *Journal of Singing* 69, No. 3 (2013): 263–65.

8. "Commercial," Merriam-Webster, last accessed June 20, 2017, https://www.merriam-webster.com/dictionary/commercial.

9. "Commerce," Merriam-Webster, last accessed June 20, 2017, www.merriam-webster.com/dictionary/commerce#h1.

10. "News and Notes on 2016 RIAA Shipment and Revenue Statistics," Recording Industry Association of America, accessed August 10, 2017, www.riaa.com/wp-content/uploads/2017/03/RIAA-2016-Year-End-News-Notes.pdf; "Live Nation Leads the Charge in Concert Business' Booming Revenue," Variety, accessed August 10, 2017, variety.com/2017/music/features/live-nation-concert-business-1201979571/.

11. "How Much Does It Cost to Make a Hit Song?" NPR, last accessed June 29, 2017, www.npr.org/sections/money/2011/07/05/137530847/how-much-does-it-cost-to-make-a-hit-song?sc=fb&cc=fp.

12. "2015 Year in Review," Opera America, last accessed June 9, 2017, operaamerica.org/Files/OADocs/Financials/FY15_AnnualReport.pdf.

13. "Statistics—Broadway in NYC," The Broadway League, last accessed June 11, 2017, www.broadwayleague.com/research/statistics-broadway-nyc/.

14. "Investing in Broadway: How We Actually Made Money," CNN Money, last accessed June 26, 2017, money.cnn.com/2016/06/11/investing/fun-home-broadway-investors/index.html.

15. See chapter 19 for additional industry data.

16. LoVetri, "Editorial," 261.

17. Stanley Green, *The World of Musical Comedy*, 4th ed. (San Diego: Da Capo Press, 1980), 1.

18. Mark N. Grant, *The Rise and Fall of the Broadway Musical* (Boston: Northeastern University Press, 2004), 203–7.

19. Allison McCracken, "'God's Gift to Us Girls': Crooning, Gender, and the Re-Creation of American Popular Song, 1928–1933," *American Music* 17, no. 4 (1999): 365–95.

20. Ibid, 367.

21. Ibid, 367.

22. Paula Lockheart, "A History of Early Microphone Singing, 1925–1939: American Mainstream Popular Singing at the Advent of Electronic Microphone Amplification," *Popular Music and Society* 26, no. 3 (2003): 367–85.

23. Grant, *The Rise and Fall of the Broadway Musical*, 191.

24. Elizabeth L. Wollman, *The Theater Will Rock* (Ann Arbor: University of Michigan Press, 2006), 100.

25. Grant, *The Rise and Fall of the Broadway Musical*, 195.

26. Personal correspondence with Ingo Titze.

27. "Share of Music Song Consumption in the United States, by Genre," Statista, last accessed June 26, 2017, www.statista.com/statistics/694862/music-song-consumption-genre/.

3

SINGING AND VOICE SCIENCE

Scott McCoy

This chapter presents a concise overview of how the voice functions as a biomechanical, acoustic instrument. We will be dealing with elements of anatomy, physiology, acoustics, and resonance. But don't panic: the things you need to know are easily accessible, even if it has been many years since you last set foot in a science or math class!

All musical instruments, including the human voice, have at least four things in common, consisting of a power source, sound source (vibrator), resonator, and a system for articulation. In most cases, the person who plays the instrument provides power by pressing a key, plucking a string, or blowing into a horn. This power is used to set the sound source in motion, which creates vibrations in the air that we perceive as sound. Musical vibrators come in many forms, including strings, reeds, and human lips. The sound produced by the vibrator, however, needs a lot of help before it becomes beautiful music—we might think of it as raw material, like a lump of clay that a potter turns into a vase. Musical instruments use resonance to enhance and strengthen the sound of the vibrator, transforming it into sounds we identify as a piano, trumpet, or guitar. Finally, instruments must have a means of articulation to create the nuanced sounds of music. Let's see how these four elements are used to create the sounds of singing.

PULMONARY SYSTEM: THE POWER SOURCE OF YOUR VOICE

The human voice has a lot in common with a trumpet: both use flaps of tissue as a sound source, both use hollow tubes as resonators, and both rely on the respiratory (pulmonary) system for power. If you stop to think about it, you quickly realize why breathing is so important for singing. First and foremost, it keeps us alive through the exchange of blood gases—oxygen in, carbon dioxide out. But it also serves as the storage depot for the air we use to produce sound. Most singers rarely encounter situations in which these two functions are in conflict, but if you are required to sustain an extremely long phrase, you could find yourself in need of fresh oxygen before your lungs are totally empty.

Misconceptions about breathing for singing are rampant. Fortunately, most are easily dispelled. We must start with a brief foray into the world of physics in the guise of Boyle's Law. Some of you no doubt remember this principle: the pressure of a gas within a container changes inversely with changes of volume. If the quantity of a gas is constant and its container is made smaller, pressure rises. But if we make the container get bigger, pressure goes down. Boyle's law explains everything that happens when we breathe, especially when we combine it with another physical law: nature abhors a vacuum. If one location has reduced pressure, air flows from an area of higher pressure to equalize the two, and vice versa. So if we can create a zone of reduced air pressure by expanding our lungs, air automatically flows in to restore balance. When air pressure in the lungs is increased, it has no choice but to flow outward.

As we all know, the air we breathe goes in and out of our lungs. Each lung contains millions and millions of tiny air sacs called alveoli, where gases are exchanged. The alveoli also function like ultra-miniature versions of the bladder for a bag pipe, storing the air that will be used to set the vocal folds into vibration. To get the air in and out of them, all we need to do is make the lungs larger for inhalation and smaller for exhalation. Always remember this relationship between cause and effect during breathing: we inhale because we make ourselves large; we exhale because we make ourselves smaller. Unfortunately, the lungs are organs, not muscles, and have no ability on their own to accomplish this feat. For this reason, your bodies came from the factory with special

SINGING AND VOICE SCIENCE   35

muscles designed to enlarge and compress your entire thorax (rib cage), while simultaneously moving your lungs. We can classify these muscles in two main categories: any muscle that has the ability to increase the volume capacity of the thorax serves an inspiratory function; any muscle that has the ability to decrease the volume capacity of the thorax serves an expiratory function.

Your largest muscle of inspiration is called the diaphragm (figure 3.1). This dome-shaped muscle originates from the bottom of your sternum (breastbone) and completely fills the area from that point around your ribs to your spine. It's the second-largest muscle in your body, but you probably have no conscious awareness of it or ability to directly control

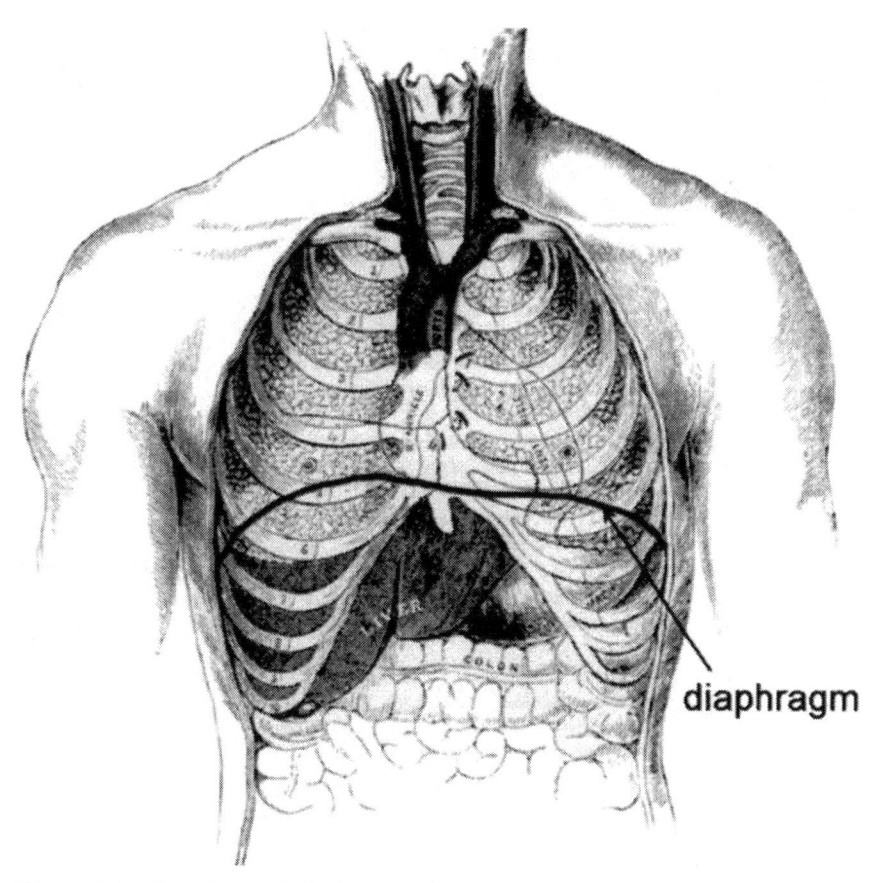

Figure 3.1. Location of diaphragm. *Courtesy of Scott McCoy*

it. When we take a deep breath, the diaphragm contracts and the central portion flattens out and drops downward a couple of inches into your abdomen, pressing against all of your internal organs. If you release tension from your abdominal muscles as you inhale, you will feel a gentle bulge in your upper or lower belly, or perhaps in your back, resulting from the displacement of your innards by the diaphragm. This is a good thing and can be used to let you know you have taken a good inhalation.

The diaphragm is important, but we must remember that it cannot function in isolation. After you inhale, it relaxes and gently returns to its resting position through an action called elastic recoil. This movement, however, is entirely passive and makes no significant contribution to generating the pressure required to sustain phonation. Therefore, it makes no sense at all to try to "sing from your diaphragm"—unless you intend to sing while you inhale, not exhale!

Eleven pairs of muscles assist the diaphragm in its inhalatory efforts, which are called the external intercostal muscles (figure 3.2). These muscles start from ribs one through eleven and connect at a slight angle downward to ribs two through twelve. When they contract, the entire thorax moves up and out, somewhat like moving a bucket handle. With the diaphragm and intercostals working together, you are able to increase the capacity of your lungs by about three to six liters, depending on your gender and overall physical stature; thus, we have quite a lot of air available to power our voices.

Eleven additional pairs of muscles are located directly under the external intercostals, which, not surprisingly, are called the internal intercostals (figure 3.2). These muscles start from ribs two through twelve and connect upward to ribs one through eleven. When they contract, they induce the opposite action of their external partners: the thorax is made smaller, inducing exhalation. Four additional pairs of expiratory muscles are located in the abdomen, beginning with the rectus (figure 3.2). The two rectus abdominis muscles run from your pubic bone to your sternum and are divided into four separate portions, called bellies of the muscle (lots of muscles have multiple bellies; it is coincidental that the bellies of the rectus are found in the location we colloquially refer to as our belly). Definition of these bellies results in the so-called ripped abdomen or six-pack of body builders and others who are especially fit.

SINGING AND VOICE SCIENCE

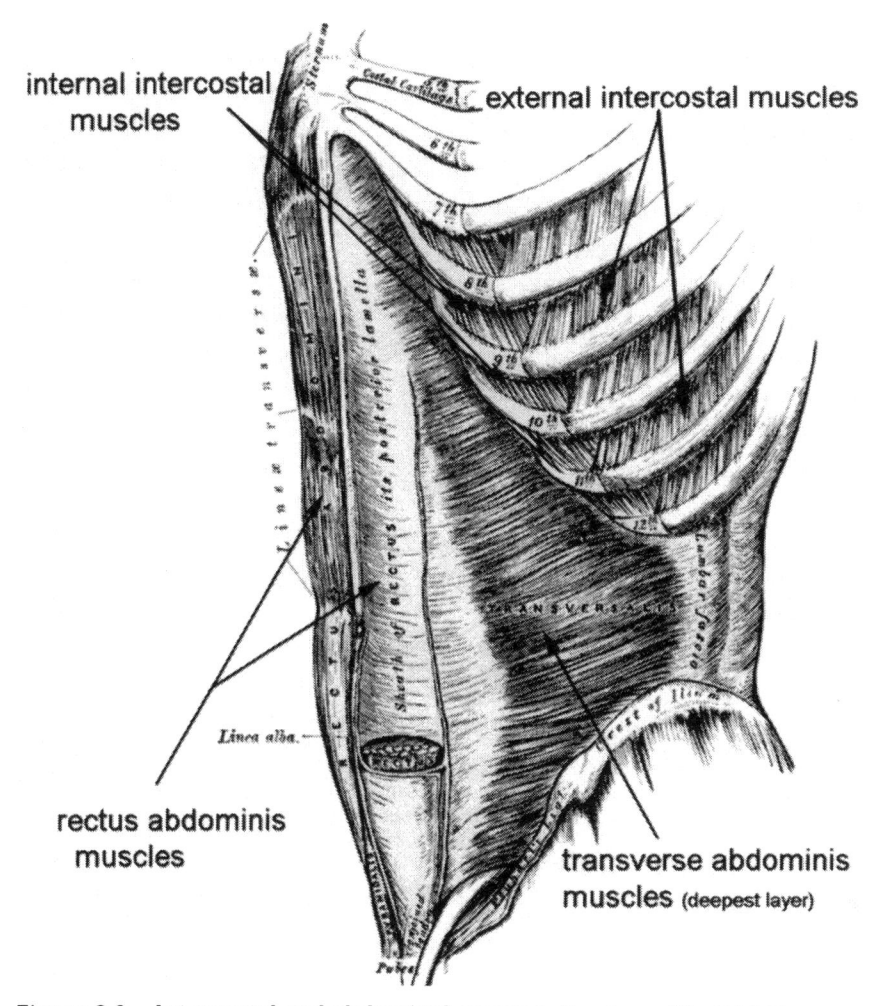

Figure 3.2. Intercostal and abdominal muscles. *Courtesy of Scott McCoy*

The largest muscles of the abdomen are called the external obliques (figure 3.3), which run at a downward angle from the sides of the rectus, covering the lower portion of the thorax, and extend all the way to the spine. The internal obliques lie immediately below, oriented at an angle that crisscrosses the external muscles. They are slightly smaller, beginning at the bottom of the thorax, rather than extending over it. The deepest muscle layer is the transverse abdominis (figure 3.2), which is

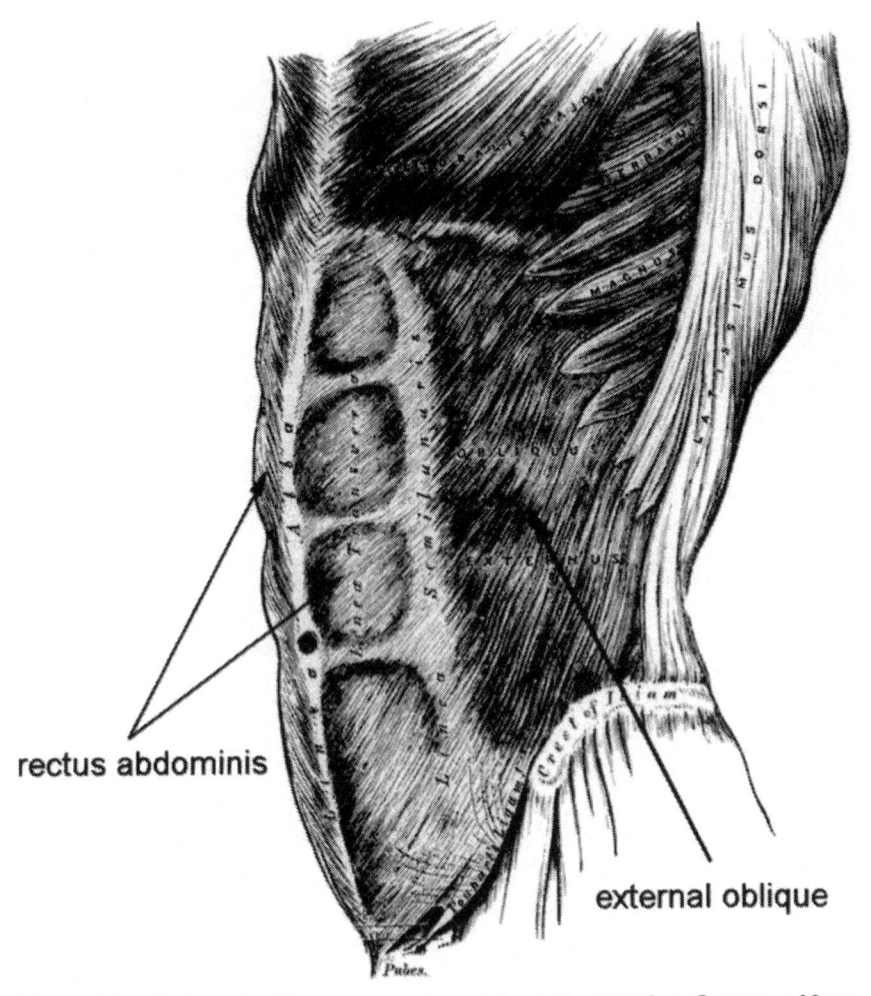

Figure 3.3. External oblique and rectus abdominis muscles. *Courtesy of Scott McCoy*

oriented with fibers that run horizontally. These four muscle pairs completely encase the abdominal region, holding your organs and digestive system in place while simultaneously helping you breathe.

Your expiratory muscles are quite large and can produce a great deal of pulmonary or air pressure. In fact, they easily can overpower the larynx. Healthy adults generally can generate more than twice the pressure that is required to produce even the loudest sounds; therefore, singers must develop a system for moderating and controlling airflow and breath pressure. This practice goes by many names, including breath support, breath control, and breath management, all of which rely on the principle of muscular antagonism. Muscles are said to have an antagonistic relationship when they work in opposing directions, usually pulling on a common point of attachment, for the sake of increasing stability or motor control. You can see a clear example of muscular antagonism in the relationship between your biceps (flexors) and triceps (extensors) when you hold out your arm. In breathing for singing, we activate inspiratory muscles (e.g., diaphragm and external intercostals) during exhalation to help control respiratory pressure and the rate at which air is expelled from the lungs.

One of the things you will notice when watching a variety of singers is that they tend to breathe in many different ways. You might think that voice teachers and scientists, who have been teaching and studying singing for hundreds, if not thousands of years, would have come to agreement on the best possible breathing technique. But for many reasons, this is not the case. For one, different musical and vocal styles place varying demands on breathing. For another, humans have a huge variety of body types, sizes, and morphologies. A breathing strategy that is successful for a tall, slender woman might be completely ineffective in a short, robust man. Our bodies actually contain a large number of muscles beyond those we've already discussed that are capable of assisting with respiration. For an example, consider your latissimi dorsi muscles. These large muscles of the arm enable us to do pull-ups (or pull-downs, depending on which exercise you perform) at the fitness center. But because they wrap around a large portion of the thorax, they also exert an expiratory force. We have at least two dozen such muscles that have secondary respiratory functions, some for exhalation and some for inhalation. When we consider all these possibilities, it is no surprise at all that there are many ways to breathe that can produce beautiful singing. Just remember to practice some muscular antagonism—maintaining a degree of inhalation posture during exhalation—and you should do well.

LARYNX: THE VIBRATOR OF YOUR VOICE

The larynx, sometimes known as the voice box or Adam's apple, is a complex physiologic structure made of cartilage, muscle, and tissue.

Biologically, it serves as a sphincter valve, closing off the airway to prevent foreign objects from entering the lungs. When firmly closed, it also is used to increase abdominal pressure to assist with lifting heavy objects, childbirth, and defecation. But if we gently close this valve while we exhale, tissue in the larynx begins to vibrate and produce the sounds that become speech and singing.

The human larynx is a remarkably small instrument, typically ranging from the size of a pecan to a walnut for women and men, respectively. Sound is produced at a location called the glottis, which is formed by two flaps of tissue called the vocal folds (aka vocal cords). In women, the glottis is about the size of a dime; in men, it can approach the diameter of a quarter. The two folds are always attached together at their front point but open in the shape of the letter V during normal breathing, an action called abduction. To phonate, we must close the V while we exhale, an action called adduction (just like the machines you use at the fitness center to exercise your thigh and chest muscles).

Phonation only is possible because of the unique multilayer structure of the vocal folds (figure 3.4). The core of each fold is formed by muscle,

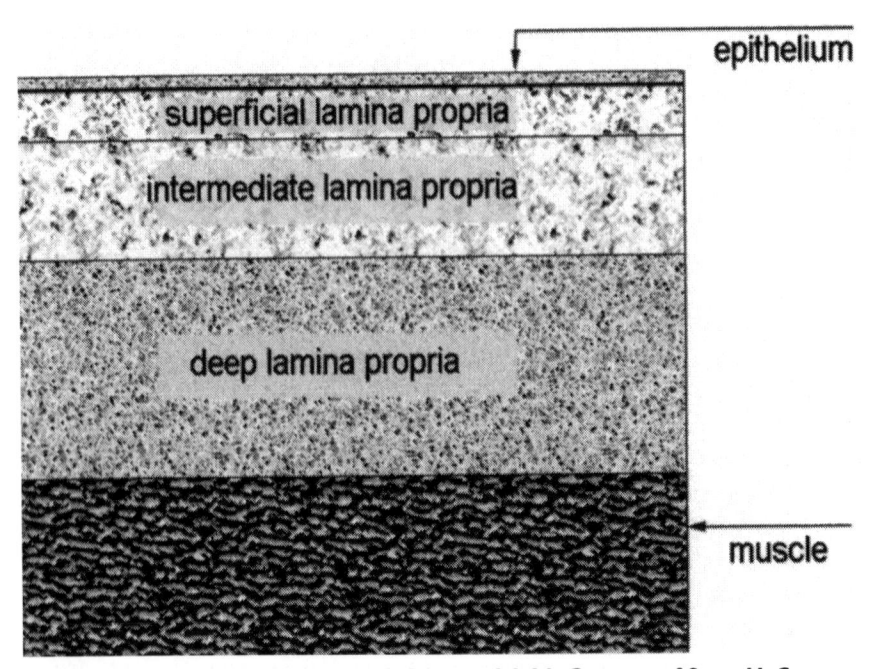

Figure 3.4. Layered structure of the vocal fold. *Courtesy of Scott McCoy*

which is surrounded by a layer of gelatinous material called the lamina propria. The vocal ligament also runs through the lamina propria, which helps to prevent injury by limiting how far the folds can be stretched for high pitches. A thin, hairless epithelial layer that is constantly kept moist with mucus secreted by the throat, larynx, and trachea surrounds all of this. During phonation, the outer layer of the fold glides independently over the inner layer in a wavelike motion, without which phonation is impossible.

We can use a simple demonstration to better understand the independence of the inner and outer portions of the folds. Explore the palm of your hand with your other index finger. Note that the skin is attached quite firmly to the flesh beneath it. If you poke at your palm, that flesh acts as padding, protecting the underlying bone. Now explore the back of your hand. You will observe that the skin is attached quite loosely—you easily can move it around with your finger. And if you poke at the back of your hand, it is likely to hurt; there is very little padding between the skin and your bones. Your vocal folds combine the best attributes of both sides of your hand. They provide sufficient padding to help reduce impact stress, while permitting the outer layer to slip like the skin on the back of your hand, enabling phonation to occur. When you are sick with laryngitis and lose your voice (a condition called aphonia), inflammation in the vocal folds couples the layers of the folds tightly together. The outer layer no longer can move independently over the inner, and phonation becomes difficult or impossible.

The vocal folds are located within the five cartilaginous structures of the larynx (figure 3.5). The largest is called the thyroid cartilage, which is shaped like a small shield. The thyroid connects to the cricoid cartilage below it, which is shaped like a signet ring—broad in the back and narrow in the front. Two cartilages that are shaped like squashed pyramids sit atop the cricoid, called the arytenoids. Each vocal fold runs from the thyroid cartilage in front to one of the arytenoids at the back. Finally, the epiglottis is located at the top of the larynx, flipping backward each time we swallow to prevent food and liquid from entering our lungs. Muscles connect between the various cartilages to open and close the glottis and to lengthen and shorten the vocal folds for ascending and descending pitch, respectively. Because they sometimes are used to identify vocal function, it is a good idea to know the names of the muscles

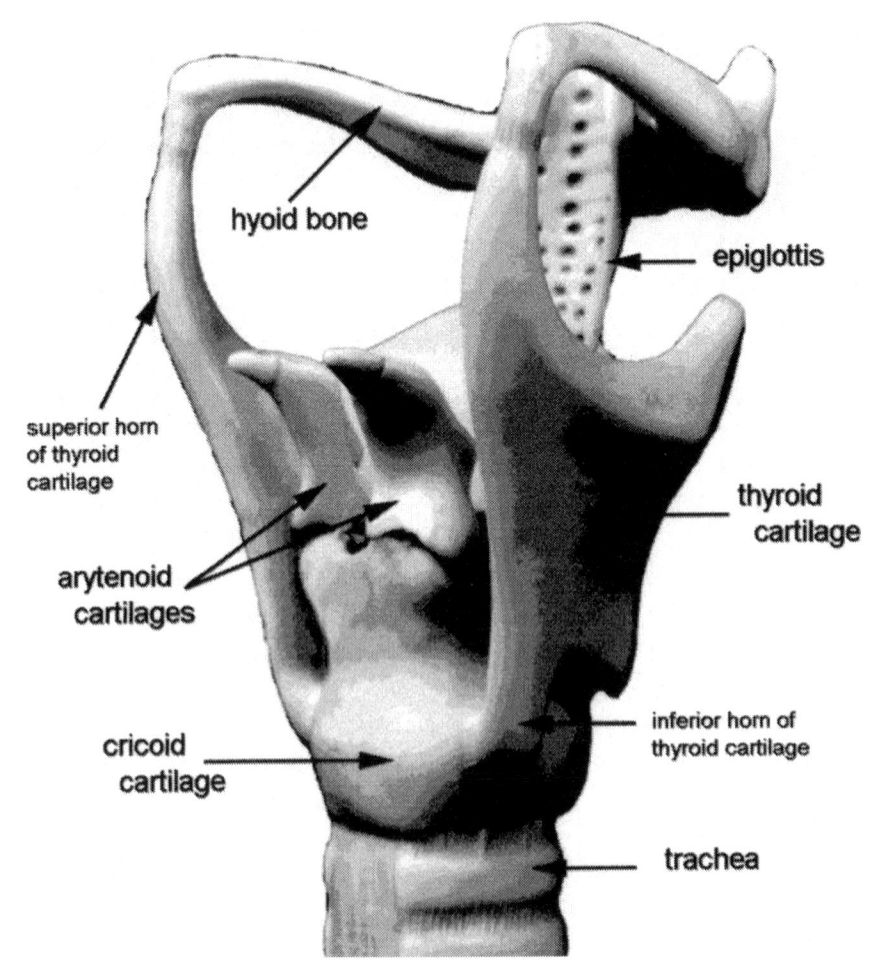

Figure 3.5. Cartilages of the larynx, viewed at an angle from the back.
Courtesy of Scott McCoy

that control the length of the folds. We've already mentioned that a muscle forms the core of each fold. Because it runs between the thyroid cartilage and an arytenoid, it is named the thyroarytenoid muscle (formerly known as the vocalis muscle). When the thyroarytenoid, or TA muscle, contracts, the fold is shortened and pitch goes down. The folds are elongated through the action of the cricothyroid, or CT muscles, which run from the thyroid to cricoid cartilage.

Vocal color (timbre) is created by the combined effects of the sound produced by the vocal folds and the resonance provided by the vocal

SINGING AND VOICE SCIENCE   43

tract. While these elements can never be completely separated, it is useful to consider the two primary modes of vocal fold vibration and their resulting sound qualities. The main differences are related to the relative thickness of the folds and their cross-sectional shape (figure 3.6). The first option depends on short, thick folds that come together with nearly square-shaped edges. Vibration in this configuration is given a variety of names, including mode 1, thyroarytenoid (TA) dominant, chest mode, or modal voice. The alternate configuration uses longer, thinner folds that only make contact at their upper margins. Common names include mode 2, cricothyroid (CT) dominant, falsetto mode, or loft voice. Singers vary the vibrational mode of the folds according to the quality of sound they wish to produce.

Before we move on to a discussion of resonance, we must consider the quality of the sound that is produced by the larynx. At the level of the glottis, we create a sound not unlike the annoying buzz of a duck call. That buzz, however, contains all the raw material we need to create speech and singing. Vocal or glottal sound is considered to be complex, meaning it consists of many simultaneously sounding frequencies (pitches). The lowest frequency within any tone is called the fundamental, which corresponds to its named pitch in the musical scale. Orchestras tune to a pitch called A-440, which means it has a frequency of 440 vibrations per second, or 440 Hertz (abbreviated Hz). Additional frequencies are included above the fundamental, which are called overtones. Overtones in the glottal sound are quieter than the fundamental. In voices, the overtones usually are whole number multiples of the fundamental, creating a pattern called the harmonic series (e.g., 100 Hz,

Glottis configuration
in mode 1 (chest voice)

Glottis configuration
in mode 2 (falsetto)

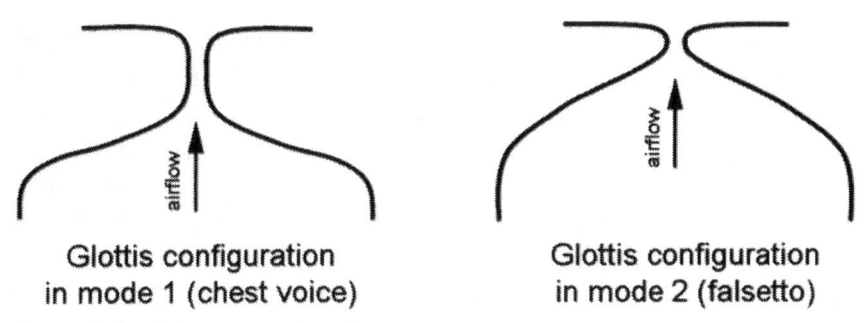

Figure 3.6. Primary modes of vocal fold vibration. *Courtesy of Scott McCoy*

200 Hz, 300 Hz, 400 Hz, 500 Hz, etc. or G2, G3, D4, G4, B4—note that pitches are named by the international system in which the lowest C of the piano keyboard is C1; middle-C therefore becomes C4, the fourth C of the keyboard) (figure 3.7).

Singers who choose to make coarse or rough sounds as might be appropriate for rock or blues often add overtones that are inharmonic, or not part of the standard numerical sequence. Inharmonic overtones also are common in singers with damaged or pathological voices.

Under most circumstances, we are completely unaware of the presence of overtones—they simply contribute to the overall timbre of a voice. In some vocal styles, however, harmonics become a dominant feature. This is especially true in throat singing or overtone singing, as is found in places like Tuva. Throat singers tune their vocal tracts so precisely that single harmonics are highlighted within the harmonic spectrum as a separate, whistle-like tone. These singers sustain a low-pitched drone and then create a melody by moving from tone to tone within the natural harmonic series. You can learn to do this too. Sustain a comfortable pitch in your range and slowly morph between the vowels [i] and [u]. If you listen carefully, you will hear individual harmonics pop out of your sound.

The mode of vocal fold vibration has a strong impact on the overtones that are produced. In mode 1, high-frequency harmonics are relatively strong; in mode 2, they are much weaker. As a result, mode 1 tends to yield a much brighter, brassier sound.

VOCAL TRACT: YOUR SOURCE OF RESONANCE

Resonance typically is defined as the amplification and enhancement (or enrichment) of musical sound through supplemental vibration. What does this really mean? In layman's terms, we could say that resonance makes instruments louder and more beautiful by reinforcing the original vibrations of the sound source. This enhancement occurs in two primary ways, which are known as forced and free resonance (there is nothing pejorative in these terms: free resonance is not superior to forced resonance). Any object that is physically connected to a vibrator can serve as a forced resonator. For a piano, the resonator is the soundboard (on the

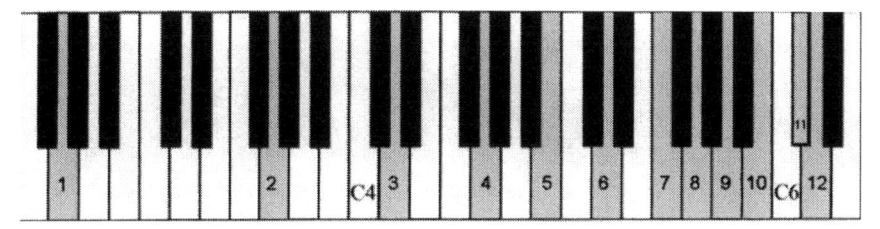

Figure 3.7. Natural harmonic series, beginning at G2. *Courtesy of Scott McCoy*

underside of a grand or on the back of an upright); the vibrations of the strings are transmitted directly to the soundboard through a structure known as the bridge, which also is found on violins and guitars. Forced resonance also plays a role in voice production. Place your hand on your chest and say [a] at a low pitch. You almost certainly felt the vibrations of forced resonance. In singing, this might best be considered your private resonance; you can feel it and it might impact your self-perception of sound, but nobody else can hear it. To understand why this is true, imagine what a violin would sound like if it were encased in a thick layer of foam rubber. The vibrations of the string would be damped out, muting the instrument. Your skin, muscles, and other tissues do the same thing to the vibrations of your vocal folds.

By contrast, free resonance occurs when sound travels through a hollow space, such as the inside of a trumpet, an organ pipe, or your vocal tract, which consists of the pharynx (throat), oral cavity (mouth), and nasal cavity (nose). As sound travels through these regions, a complex pattern of echoes is created; every time sound encounters a change in the shape of the vocal tract, some of its energy is reflected backward, much like an echo in a canyon. If these echoes arrive back at the glottis at the precise moment a new pulse of sound is created, the two elements synchronize, resulting in a significant increase in intensity. All of this happens very quickly—remember that sound is traveling through your vocal tract at more than seven hundred miles per hour.

Whenever this synchronization of the vocal tract and sound source occurs, we say that the system is in resonance. The phenomenon occurs at specific frequencies (pitches), which can be varied by changing the position of the tongue, lips, jaw, palate, and larynx. These resonant frequencies, or areas in which strong amplification occurs, are called formants. Formants provide the specific amplification that changes the raw, buzzing sound produced by your vocal folds into speech and singing. The vocal tract is capable of producing many formants, which are labeled sequentially by ascending pitch. The first two, F1 and F2, are used to create vowels; higher formants contribute to the overall timbre and individual characteristics of a voice. In some singers, especially those who train to sing in opera, formants three through five are clustered together to form a super formant, eponymously called the singer's formant, which creates a ringing sound and enables a voice to be heard in a large theater without electronic amplification.

Formants are vitally important in singing, but they can be a bit intimidating to understand. An analogy that works really well for me is to think of formants like the wind. You cannot see the wind, but you know it is present when you see leaves rustling in a tree or feel a breeze on your face. Formants work in the same manner. They are completely invisible and directly inaudible. But just as we see the rustling leaf, we can hear, and perhaps even feel, the action of formants through how they change our sound. Try a little experiment. Sing an ascending scale beginning at B♭3, sustaining the vowel [i]. As you approach the D♮ or E♭ of the scale, you likely will feel (and hear) that your sound becomes a bit stronger and easier to produce. This occurs because the scale tone and formant are on the same pitch, providing additional amplification. If you change to an [u] vowel, you will feel the same thing at about the same place in the scale. If you sing to an [o] or [e] and continue up the scale, you'll feel a bloom in the sound somewhere around C5 (an octave above middle C); [a] is likely to come into its best focus at about G5.

To remember the approximate pitches of the first formants for the main vowels, [i]-[e]-[a]-[o]-[u], just think of a C-major triad in first inversion, open position, starting at E4: [i] = E4, [e] = C5, [a] = G5, [o] = C5, and [u] = E4 (figure 3.8). If your music theory isn't strong, you could use the mnemonic "every child gets candy eagerly." These pitches might vary by as much as a minor third higher and lower but no farther: once a formant changes by more than that interval, the vowel that is produced must change.

Formants have absolutely no preference for what they amplify—they are indiscriminate lovers, just as happy to bond with the first harmonic as the fifth. When men or women sing low pitches, there almost always

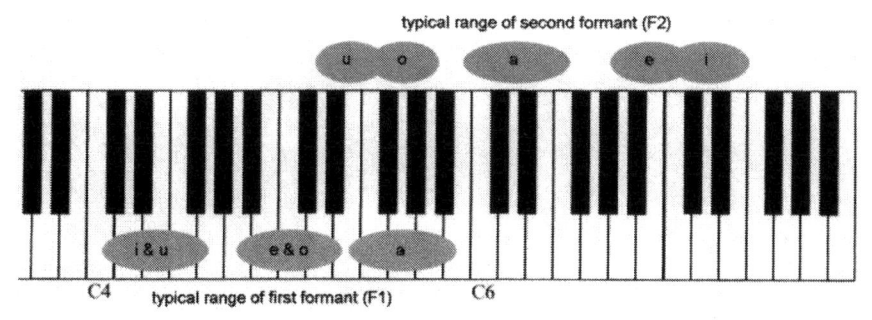

Figure 3.8. Typical range of first and second formants for primary vowels.
Courtesy of Scott McCoy

will be at least one harmonic that comes close enough to a formant to produce a clear vowel sound. The same is not true for women with high voices, especially sopranos, who routinely must sing pitches that have a fundamental frequency higher than the first formant of many vowels. Imagine what happens if she must sing the phrase "and I'll leave you forever," with the word "leave" set on a very high, climactic note. The audience won't be able to tell if she is singing *leave* or *love*; the two will sound identical. This happens because the formant that is required to identify the vowel [i] is too far below the pitch being sung. Even if she tries to sing *leave*, the sound that comes out of her mouth will be heard as some variation of [a].

Fortunately, this kind of mismatch between formants and musical pitches rarely causes problems for anyone but opera singers, choir sopranos, and perhaps ingénues in classic music theater shows. Almost everyone else generally sings low enough in their respective voice ranges to produce easily identifiable vowels.

Second formants also can be important, but more so for opera singers than everyone else. They are much higher in pitch, tracking the pattern [u] = E5, [o] = G5, [a] = D6, [e] = B6, [i] = D7 (you can use the mnemonic "every good dad buys diapers" to remember these pitches) (figure 3.8). Because they can extend so high, into the top octave of the piano keyboard for [i], they interact primarily with higher tones in the natural harmonic series. Unless you are striving to produce the loudest unamplified sound possible, you probably never need to worry about the second formant; it will steadfastly do its job of helping to produce vowel sounds without any conscious thought or manipulation on your part.

If you are interested in discovering more about resonance and how it impacts your voice, you might want to install a spectrum analyzer on your computer. Free (or inexpensive) programs are readily available for download over the Internet that will work with either a PC or Mac computer. You don't need any specialized hardware—if you can use Skype or FaceTime, you already have everything you need. Once you've installed something, simply start playing with it. Experiment with your voice to see exactly how the analysis signal changes when you change the way your voice sounds. You'll be able to see how harmonics change in intensity as they interact with your formants. If you sing with vibrato, you'll see how consistently you produce your variations in pitch and amplitude. You'll even be able to see if your tone is excessively nasal for the kind of singing you want to do. Other programs are available that will help you improve your intonation (how well you sing in tune) or enhance your basic musicianship skills. Technology truly has advanced sufficiently to help us sing more beautifully.

MOUTH, LIPS, AND TONGUE: YOUR ARTICULATORS

The articulatory life of a singer is not easy, especially when compared to the demands placed on other musicians. Like a pianist or brass player, we must be able to produce the entire spectrum of musical articulation, including dynamic levels from hushed pianissimos to thunderous fortes, short notes, long notes, accents, crescendos, diminuendos, and so on. We produce most of these articulations the same way instrumentalists do, which is by varying our power supply. But singers have another layer of articulation that makes everything much more complicated; we must produce these musical gestures while simultaneously singing words.

As we learned in our brief examination of formants, altering the resonance characteristics of the vocal tract creates the vowel sounds of language. We do this by changing the position of our tongue, jaw, lips, and sometimes palate. Slowly say the vowel pattern [i]-[e]-[a]-[o]-[u]. Can you feel how your tongue moves in your mouth? For [i], it is high in the front and low in the back, but it takes the opposite position for

[u]. Now slowly say the word Tuesday, noting all the places your tongue comes into contact with your teeth and palate and how it changes shape as you produce the vowels and diphthongs. There is a lot going on in there—no wonder it takes so long for babies to learn to speak!

Our articulatory anatomy is extraordinarily complex, in large part because our bodies use the same passageway for food, water, air, and sound. As a result, our tongue, larynx, throat, jaw, and palate are all interconnected with common physical and neurologic points of attachment. Our anatomical Union Station in this regard is a small structure called the hyoid bone. The hyoid is one of only three bones in your entire body that do not connect to other bones via a joint (the other two are your patellae, or kneecaps). This little bone is suspended below your jaw, freely floating up and down every time you swallow. It is a busy place, serving as the upper suspension point for the larynx, the connection for the root of the tongue, and the primary location of the muscles that open your mouth by dropping your jaw.

There is one more significant pitfall to the close proximity of all these articulators: tension in one area is easily passed along to another. If your jaw muscles are too tight while you sing, that hyperactivity will likely be transferred to the larynx and tongue—remember, they all are interconnected through the hyoid bone. It can be tricky to determine the primary offender in this kind of chain reaction of tension. A tight tongue could just as easily be making your jaw stiff, or an elevated, rigid larynx could make both tongue and jaw suffer.

Neurology complicates matters even further. You have sixteen muscles in your tongue, fourteen in your larynx, twenty-two in your throat and palate, and another sixteen that control your jaw. Many of these are very small and lie directly adjacent to each other, and you often are required to contract one quite strongly while its next-door neighbor must remain totally relaxed. Our brains need to develop laser-like control, sending signals at the right moment with the right intensity to the precise spot where they are needed. When we first start singing, these brain signals come more like a blast from a shotgun, spreading the neurologic impulse over a broad area to multiple muscles, not all of which are the intended target. Again, with practice and training, we learn to refine our control, enabling us to use only those muscles that will help, while disengaging those that would get in the way of our best singing.

FINAL THOUGHTS

This brief chapter has only scratched the surface of the huge field of voice science. To learn more, you might visit the websites of the National Association of Teachers of Singing (NATS), the Voice Foundation (TVF), or the National Center for Voice and Speech (NCVS). You can easily locate the appropriate addresses through any Internet search engine. Remember: knowledge is power. Occasionally, people are afraid that if they know more about the science of how they sing, they will become so analytical that all spontaneity will be lost or they will become paralyzed by too much information and thought. In my forty-plus years as a singer and teacher, I've never encountered somebody who actually suffered this fate. To the contrary, the more we know, the easier—and more joyful—singing becomes. ♪

4

VOCAL HEALTH FOR THE CONTEMPORARY COMMERCIAL MUSIC (CCM) SINGER

Wendy LeBorgne

GENERAL PHYSICAL WELL-BEING

All singers, regardless of genre, should consider themselves as "vocal athletes." The physical, emotional, and performance demands necessary for optimal output require that the artist consider training and maintaining their instrument as an athlete trains for an event. With increased vocal and performance demands, it is unlikely that a vocal athlete will have an entire performing career completely injury free. This may not be the fault of the singer, as many injuries occur due to circumstances beyond the singer's control such as singing through an illness or being on a new medication seemingly unrelated to the voice.

Vocal injury has often been considered taboo to talk about in the performing world as it has been considered to be the result of faulty technique or poor vocal habits. In actuality, the majority of vocal injuries presenting in the elite performing population tend to be overuse and/or acute injury. From a clinical perspective over the past seventeen years, younger, less experienced singers with fewer years of training (who tend to be quite talented) generally are the ones who present with issues related to technique or phonotrauma (nodules, edema, contact ulcers), while more mature singers with professional performing careers tend to present with acute injuries (hemorrhage) or overuse and misuse injuries (muscle tension dysphonia, edema, GERD) or injuries following an illness. There are no current studies documenting use and training in correlation to laryngeal pathologies. However, there are studies that document that somewhere between 35 percent and 100 percent of professional vocal athletes have abnormal vocal fold findings on stroboscopic evaluation. Many times these "abnormalities" are in singers who have no vocal complaints or symptoms of vocal problems. From a performance perspective, uniqueness in vocal quality often gets hired and perhaps a slight aberration in the way a given larynx functions may become quite marketable. Regardless of what the vocal folds may look like, the most integral part of performance is that the singer must maintain agility, flexibility, stamina, power, and inherent beauty (genre appropriate) for their current level of performance, taking into account physical, vocal, and emotional demands.

Unlike sports medicine and the exercise physiology literature where much is known about the types and nature of given sports injuries, there is no common parallel for the vocal athlete model. However, because the vocal athlete utilizes the body systems of alignment, respiration, phonation, and resonance with some similarities to physical athletes, a parallel protocol for vocal wellness may be implemented/considered for vocal athletes to maximize injury prevention knowledge for both the singer and teacher. This chapter aims to provide information on vocal wellness and injury prevention for the vocal athlete.

CONSIDERATIONS FOR WHOLE BODY WELLNESS

Nutrition

You have no doubt heard the saying "You are what you eat." Eating is a social and psychological event. For many people, food associations and eating have an emotional basis resulting in either overeating or being malnourished. Eating disorders in performers and body image issues may have major implications and consequences for the performer on both ends of the spectrum (obesity and anorexia). Singers should be encouraged to reprogram the brain and body to consider food as fuel. You want to use high-octane gas in your engine, as pouring water in your car's gas tank won't get you very far. Eating a poor diet or a diet that lacks appropriate nutritional value will have negative physical and vocal effects on the singer. Effects of poor dietary choices for the vocal athlete may result in physical and vocal effects ranging from fatigue to life-threatening disease over the course of a lifetime. Encouraging and engaging in healthy eating habits from a young age will potentially prevent long-term negative effects from poor nutritional choices. It is beyond the scope of this chapter to provide a complete overview of all the dietary guidelines for pediatrics, adolescents, adults, and the mature adult; however, a listing of additional references to help guide your food and beverage choices for making good nutritional choices can be found online at websites such as Dietary Guidelines for Americans, Nutrition. gov Guidelines for Tweens and Teens, and Fruits and Veggies Matter. See the online companion web page on the NATS website for links to these and other resources. ♪

Hydration

"Sing wet, pee pale." This phrase was echoed in the studio of Van Lawrence regarding how his students would know if they were well hydrated. Generally, this rule of pale urine during your waking hours is a good indicator that you are well hydrated. Medications, vitamins, and certain foods may alter urine color despite adequate hydration. Due to the varying levels of physical and vocal activity of many performers, in order to maintain adequate oral hydration, the use of a hydration calculator based on activity level may be a better choice. These hydration calculators are easily accessible online and take into account the amount and level of activity the performer engages in on a daily basis. In a recent study of the vocal habits of musical theater performers, one of the findings indicated a significantly underhydrated group of performers.[1]

Laryngeal and pharyngeal dryness as well as "thick, sticky mucus" are often complaints of singers. Combating these concerns and maintaining an adequate viscosity of mucus for performance has resulted in some research. As a reminder of laryngeal and swallowing anatomy, nothing that is swallowed (or gargled) goes over or touches the vocal folds directly (or one would choke). Therefore, nothing that a singer eats or drinks ever touches the vocal folds, and in order to adequately hydrate the mucous membranes of the vocal folds, one must consume enough fluids for the body to produce a thin mucus. Therefore, any "vocal" effects from swallowed products are limited to potential pharyngeal and oral changes, not the vocal folds themselves.

The effects of systemic hydration are well documented in the literature. There is evidence to suggest that adequate hydration will provide some protection of the laryngeal mucosal membranes when they are placed under increased collision forces as well as reducing the amount of effort (phonation threshold pressure) to produce voice. This is important for the singer because it means that with adequate hydration and consistency of mucus, the effort to produce voice is less and your vocal folds are better protected from injury. Imagine the friction and heat produced when two dry hands rub together and then what happens if you put lotion on your hands. The mechanisms in the larynx to provide appropriate mucus production are not fully understood, but there is enough evidence at this time to support oral hydration as a vital component of every singer's vocal health regime to maintain appropriate mucosal viscosity.

Although very rare, overhydration (hyperhidrosis) can result in dehydration and even illness or death. An overindulgence of fluids essentially makes the kidneys work "overtime" and flushes too much water out of the body. This excessive fluid loss in a rapid manner can be detrimental to the body.

In addition to drinking water to systemically monitor hydration, there are many nonregulated products on the market for performers that lay claim to improving the laryngeal environment (e.g., Entertainer's Secret, Throat Coat Tea, Greathers Pastilles, Slippery Elm, etc.). Although there may be little detriment in using these products, quantitative research documenting change in laryngeal mucosa is sparse. One study suggests that the use of Throat Coat when compared to a placebo treatment for pharyngitis did show a significant difference in decreasing the perception of sore throat.[2] Another study compared the use of Entertainer's Secret to two other nebulized agents and its effect on phonation threshold pressure (PTP).[3] There was no positive benefit in decreasing PTP with Entertainer's Secret.

Many singers use personal steam inhalers and/or room humidification to supplement oral hydration and aid in combating laryngeal dryness.

There are several considerations for singers who choose to use external means of adding moisture to the air they breathe. Personal steam inhalers are portable and can often be used backstage or in the hotel room for the traveling performer. Typically, water is placed in the steamer and the face is placed over the steam for inhalation. Because the mucus membranes of the larynx are composed of a saltwater solution, one study looked at the use of nebulized saline in comparison to plain water and its potential effects on effort or ease to sound production in classically trained sopranos.[4] Data suggested that perceived effort to produce voice was less in the saline group than the plain water group. This indicated that the singers who used the saltwater solution reported less effort to sing after breathing in the saltwater than singers who used plain water. The researchers hypothesized that because the body's mucus is not plain water (rather it is a saltwater—think about your tears), when you use plain water for steam inhalation, it may actually draw the salt from your own saliva, resulting in a dehydrating effect.

In addition to personal steamers, other options for air humidification come in varying sizes of humidifiers from room size to whole house humidifiers. When choosing between a warm air or cool mist humidifier, considerations include both personal preference and needs. One of the primary reasons warm mist humidifiers are not recommended for young children is due to the risk of burns from the heating element. Both the warm mist and cool air humidifiers act similarly in adding moisture to the environmental air. External air humidification may be beneficial and provide a level of comfort for many singers. Regular cleaning of the humidifier is vital to prevent bacteria and mold buildup. Also, depending on the hardness of the water, it is important to avoid mineral buildup on the device and distilled water may be recommended for some humidifiers.

For traveling performers who often stay in hotels, fly on airplanes, or are generally exposed to other dry-air environments, there are products on the market designed to help minimize drying effects. One such device is called a Humidflyer, which is a face mask designed with a filter to recycle the moisture of a person's own breath and replenish moisture on each breath cycle.

For dry nasal passages or to clear sinuses, many singers use Neti pots. Many singers use this homeopathic flushing of the nasal passages regularly. Research supports the use of a Neti pot as a part of allergy relief and chronic rhinosinusitis control when utilized properly, sometimes in combination with medical management.[5] Conversely, long-term use of nasal irrigation (without taking intermittent breaks from daily use) may result in washing out the "good" mucus of the nasal passages, which naturally help to rid the nose of infections. A study presented at the 2009 American College of Allergy, Asthma, and Immunology (ACAAI) annual scientific meeting reported that when a group of individuals who were using twice-daily nasal irrigation for one year discontinued using it, they had an increase in acute rhinosinusitis.[6]

Tea, Honey, and Gargle to Keep the Throat Healthy

Regarding the use of general teas (which many singers combine with honey or lemon), there is likely no harm in the use of decaffeinated tea (caffeine may cause systemic dryness). The warmth of the tea may provide a soothing sensation to the pharynx and the act of swallowing can be relaxing for the muscles of the throat. Honey has shown promising results as an effective cough suppressant in the pediatric population.[7] The dose of honey given to the children in the study was two teaspoons. Gargling with salt or apple cider vinegar and water are also popular home remedies for many singers with the uses being from soothing the throat to curing reflux. Gargling plain water has been shown to be efficacious in reducing the risk of contracting upper respiratory infections. I suggest that when gargling, the singer only "bubble" the water with air and avoid engaging the vocal folds in sound production. Saltwater as a gargle has long been touted as a sore throat remedy and can be traced back to 2700 BCE in China for treating gum disease. The science behind a saltwater rinse for everything from oral hygiene to sore throat is that salt (sodium chloride) may act as a natural analgesic (pain killer) and may also kill bacteria. Similar to the effects that not enough salt in the water may have on drawing the salt out of the tissue in the steam inhalation, if you oversaturate the water solution with excess salt and gargle it, it may act to draw water out of the oral mucosa, thus reducing inflammation.

Another popular home remedy reported by singers is the use of apple cider vinegar to help with everything from acid reflux to sore throats. Dating back to 3300 BCE, apple cider vinegar was reported as a medicinal remedy, and it became popular in the 1970s as a weight loss diet cocktail. Popular media reports apple cider vinegar can improve conditions from acne and arthritis to nosebleeds and varicose veins. Specific efficacy data regarding the beneficial nature of apple cider vinegar for the purpose of sore throat, pharyngeal inflammation, and/or reflux has not been reported in the literature at this time. Of the peer-reviewed studies found in the literature, one discussed possible esophageal erosion and inconsistency of actual product in tablet form.[8] Therefore, at this time, strong evidence supporting the use of apple cider vinegar is not published.

Medications and the Voice

Medications (over the counter, prescription, and herbal) may have resultant drying effects on the body and often the laryngeal mucosa. General classes of drugs with potential drying effects include: antidepressants, antihypertensives, diuretics, ADD/ADHD medications, some oral acne medications, hormones, allergy drugs, and vitamin C in high doses. The National Center for Voice and Speech (NCVS) provides a listing of some common medications with potential voice side effects including laryngeal dryness. This listing does not take into account all medications, so singers should always ask their pharmacist about the potential side effects of a given medication. Due to the significant number of drugs on the market, it is safe to say that most pharmacists will not be acutely aware of "vocal side effects," but if dryness is listed as a potential side effect of the drug, you may assume that all body systems could be affected. Under no circumstances should you stop taking a prescribed medication without consulting your physician first. As every person has a different body chemistry and reaction to medication, just because a medication lists dryness as a potential side effect, it does not necessarily mean you will experience that side effect. Conversely, if you begin a new medication and notice physical or vocal changes that are unexpected, you should consult with your physician. Ultimately, the goal of medical management for any condition is to achieve the most benefits with the least side effects. Please see the companion page on the NATS website for a list of possible resources for the singer regarding prescription drugs and herbs. ♪

In contrast to medications that tend to dry, there are medications formulated to increase saliva production or alter the viscosity of mucus. Medically, these drugs are often used to treat patients who have had a loss of saliva production due to surgery or radiation. Mucolytic agents are used to thin secretions as needed. As a singer, if you feel that you need to use a mucolytic agent on a consistent basis, it may be worth considering getting to the root of the laryngeal dryness symptom and seeking a professional opinion from an otolaryngologist.

Reflux and the Voice

Gastroesophageal reflux (GERD) and/or laryngopharyngeal reflux (LPR) can have a devastating impact on the singer if not recognized and treated appropriately. Although GERD and LPR are related, they are considered as slightly different diseases. GERD (Latin root meaning "flowing back") is the reflux of digestive enzymes, acids, and other stomach contents into the esophagus (food pipe). If this backflow is propelled through the upper esophagus and into the throat (larynx and pharynx), it is referred to as LPR. It is not uncommon to have both GERD and LPR, but they can occur independently.

More frequently, people with GERD have decreased esophageal clearing. Esophagitis, or inflammation of the esophagus, is also associated with GERD. People with GERD often feel heartburn. LPR symptoms are often "silent" and do not include heartburn. Specific symptoms of LPR may include some or all of the following: lump in the throat sensation, feeling of constant need to clear the throat/postnasal drip, longer vocal warm-up time, quicker vocal fatigue, loss of high frequency range, worse voice in the morning, sore throat, and bitter/raw/brackish taste in the mouth. If you experience these symptoms on a regular basis, it is advised that you consider a medical consultation for your symptoms. Prolonged, untreated GERD or LPR can lead to permanent changes in both the esophagus and/or larynx. Untreated LPR also provides a laryngeal environment that is conducive for vocal fold lesions to occur as it inhibits normal healing mechanisms.

Treatment of LPR and GERD generally includes both dietary and lifestyle modifications in addition to medical management. Some of the dietary recommendations include: elimination of caffeinated and carbonated beverages, smoking cessation, no alcohol use, and limiting tomatoes, acidic foods and drinks, and raw onions or peppers, to name a few. Also, avoidance of high-fat foods is recommended. From a lifestyle perspective, suggested changes include not eating within three hours of lying down, eating small meals frequently (instead of large meals), elevating the head of your bed, avoiding tight clothing around the belly, and not bending over or exercising too soon after you eat.

Reflux medications fall in three general categories: antacids, H2 blockers, and proton pump inhibitors (PPI). There are now combination drugs that include both an H2 blocker and proton pump inhibitor. Every medication has both associated risks and benefits, and singers should be aware of the possible benefits and side effects of the medications they take. In general terms, antacids (e.g., Tums, Mylanta, Gaviscon) neutralize stomach acid. H2 (histamine) blockers, such as Axid (nizatidine), Tagamet (cimetidine), Pepcid (famotidine), and Zantac (ranitidine), work to decrease acid production in the stomach by preventing histamine from triggering the H2 receptors to produce more acid. Then there are the PPIs: Nexium (esomeprazole), Prevacid (lansoprazole), Protonix (pantoprazole), AcipHex (rabeprazole), Prilosec (omeprazole), and Dexilant (dexlansoprazole). PPIs act as a last line of defense to decrease acid production by blocking the last step in gastric juice secretion. Some of the most recent drugs to combat GERD/LPR are combination drugs (e.g., Zegrid [sodium bicarbonate plus omeprazole]), which provide a short-acting response (sodium bicarbonate) and a long release (omeprazole). Because some singers prefer a holistic approach to reflux management, strict dietary and lifestyle compliance is recommended and consultation with both your primary care physician and naturopath are warranted in that situation. Efficacy data on nonregulated herbs, vitamins, and supplements is limited, but some data does exist.

Physical Exercise

Vocal athletes, like other physical athletes, should consider how and what they do to maintain both cardiovascular fitness and muscular strength. In today's performance culture, it is rare that a performer stands still and sings, unless in a recital or choral setting. The range of physical activity can vary from light movement to high-intensity choreography with acrobatics. As performers are being required to increase their on-stage physical activity level from the operatic stage to the pop-star arena, overall physical fitness is imperative to avoid compromise in the vocal system. Breathlessness will result in compensation by the larynx, which is now attempting to regulate the air. Compensatory vocal behaviors over time may result in a change in vocal performance. The health benefits of both cardiovascular training and strength training are well documented for physical athletes but relatively rare in the literature for vocal performers.

Mental Wellness

Vocal performers must maintain a mental focus during performance and a mental toughness during auditioning and training. Rarely during vocal performance training programs is this important aspect of performance addressed, and it is often left to the individual performer to develop their own strategy or coping mechanism. Yet, many performers are on antianxiety or antidepressant drugs (which may be the direct result of performance-related issues). If the sports world is again used as a parallel for mental toughness, there are no elite-level athletes (and few junior-level athletes) who don't utilize the services of a performance/sports psychologist to maximize focus and performance. I recommend that performers consider the potential benefits of a performance psychologist to help maximize vocal performance. Several references that may be of interest to the singer include: Joanna Cazden's *Visualization for Singers* (1992) and Shirlee Emmons and Alma Thomas's *Power Performance for Singers: Transcending the Barriers* (1998). ♪

Unlike instrumentalists, whose performance is dependent on accurate playing of an external musical instrument, the singer's instrument is uniquely intact and subject to the emotional confines of the brain and body in which it is housed. Musical performance anxiety (MPA) can be career threatening for all musicians, but perhaps the vocal athlete is more severely impacted. The majority of literature on MPA is dedicated to instrumentalists, but the basis of definition, performance effects, and treatment options can be considered for vocal athletes. Fear is a natural reaction to a stressful situation, and there is a fine line between emotional excitation and perceived threat (real or imagined). The job of a performer is to convey to an audience through vocal production, physical gestures, and facial expression a most heightened state of emotion. Otherwise, why would audience members pay top dollar to sit for two or three hours for a mundane experience? Not only is there the emotional conveyance of the performance, but also the internal turmoil often experienced by the singers themselves in preparation for elite performance. It is well documented in the literature that even the most elite performers have experienced debilitating performance anxiety. MPA is defined on a continuum with anxiety levels ranging from low to high and has been reported to comprise four distinct components: affect, cognition, behavior, and physiology. Affect comprises feelings (e.g., doom, panic, anxiety). Affected cognition will result in altered levels of concentration, while the behavior component results in postural shifts, quivering, and trembling. Finally physiologically the body's autonomic nervous system (ANS) will activate, resulting in the "fight or flight" response.

In recent years, researchers have been able to define two distinct neurological pathways for MPA. The first pathway happens quickly and without conscious input (ANS), resulting in the same fear stimulus as if a person were put into an emergent, life-threatening situation. In those situations, the brain releases adrenaline, resulting in physical changes of increased heart rate, increased respiration, shaking, pale skin, dilated pupils, slowed digestion, bladder relaxation, dry mouth, and dry eyes, all of which severely affect vocal performance. The second pathway that has been identified results in a conscious identification of the fear/threat and a much slower physiologic response. With the second neuromotor response, the performer has a chance to recognize the fear, process how to deal with the fear, and respond accordingly.

Treatment modalities to address MPA include psycho-behavioral therapy (including biofeedback) and drug therapies. Elite physical performance athletes have been shown to benefit from visualization techniques and psychological readiness training, yet within the performing arts community, stage fright may be considered a weakness or character flaw precluding readiness for professional performance. On the contrary, vocal athletes, like physical athletes, should mentally prepare themselves for optimal competition (auditions) and performance. Learning to convey emotion without eliciting an internal emotional response by the vocal athlete may take the skill of an experienced psychologist to help change ingrained neural pathways. Ultimately, control and understanding of MPA will enhance performance and prepare the vocal athlete for the most intense performance demands without vocal compromise.

VOCAL WELLNESS: INJURY PREVENTION

In order to prevent vocal injury and understand vocal wellness in the singer, general knowledge of common causes of voice disorders is imperative. One common cause of voice disorders is vocally abusive behaviors or misuse of the voice to include phonotraumatic behaviors such as yelling, screaming, loud talking, talking over noise, throat clearing, coughing, harsh sneezing, and boisterous laughing. Chronic or less than optimal vocal properties such as poor breathing techniques, inappropriate phonatory habits during conversational speech (glottal fry, hard glottal attacks), inapt pitch, loudness, rate of speech, and/or hyperfunctional laryngeal-area muscle tone may also negatively impact vocal function. Medically related etiologies, which also have the potential to impact vocal function, range from untreated chronic allergies and sinusitis to endocrine dysfunction and hormonal imbalance. Direct trauma, such as a blow to the neck or the risk of vocal fold damage during intubation, can impact optimal performance in vocal athletes depending on the nature and extent of the trauma. Finally, external irritants ranging from cigarette smoke to reflux directly impact the laryngeal mucosa and ultimately can lead to laryngeal pathology.

Vocal hygiene education and compliance may be one of the primary essential components for maintaining the voice throughout a career. This section will provide the singer with information on prevention of vocal injury. However, just like a professional sports athlete, it is unlikely that a professional vocal athlete will go through an entire career without some compromise in vocal function. This may be a common upper respiratory infection that creates vocal fold swelling for a short time, or it may be a "vocal accident" that is career threatening. Regardless, the knowledge of how to take care of your voice is essential for any vocal athlete.

Train Like an Athlete for Vocal Longevity

Performers seek instant gratification in performance sometimes at the cost of gradual vocal building for a lifetime of healthy singing. Historically, voice pedagogues required their students to perform vocalises exclusively for up to two years before beginning any song literature. Singers gradually built their voices by ingraining appropriate muscle memory and neuromotor patterns through development of aesthetically pleasing tones, onsets, breath management, and support. There was an intensive master-apprentice relationship and rigorous vocal guidelines to maintain a place within a given studio. Time off was taken if a vocal injury ensued or careers potentially were ended, and students were asked to leave a given singing studio if their voices were unable to withstand the rigors of training. Training vocal athletes today has evolved and appears driven to create a "product" quickly, perhaps at the expense of the longevity of the singer. Pop stars emerging well before puberty are doing international concert tours, yet many young artist programs in the classical arena do not consider singers for their programs until they are in their mid- to late twenties.

Each vocal genre presents with different standards and vocal demands. Therefore, the amount and degree of vocal training are varied. Some would argue that performing extensively without adequate vocal training and development is ill-advised, yet singers today are thrust onto the stage at very young ages. Dancers, instrumentalists, and physical athletes all spend many hours per day developing muscle strength, memory, and proper technique for their craft. The more advanced the artist or athlete, generally the more specific the training protocol becomes. Consideration of training vocal athletes in this same fashion is recommended. One would generally not begin a young, inexperienced singer on a Wagner aria without previous vocal training. Similarly, in nonclassical vocal music, there are easy, moderate, and difficult pieces to consider pending level of vocal development and training.

Basic pedagogical training of alignment, breathing, voice production, and resonance are essential building blocks for development of good voice production. Muscle memory and development of appropriate muscle patterns happen slowly over time with appropriate repetitive practice. Doing too much, too soon for any athlete (physical or vocal) will result in an increased risk for injury. When the singer is being asked to do "vocal gymnastics," they must be sure to have a solid basis of strength and stamina in the appropriate muscle groups to perform consistently with minimal risk of injury.

Vocal Fitness Program

One generally does not get out of bed first thing in the morning and try to do a split. Yet many singers go directly into a practice session or audition without proper warm-up. Think of your larynx like your knee, made up of cartilage, ligaments, and muscles. Vocal health is dependent upon appropriate warm-ups (to get things moving), drills for technique, and then cooldowns (at the end of your day). Consider vocal warm-ups a "gentle stretch." Depending on the needs of the singer, warm-ups should include physical stretching; postural alignment self-checks; breathing exercises to promote rib cage, abdominal, and back expansion; vocal stretches (glides up to stretch the vocal folds and glides down to contract the vocal folds); articulatory stretches (yawning, facial stretches); and mental warm-ups (to provide focus for the task at hand). Vocalises, in my opinion, are designed as exercises to go beyond warm-ups and prepare the body and voice for the technical and vocal challenges of the music they sing. They are varied and address the technical level and genre of the singer to maximize performance and vocal growth. Cooldowns are a part of most athletes' workouts. However, singers often do not use cooldowns (physical, mental, and vocal) at the end of a performance. A recent study looked specifically at the benefits of vocal cooldowns in singers and found that singers who used a vocal cooldown had decreased effort to produce voice the next day.[9]

Systemic hydration as a means to keep the vocal folds adequately lubricated for the amount of impact and friction that they will undergo has been previously discussed in this chapter. Compliance with adequate oral hydration recommendations is important, and subsequently so is the minimization of agents that could potentially dry the membranes (e.g., caffeine, medications, dry air). The body produces approximately two quarts of mucus per day. If not adequately hydrated, the mucus tends to be thick and sticky. Poor hydration is similar to not putting enough oil in the car engine. Frankly, if the gears do not work as well, there is increased friction and heat, and the engine is not efficient.

Speak Well, Sing Well

Optimize the speaking voice utilizing ideal frequency range, breath, intensity, rate, and resonance. Singers generally are vocally enthusiastic individuals who talk a lot and often talk loudly. During typical conversation, the average fundamental speaking frequency (times per second the vocal folds are impacting) for a male varies from 100 to 150 Hz and 180 to 230 Hz for women. Because of the delicate structure of the vocal folds and the importance of the layered microstructure vibrating efficiently and effectively to produce voice, vocal behaviors or outside factors that compromise the integrity of the vibration patterns of the vocal folds may be considered phonotrauma.

Phonotraumatic behaviors can include yelling, screaming, loud talking, harsh sneezing, and harsh laughing. Elimination of phonotraumatic behaviors is essential for good vocal health. The louder one speaks, the farther apart the vocal folds move from midline, the harder they impact, and the longer they stay closed. A tangible example would be to take your hands, move them only six inches apart, and clap as hard and as loudly as you can for ten seconds. Now, move your hands two feet apart and clap as hard, loudly, and quickly as possible for ten seconds. The farther apart your hands are, the more air you move and the louder the clap, and the skin on the hands becomes red and ultimately swollen (if you do it long enough and hard enough). This is what happens to the vocal folds with repeated impact at increased vocal intensities. The vocal folds are approximately 17 mm in length and vibrate at 220 times per second on A3, 440 on A4, 880 on A5, and more than 1,000 per second when singing a high C. That is a lot of impact for little muscles. Consider this fact when singing loudly or in a high tessitura for prolonged periods of time. It becomes easy to see why women are more prone than men to laryngeal impact injuries due to the frequency range of the voice alone.

In addition to the amount of cycles per second (cps) the vocal folds are impacting, singers need to be aware of their vocal intensity (volume). One should be aware of the volume of the speaking and singing voice and consider using a distance of three to five feet (about an arm's-length distance) as a gauge for how loud to be in general conversation. Using cell phones and speaking on a Bluetooth device in a car generally results in greater vocal intensity than normal, and singers are advised to minimize unnecessary use of these devices.

Singers should be encouraged to take "vocal naps" during their day. A vocal nap would be a short period of time (five minutes to an hour) of complete silence. Although the vocal folds are rarely completely still (because they move when you swallow and breathe), a vocal nap minimizes impact and vibration for a short window of time. A physical nap can also be refreshing for the singer mentally and physically.

Avoid Environmental Irritants: Alcohol, Smoking, Drugs

Arming singers with information on the actual effects of environmental irritants so that they can make informed choices on engaging in exposure to these potential toxins is essential. The glamour that continues to be associated with smoking, drinking, and drugs can be tempered with the deaths of popular stars such as Amy Winehouse and Cory Monteith who engaged in life-ending choices. There is extensive documentation about the long-term effects of toxic and carcinogenic substances, but here are a few key facts to consider when choosing whether to partake.

Alcohol, although it does not go over the vocal folds directly, does have a systemic drying effect. Due to the acidity in alcohol, it may increase the likelihood of reflux, resulting in hoarseness and other laryngeal pathologies. Consuming alcohol generally decreases one's inhibitions, and therefore you are more likely to sing and do things that you would not typically do under the influence of alcohol.

Beyond the carcinogens in nicotine and tobacco, the heat at which a cigarette burns is well above the boiling temperature of water (water boils at 212°F; cigarettes burn at over 1400°F). No one would consider pouring a pot of boiling water on their hand, and yet the burning temperature for a cigarette results in significant heat over the oral mucosa and vocal folds. The heat alone can create a deterioration in the lining, resulting in polypoid degeneration. Obviously, cigarette smoking has been well documented as a cause for laryngeal cancer.

Marijuana and other street drugs are not only addictive but can cause permanent mucosal lining changes depending on the drug used and the method of delivery. If you or one of your singer colleagues is experiencing a drug or alcohol problem, research or provide information and support on getting appropriate counseling and help.

SMART PRACTICE STRATEGIES FOR SKILL DEVELOPMENT AND VOICE CONSERVATION

Daily practice and drills for skill acquisition are an important part of any singer's training. However, overpracticing or inefficient practicing may be detrimental to the voice. Consider practice sessions of athletes: they may practice four to eight hours per day broken into one- to two-hour training sessions with a period of rest and recovery in between sessions. Although we cannot parallel the sports model without adequate evidence in the vocal athlete, the premise of short, intense, focused practice sessions is logical for the singer. Similar to physical exercise, it is suggested that practice sessions do not have to be all "singing." Rather, structuring sessions so that one-third of the session is spent on warm-up; one-third on vocalises, text work, rhythms, character development, and so on; and one-third on repertoire will allow the singer to function in a more efficient vocal manner. Building the amount of time per practice session—increasing duration by five minutes per week, building to sixty to ninety minutes—may be effective (e.g., Week 1: twenty minutes three times per day; Week 2: twenty-five minutes three times per day, etc.).

Vary the "vocal workout" during your week. For example, if you do the same physical exercise in the same way day after day with the same intensity and pattern, you will likely experience repetitive strain–type injuries. However, cross-training or varying the type and level of exercise aids in injury prevention. So when planning your practice sessions for a given week (or rehearsal process for a given role), consider varying your vocal intensity, tessitura, and exercises to maximize your training sessions, building stamina, muscle memory, and skill acquisition. For example, one day you may spend more time on learning rhythms and translation and the next day you spend thirty minutes performing coloratura exercises to prepare for a specific role. Take one day a week off from vocal training and give your voice a break. This does not mean complete vocal rest (although some singers find this beneficial), but rather a day without singing and limited talking.

Practice Your Mental Focus

Mental wellness and stress management are equally as important as vocal training for vocal athletes. Addressing any mental health issues is paramount to developing the vocal artist. This may include anything from daily mental exercises/meditation/focus to overcoming performance anxiety to more serious mental health issues/illness. Every person can benefit from improved focus and mental acuity.

SPECIFIC VOCAL WELLNESS CONCERNS FOR CCM SINGERS

General vocal wellness guidelines for all singers hold true for the CCM singer. Because CCM singing encompass styles from hip-hop, rap, jazz, R&B, and country to Broadway musicals (and everything in between), there is potential increased need for attention to vocal health and wellness in the CCM artist. There are a multitude of studies discussing the vocal health and wellness of artists that fall within varying categories of CCM. It is often the slightly abnormal and sometimes pathologic voice that gets hired within the CCM market because of the unique vocal quality. Vocal wellness with a pathologic or abnormal voice includes maintaining flexibility, agility, stamina, power, and consistent performance to meet market demands. If any of the above elements are compromised, the CCM artist is no longer functioning in a vocally healthy manner. Contemporary commercial music singers may or may not have formal vocal training but are required to keep vocally demanding and extensive performing and recording schedules often while touring and/or sleeping in hotels, buses, planes, and trains.

Vocal Wellness Tips for the CCM Artist

For the CCM artist, the most common presentation in my voice clinic relates to vocal fatigue, acute vocal injury, and loss of high frequency range. Vocal fatigue complaints are generally related to the duration of their rehearsals, recording sessions, "meet and greets," and performances; vocal gymnastics; general lack of sleep; and the vocal requirements to traverse their entire range (and occasionally outside of physiological comfort range). Depending on the genre performed, CCM singing includes a high vocal load with the associated risk of repetitive strain and increased collision force injuries. Acute vocal injuries within this population include phonotraumatic lesions (hemorrhages, vocal fold polyps, vocal fold nodules, reflux, and general vocal fold edema/erythema). Often these are not injuries related to problematic vocal technique but rather due to "vocal accidents" and/or overuse (due to required performance/contract demands). CCM singers are required to connect with the audience from a vocal and emotional standpoint. Physical performance demands—dependent on the subgenre within CCM—may be extreme and at times highly cardiovascular and/or acrobatic. Both physical and vocal fitness should be foremost in the minds of anyone desiring to perform CCM music today, and these singers should be physically and vocally in shape to meet the necessary performance demands.

Performance of CCM music requires that the singer has a flexible, agile, and dynamic instrument with appropriate stamina. The singer must have a good command of their instrument as well as exceptional underlying intention to what they are singing as it is about relaying a message, characteristic sound, and connecting with the audience. The singers that perform CCM must reflect the mood and intent of the composer, requiring dynamic control, vocal control/power, and an emotional connection to the text.

All commercial music singers use microphones and personal amplification to their maximal capacity. If used correctly, amplification can be used to maximize vocal health by allowing the singer to produce voice in an efficient manner while the sound engineer is effectively able to mix, amplify, and add effects to the voice. Understanding both the utility and limits of a given microphone and sound system is essential for the singer both for live and studio performances. Using an appropriate microphone can not only enhance the singer's performance, but can also reduce vocal load. Emotional extremes (intimacy and exultation) can be enhanced by appropriate microphone choice, placement, and acoustical mixing, thus saving the singer's voice.

Not everything a singer does is "vocally healthy," sometimes because the emotional expression may be so intense that it results in vocal collision forces that are extreme. Even if the singer does not have formal vocal training, the concept of "vocal cross-training"—which can mean singing in both high and low registers with varying intensities and resonance options—before and after practice sessions and services is likely a vital component to minimizing vocal injury.

FINAL THOUGHTS

Ultimately, the singer must learn to provide the most output with the least "cost" to the system. Taking care of the physical instrument through daily physical exercise, adequate nutrition and hydration, and focused attention on performance will provide a necessary basis for vocal health during performance. Small doses of high-intensity singing (or speaking) will limit impact stress on the vocal folds. Finally, attention to the mind, body, and voice will provide the singer with an awareness when something is wrong. This awareness and knowledge of when to rest or seek help will promote vocal well-being for the singer throughout his or her career.

NOTES

1. W. LeBorgne et al., "Prevalence of Vocal Pathology in Incoming Freshman Musical Theatre Majors: A 10-year Retrospective Study," Fall Voice Conference, New York, 2012.

2. J. Brinckmann et al., "Safety and Efficacy of a Traditional Herbal Medicine (Throat Coat) in Symptomatic Temporary Relief of Pain in Patients with Acute Pharyngitis: A Multicenter, Prospective, Randomized, Double-Blinded, Placebo-Controlled Study," *Journal of Alternative and Complementary Medicine* 9, no. 2 (2003): 285–98.

3. N. Roy et al., "An Evaluation of the Effects of Three Laryngeal Lubricants on Phonation Threshold Pressure (PTP)," *Journal of Voice* 17, no. 3 (2003): 331–42.

4. K. Tanner et al., "Nebulized Isotonic Saline versus Water Following a Laryngeal Desiccation Challenge in Classically Trained Sopranos," *Journal of Speech Language and Hearing Research* 53, no. 6 (2010): 1555–66.

5. C. Brown and S. Graham, "Nasal Irrigations: Good or Bad?" *Current Opinion in Otolaryngology, Head and Neck Surgery* 12, no. 1 (2004): 9–13.

6. T. Nsouli, "Long-Term Use of Nasal Saline Irrigation: Harmful or Helpful?" American College of Allergy, Asthma and Immunology Annual Scientific Meeting, Abstract 32, 2009.

7. M. Shadkam et al., "A Comparison of the Effect of Honey, Dextromethorphan, and Diphenhydramine on Nightly Cough and Sleep Quality in Children and Their Parents," *Journal of Alternative and Complementary Medicine* 16, no. 7 (2010): 787–93.

8. L. Hill et al., "Esophageal Injury by Apple Cider Vinegar Tablets and Subsequent Evaluation of Products," *Journal of the American Dietetic Association* 105, no. 7 (2005): 1141–44.

9. R. O. Gottliebson, "The Efficacy of Cooldown Exercises in the Practice Regimen of Elite Singers," PhD dissertation, University of Cincinnati, 2011.

USING AUDIO ENHANCEMENT TECHNOLOGY

Matthew Edwards

In the early days of popular music, musicians performed without electronic amplification. Singers learned to project their voices in the tradition of vaudeville performers with a technique similar to operatic and operetta performers who had been singing unamplified for centuries. When microphones began appearing on stage in the 1930s, vocal performance changed forever since the loudness of a voice was no longer a factor in the success of a performer. In order to be successful, all a singer needed was an interesting vocal quality and an emotional connection to what he or she was singing. The microphone would take care of projection.[1]

Vocal qualities that may sound weak without a microphone can sound strong and projected when sung with one. At the same time, a singer with a voice that is acoustically beautiful and powerful can sound harsh and pushed if he or she lacks microphone technique. Understanding how to use audio equipment to get the sounds a singer desires without harming the voice is crucial. The information in this chapter will help the reader gain a basic knowledge of terminology and equipment commonly used when amplifying or recording a vocalist as well as provide tips for singing with a microphone.

THE FUNDAMENTALS OF SOUND

In order to understand how to manipulate an audio signal, you must first understand a few basics of sound including frequency, amplitude, harmonics, and resonance.

Frequency

Sound travels in waves of compression and rarefaction within a medium, which for our purposes is air (see figure 5.1). These waves travel through the air and into our inner ears via the ear canal. There they are converted via the eardrums into nerve impulses that are transmitted to the brain and interpreted as sound. The number of waves per second is measured in Hertz (Hz), which gives us the frequency of the sound that we have learned to perceive as pitch. For example, we hear 440 Hz (440 cycles of compression and rarefaction per second) as A4, the pitch A above middle C.

Amplitude

The magnitude of the waves of compression and rarefaction determines the amplitude of the sound, which we call its "volume." The larger the waves of compression and rarefaction, the louder we perceive the sound to be. Measured in decibels (dB), amplitude represents changes in air pressure from the baseline. Decibel measurements range from zero decibels (0 dB), the threshold of human hearing, to 130 dB, the upper edge of the threshold of pain.

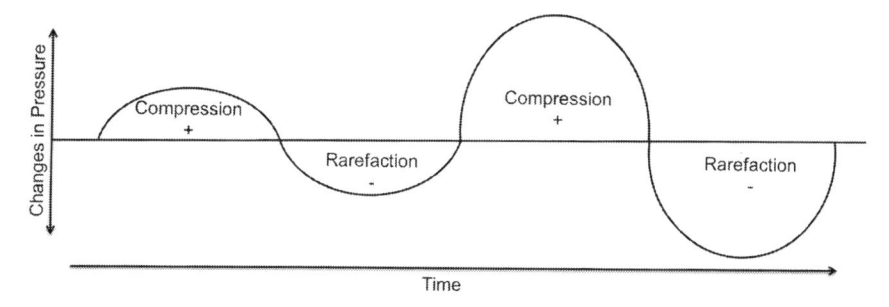

Figure 5.1. Compression and rarefaction. *Creative Commons*

Harmonics

The vibrating mechanism of an instrument produces the vibrations necessary to establish pitch (the fundamental frequency). The vibrating mechanism for a singer is the vocal folds. If an acoustic instrument, such as the voice, were to produce a note with the fundamental frequency alone, the sound would be strident and mechanical like the emergency alert signal used on television. Pitches played on acoustic instruments consist of multiple frequencies, called overtones, which are emitted from the vibrator along with the fundamental frequency. For the purposes of this chapter, the overtones that we are interested in are called harmonics. Harmonics are whole number multiples of the fundamental frequency. For example, if the fundamental is 220 Hz (A3), the harmonic overtone series would be 220 Hz, 440 Hz (fundamental frequency times two), 660 Hz (fundamental frequency times three), 880 Hz (fundamental frequency times four), and so on. Every musical note contains both the fundamental frequency and a predictable series of harmonics, each of which can be measured and identified as a specific frequency. This series of frequencies then travels through a hollow cavity (the vocal tract) where they are attenuated or amplified by the resonating frequencies of the cavity, which is how resonance occurs.

Resonance

The complex waveform created by the vocal folds travels through the vocal tract, where it is enhanced by the tract's unique resonance characteristics. Depending on the resonator's shape, some harmonics are amplified and some are attenuated. Each singer has a unique vocal tract shape with unique resonance characteristics. This is why two singers of the same voice type can sing the same pitch and yet sound very different. We can analyze these changes with a tool called a spectral analyzer as seen in figure 5.2. The slope from left to right is called the spectral slope. The peaks and valleys along the slope indicate amplitude variations of the corresponding overtones. The difference in spectral slope between instruments (or voices) is what enables a listener to aurally distinguish the difference between two instruments playing or singing the same note.

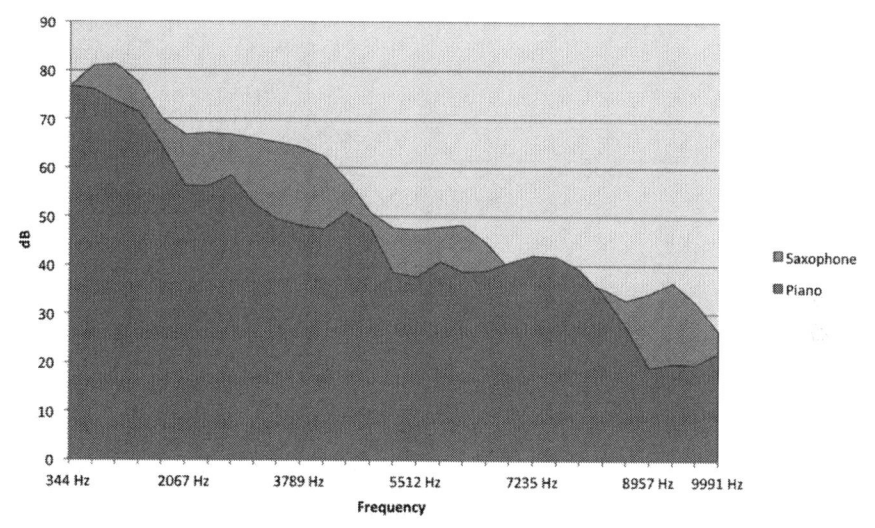

Figure 5.2. The figure shows two instruments playing the same pitch. The peak at the far left is the fundamental frequency and the peaks to the right are harmonics that have been amplified and attenuated by the instrument's resonator, resulting in a specific timbre. *Courtesy of Matthew Edwards*

Because the throat and mouth act as the resonating tube in acoustic singing, changing their size and shape is the only option for making adjustments to timbre for those who perform without microphones. In electronically amplified singing, the sound engineer can make adjustments to boost or attenuate specific frequency ranges, thus changing the singer's timbre. For this and many other reasons discussed in this chapter, it is vitally important for singers to know how audio technology can affect the quality of their voice.

SIGNAL CHAIN

The signal chain is the path an audio signal travels from the input to the output of a sound system. A voice enters the signal chain through a microphone, which transforms acoustic energy into electrical impulses. The electrical pulses generated by the microphone are transmitted through a series of components that modify the signal before the speakers transform it back into acoustic energy. Audio engineers and producers understand the intricacies of these systems and are able to make an infinite variety of alterations to the vocal signal. While some engineers strive to replicate the original sound source as accurately as possible, others use the capabilities of the system to alter the sound for artistic effect. Since more components and variations exist than can be discussed in just a few pages, this chapter will discuss only basic components and variations found in most systems.

Microphones

Microphones transform the acoustic sound waves of the voice into electrical impulses. The component of the microphone that is responsible for receiving the acoustic information is the diaphragm. The two most common diaphragm types that singers will encounter are dynamic and condenser. Each offers advantages and disadvantages depending on how the microphone is to be used.

Dynamic Dynamic microphones consist of a dome-shaped Mylar diaphragm attached to a free-moving copper wire coil that is positioned between the two poles of a magnet. The Mylar diaphragm moves in response to air pressure changes caused by sound waves. When the diaphragm moves, the magnetic coil that is attached to it also moves. As the magnetic coil moves up and down between the magnetic poles, it produces an electrical current that corresponds to the sound waves produced by the singer's voice. That signal is then sent to the soundboard via the microphone cable.

The Shure SM58 dynamic microphone is the industry standard for live performance because it is affordable, nearly indestructible, and easy to use. Dynamic microphones such as the Shure SM58 have a lower sensitivity than condenser microphones, which makes them more successful at avoiding feedback. Because of their reduced tendency to feedback, dynamic microphones are the best choice for artists who use handheld microphones when performing. ♪

Condenser Condenser microphones are constructed with two parallel plates: a rigid posterior plate and a thin, flexible anterior plate. The anterior plate is constructed of either a thin sheet of metal or a piece of Mylar that is coated with a conductive metal. The plates are separated by air, which acts as a layer of insulation. In order to use a condenser mi-

USING AUDIO ENHANCEMENT TECHNOLOGY

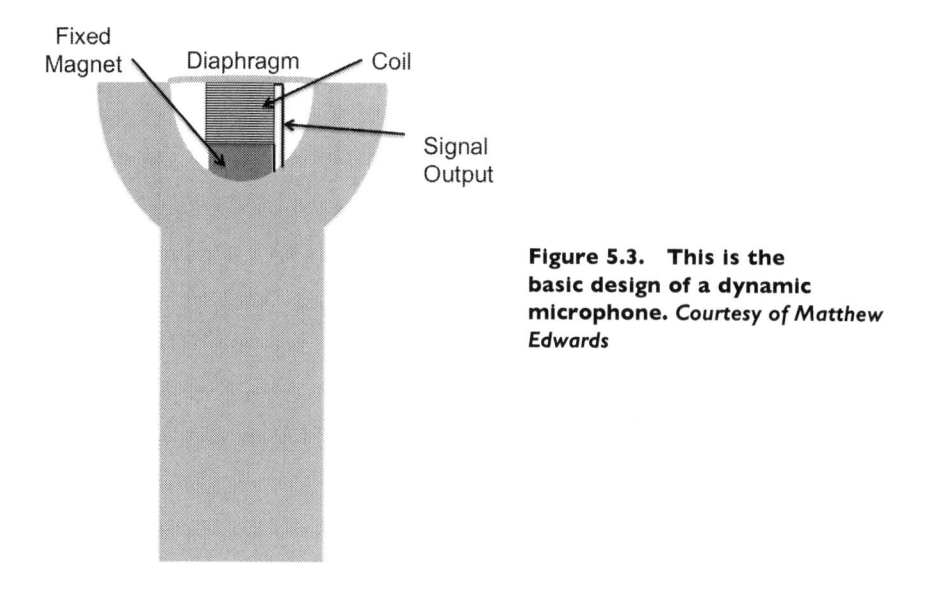

Fixed Magnet   Diaphragm   Coil

Signal Output

Figure 5.3. This is the basic design of a dynamic microphone. *Courtesy of Matthew Edwards*

crophone, it must be connected to a soundboard that supplies "phantom power." A component of the soundboard, phantom power sends a 48-volt power supply through the microphone cable to the microphone's plates. When the plates are charged by phantom power, they form a capacitor. As acoustic vibrations send the anterior plate into motion, the distance between the two plates varies, which causes the capacitor to release a small electric current. This current, which corresponds with the acoustic signal of the voice, travels through the microphone cable to the soundboard where it can be enhanced and amplified.

Electret condenser microphones are similar to condenser microphones, but they are designed to work without phantom power. The anterior plate of an electret microphone is made of a plastic film coated with a conductive metal that is electrically charged before being set into place opposite the posterior plate. The charge applied to the anterior plate will last for ten or more years and therefore eliminates the need for an exterior power source. Electret condenser microphones are often used in head-mounted and lapel microphones, laptop computers, and smartphones.

Recording engineers prefer condenser microphones for recording applications due to their high level of sensitivity. Using a condenser microphone, performers can sing at nearly inaudible acoustic levels and

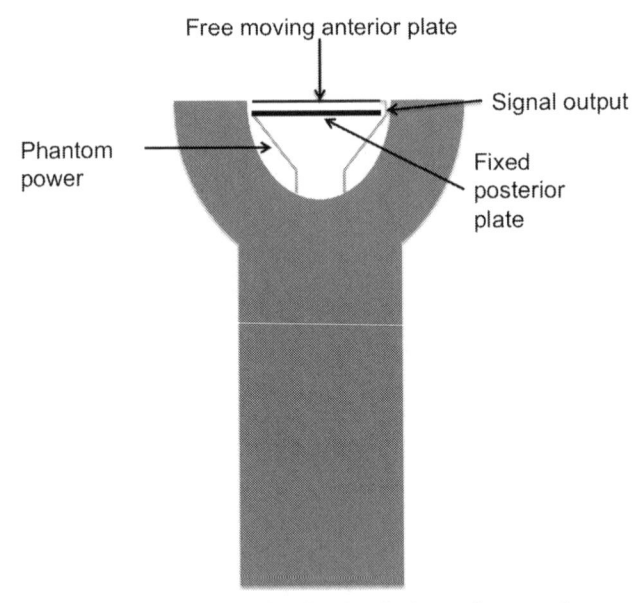

Figure 5.4. This is the basic design of a condenser microphone. *Courtesy of Matthew Edwards*

obtain a final recording that is intimate and earthy. While the same vocal effects can be recorded with a dynamic microphone, they will not have the same clarity as those produced with a condenser microphone.

Frequency Response Frequency response is a term used to define how accurately a microphone captures the tone quality of the signal. A "flat response" microphone captures the original signal with little to no signal alteration. Microphones that are not designated as "flat" have some type of amplification or attenuation of specific frequencies, also known as cut or boost, within the audio spectrum. For instance, the Shure SM58 microphone drastically attenuates the signal below 300 Hz and amplifies the signal in the 3 kHz range by 6 dB, the 5 kHz range by nearly 8 dB, and the 10 kHz range by approximately 6 dB. The Oktava 319 microphone cuts the frequencies below 200 Hz while boosting everything above 300 Hz with nearly 5 dB between 7 kHz and 10 kHz (see figure 5.5). In practical terms, recording a bass singer with the Shure SM58 would drastically reduce the amplitude of the fundamental frequency, while the Oktava 319 would produce a slightly more consistent boost in the range of the singer's formant. Either of these options could

USING AUDIO ENHANCEMENT TECHNOLOGY 79

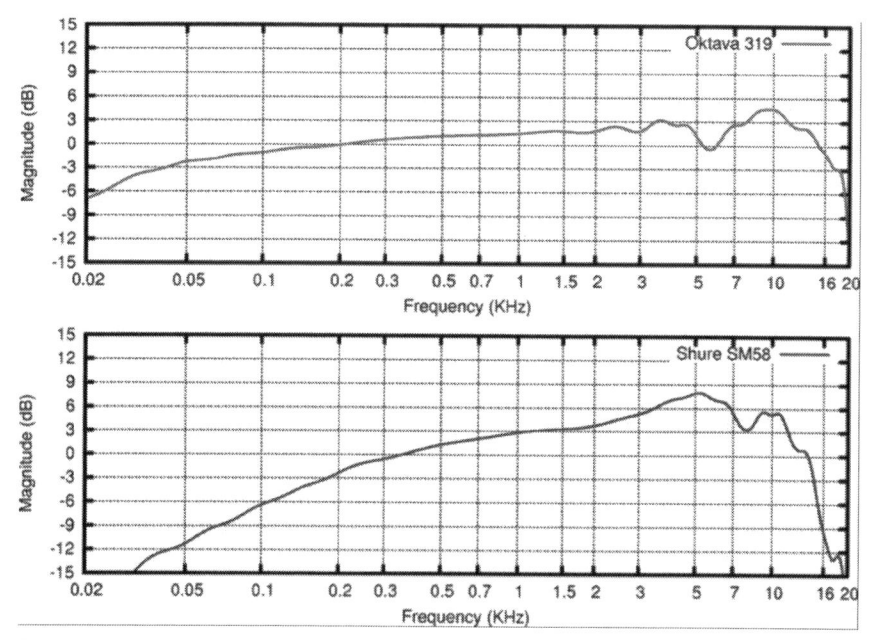

Figure 5.5. Example frequency response graphs for the Oktava 319 and the Shure SM58. *Wikimedia Commons*

be acceptable depending on the situation, but the frequency response must be considered before making a recording or performing live.

Amplitude Response The amplitude response of a microphone varies depending on the angle at which the singer is positioned in relation to the axis of the microphone. In order to visualize the amplitude response of a microphone at various angles, microphone manufacturers publish polar pattern diagrams (also sometimes called a directional pattern or a pickup pattern). Polar pattern diagrams usually consist of six concentric circles divided into twelve equal sections. The center point of the microphone's diaphragm is labeled 0° and is referred to as "on-axis" while the opposite side of the diagram is labeled 180° and is described as "off-axis."

Although polar pattern diagrams appear in two dimensions, they actually represent a three-dimensional response to acoustic energy. You can use a round balloon as a physical example to help you visualize a three-dimensional polar pattern diagram. Position the tied end of the balloon away from your mouth and the inflated end directly in front of

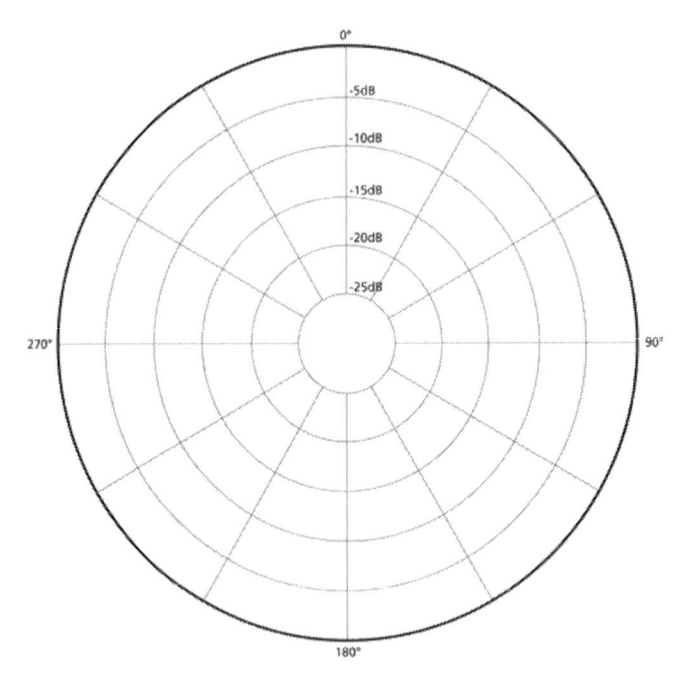

Figure 5.6. An example of a microphone polar pattern diagram. *Wikimedia Commons*

your lips. In this position, you are singing on-axis at 0° with the tied end of the balloon being 180°, or off-axis. If you were to split the balloon in half vertically and horizontally (in relationship to your lips), the point at which those lines intersect would be the center point of the balloon. That imaginary center represents the diaphragm of the microphone. If you were to extend a 45° angle in any direction from the imaginary center and then drew a circle around the inside of the balloon following that angle, you would have a visualization of the three-dimensional application of the two-dimensional polar pattern drawing.

The outermost circle of the diagram indicates that the sound pressure level (SPL) of the signal is transferred without any amplitude reduction, indicated in decibels (dB). Each of the inner circles represents a -5 dB reduction in the amplitude of the signal up to -25 dB. Figure 5.7 is an example.

Figures 5.8, 5.9, and 5.10 show the most commonly encountered polar patterns.

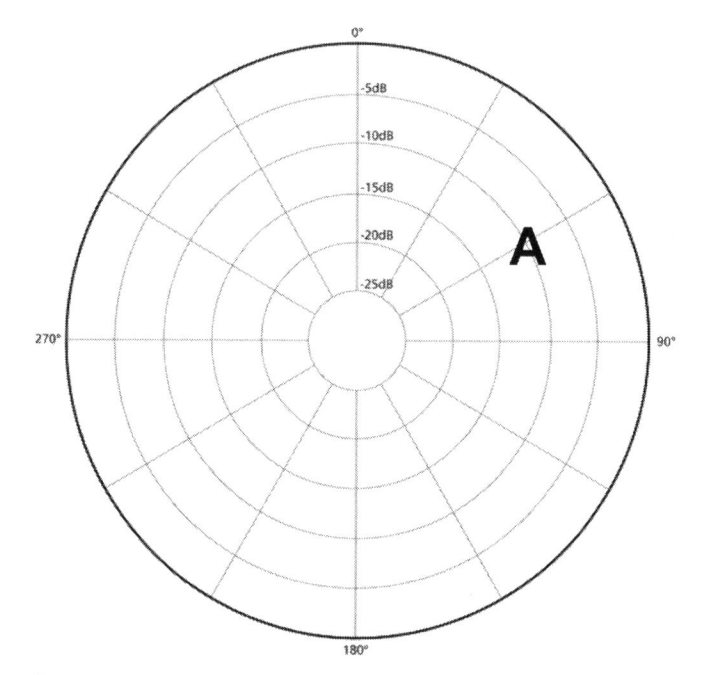

Figure 5.7. If the amplitude response curve intersected with point A, there would be a -10dB reduction in the amplitude of frequencies received by the microphone's diaphragm at that angle. *Wikimedia Commons*

When you are using a microphone with a polar pattern other than omnidirectional (a pattern that responds to sound equally from all directions), you may encounter frequency response fluctuations in addition to amplitude fluctuations. Cardioid microphones in particular are known for their tendency to boost lower frequencies at close proximity to the sound source while attenuating those same frequencies as the distance between the sound source and the microphone increases. This is known as the "proximity effect." Some manufacturers will notate these frequency response changes on their polar pattern diagrams by using a combination of various lines and dashes alongside the amplitude response curve.

Sensitivity While sensitivity can be difficult to explain in technical terms without going into an in-depth discussion of electricity and electrical terminology, a simplified explanation should suffice for most readers. Manufacturers test microphones with a standardized 1 kHz tone at

1 **2**

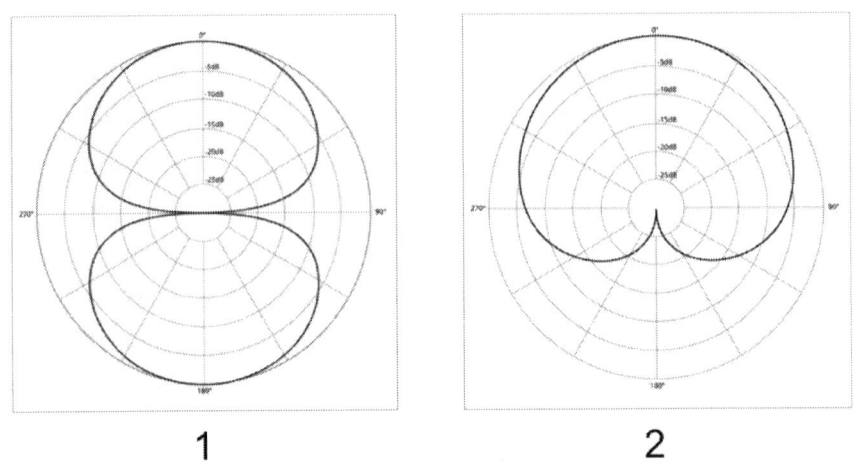

Figure 5.8. Diagram one represents a bidirectional pattern; diagram two represents a cardioid pattern. *Creative Commons*

94 dB in order to determine how sensitive the microphone's diaphragm will be to acoustic energy. Microphones with greater sensitivity can be placed farther from the sound source without adding excessive noise to the signal. Microphones with lower sensitivity will need to be placed closer to the sound source in order to keep excess noise at a minimum.

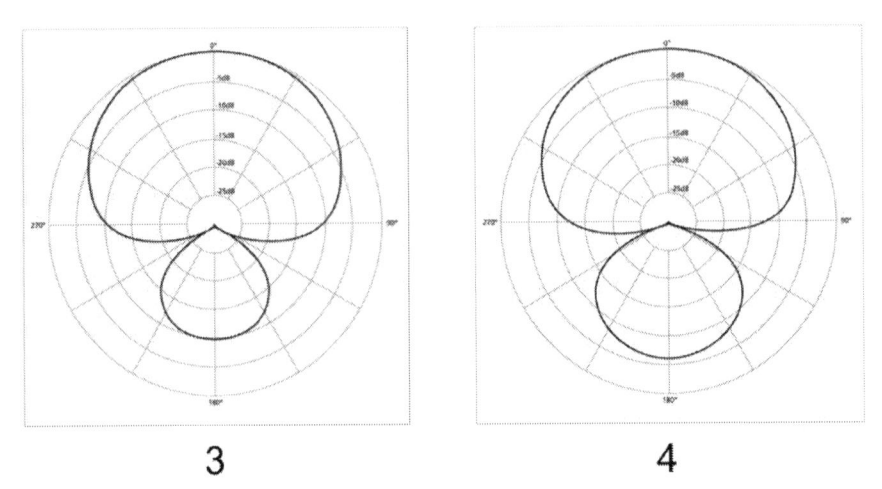

3 **4**

Figure 5.9. Diagram three represents a supercardioid pattern; diagram four represents a hypercardioid pattern. *Creative Commons*

USING AUDIO ENHANCEMENT TECHNOLOGY

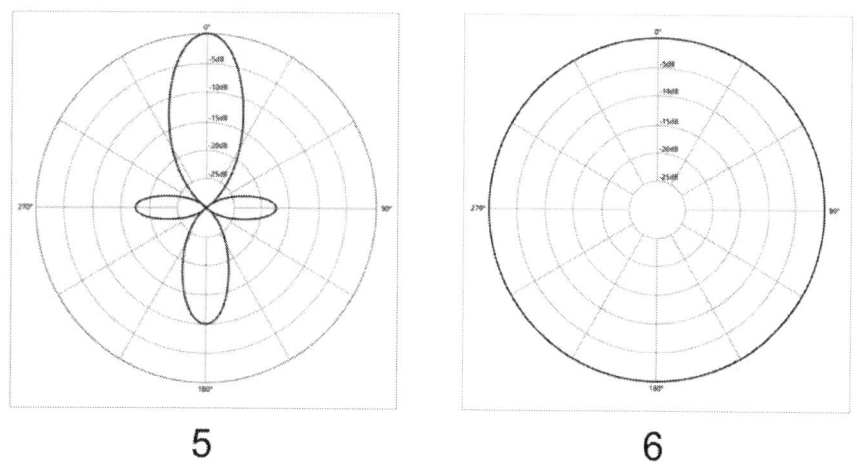

5   6

Figure 5.10. Diagram five represents a shotgun pattern, and diagram six represents an omnidirectional pattern. *Creative Commons*

When shopping for a microphone, the performer should audition several next to each other, plugged into the same soundboard, with the same volume level for each. When singing on each microphone, at the same distance, the performer will notice that some models replicate the voice louder than others. This change in output level is due to differences in each microphone's sensitivity. If a performer has a loud voice, they may prefer a microphone with lower sensitivity (one that requires more acoustic energy to respond). If a performer has a lighter voice, they may prefer a microphone with higher sensitivity (one that responds well to softer signals).

Equalization (EQ)

Equalizers enable the audio engineer to alter the audio spectrum of the sound source and make tone adjustments with a simple electronic interface. Equalizers come in three main types: shelf, parametric, and graphic.

Shelf Shelf equalizers cut or boost the uppermost and lowermost frequencies of an audio signal in a straight line (see figure 5.11). While this style of equalization is not very useful for fine-tuning a singer's tone quality, it can be very effective in removing room noise. For example,

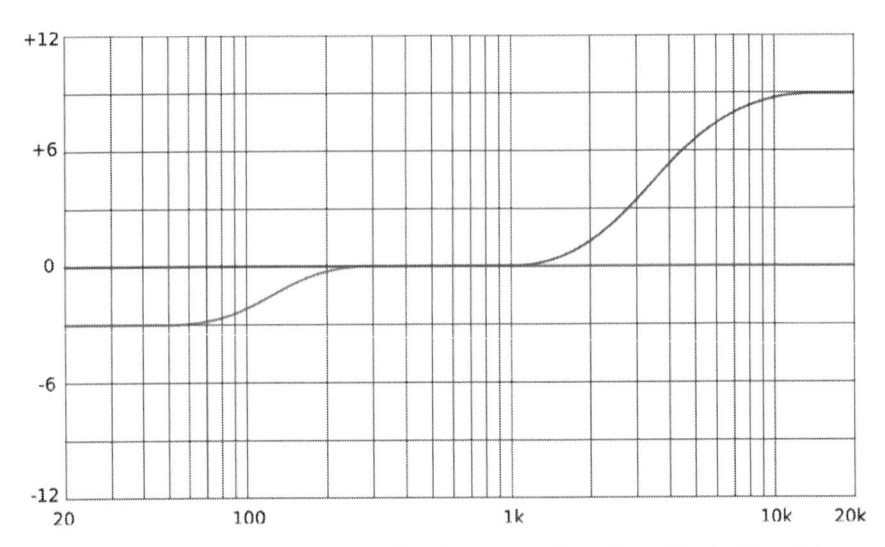

[Graph showing frequency amplitude curve from 20 Hz to 20k Hz, with amplitude from -12 to +12 dB, displaying a shelf EQ curve that rises around 1k to 10k]

Figure 5.11. The frequency amplitude curves show the effect of applying a shelf EQ to an audio signal. *Wikimedia Commons*

if an air conditioner creates a 60-Hz hum in the recording studio, the shelf can be set at 65 Hz, with a steep slope. This setting eliminates frequencies below 65 Hz and effectively removes the hum from the microphone signal.

Parametric Parametric units simultaneously adjust multiple frequencies of the audio spectrum that fall within a defined parameter. The engineer selects a center frequency and adjusts the width of the bell curve surrounding that frequency by adjusting the "Q" (see figure 5.12). He or she then boosts or cuts the frequencies within the bell curve to alter the audio spectrum. Parametric controls take up minimal space on a soundboard and offer sufficient control for most situations. Therefore, most live performance soundboards have parametric EQs on each individual channel. With the advent of digital workstations, engineers can now use computer software to fine-tune the audio quality of each individual channel using a more complex graphic equalizer in both live and recording studio settings without taking up any additional physical space on the board. However, many engineers still prefer to use parametric controls during a live performance since they are usually sufficient and are easier to adjust mid-performance.

Parametric adjustments on a soundboard are made with rotary knobs similar to those in figure 5.13. In some cases, you will find a button

USING AUDIO ENHANCEMENT TECHNOLOGY

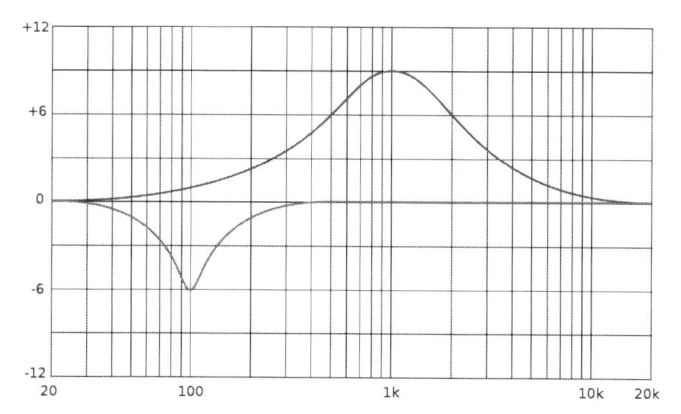

Figure 5.12. The frequency amplitude curves above display two parametric EQ settings. The top curve represents a boost of +8 dB set at 1 kHz with a relatively large bell curve—a low Q. The lower curve represents a high Q set at 100 Hz with a cut of -6 dB. *Wikimedia Commons*

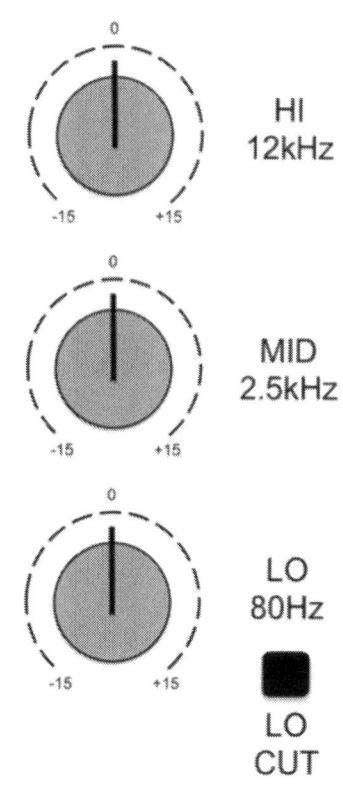

Figure 5.13. This is an example of a parametric EQ interface. The "LO CUT" button applies a shelf EQ at 80 Hz when depressed. *Courtesy of Matthew Edwards*

labeled "low cut" or "high pass" that will automatically apply a shelf filter to the bottom of the audio spectrum at a specified frequency. On higher-end boards, you may also find a knob that enables you to select the high pass frequency.

Graphic Graphic equalizers enable engineers to identify a specific frequency for boost or cut with a fixed frequency bandwidth. For example, a ten-band equalizer enables the audio engineer to adjust ten specific frequencies (in Hz): 31, 63, 125, 250, 500, 1K, 2K, 4K, 8K, and 16K. Graphic equalizers are often one of the final elements of the signal chain, preceding only the amplifier and speakers. In this position, they can be used to adjust the overall tonal quality of the entire mix.

Utilizing Equalization Opinions on the usage of equalization vary among engineers. Some prefer to only use equalization to remove or reduce frequencies that were not a part of the original sound signal. Others will use EQ if adjusting microphone placement fails to yield acceptable results. Some engineers prefer a more processed sound and may use equalization liberally to intentionally change the vocal quality of the singer. For instance, if the singer's voice sounds dull, the engineer could add "ring" or "presence" to the voice by boosting the equalizer in the 2–10 kHz range.

Compression

Many singers are capable of producing vocal extremes in both frequency and amplitude levels that can prove problematic for the sound team. To help solve this problem, engineers often use compression.

Compressors limit the output of a sound source by a specified ratio. The user sets the maximum acceptable amplitude level for the output, called the "threshold," and then sets a ratio to reduce the output once it surpasses the threshold. The typical ratio for a singer is usually between 3:1 and 5:1. A 4:1 ratio indicates that for every 4 dB beyond the threshold level, the output will only increase by 1 dB. For example, if the singer went 24 dB beyond the threshold with a 4:1 ratio, the output would only be 6 dB beyond the threshold level (see figure 5.15).

Adjusting the sound via microphone technique can provide some of the same results as compression and is preferable for the experienced artist. However, compression tends to be more consistent and also gives

USING AUDIO ENHANCEMENT TECHNOLOGY   87

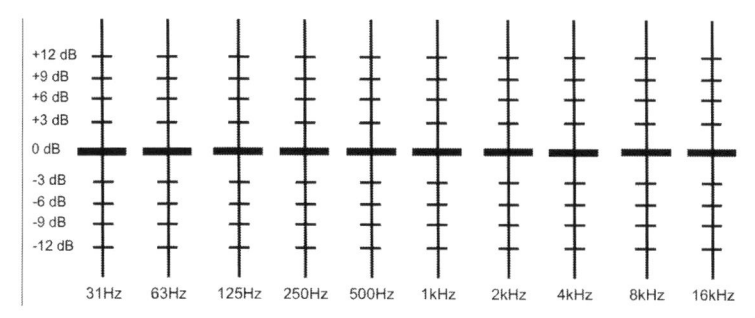

Figure 5.14.   This is an example of a graphic equalizer interface.
Courtesy of Matthew Edwards

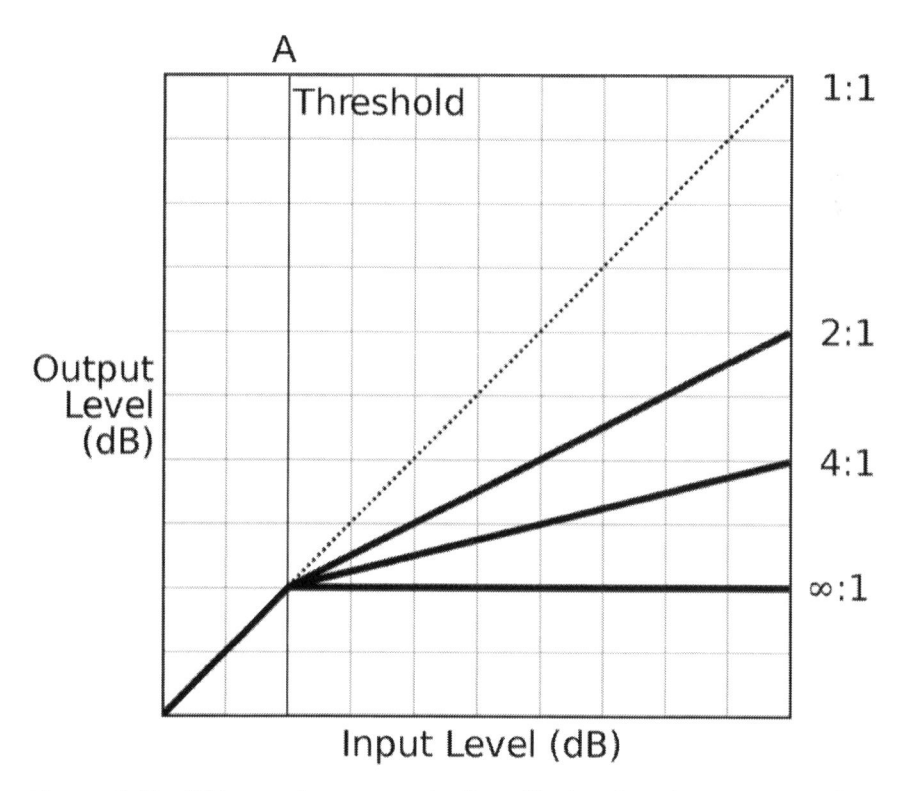

Figure 5.15. This graph represents the effects of various compression ratios applied to a signal. The 1:1 angle represents no compression. The other ratios represent the effect of compression on an input signal with the threshold set at line A. *Wikimedia Commons*

the singer freedom to focus on performing and telling a story. The additional artistic freedom provided by compression is especially beneficial to singers who use head-mounted microphones, performers who switch between vocal extremes such as falsetto and chest voice, and those who are new to performing with a microphone. Compression can also be helpful for classical singers whose dynamic abilities, while impressive live, are often difficult to record in a manner that allows for consistent listening levels through a stereo system.

If a standard compressor causes unacceptable alterations to the tone quality, engineers can turn to a multiband compressor. Rather than affecting the entire spectrum of sound, multiband compressors allow the engineer to isolate a specific frequency range within the audio signal and then set an individual compression setting for that frequency range. For example, if a singer creates a dramatic boost in the 4-kHz range every time they sing above an A4, a multiband compressor can be used to limit the amplitude of the signal in only that part of the voice. By setting a 3:1 ratio in the 4-kHz range at a threshold that corresponds to the amplitude peaks that appear when the performer sings above A4, the engineer can eliminate vocal "ring" from the sound on only the offending notes while leaving the rest of the signal untouched. These units are available for both live and studio use and can be a great alternative to compressing the entire signal.

Reverb

Reverb is one of the easier effects for singers to identify; it is the effect you experience when singing in a cathedral. An audience experiences natural reverberation when they hear the direct signal from the singer and then, milliseconds later, they hear multiple reflections as the acoustical waves of the voice bounce off the side walls, floor, and ceiling of the performance hall.

Many performance venues and recording studios are designed to inhibit natural reverb. Without at least a little reverb added to the sound, even the best singer can sound harsh and even amateurish. Early reverb units transmitted the audio signal through a metal spring, which added supplementary vibrations to the signal. While some engineers still use spring reverb to obtain a specific effect, most now use digital units.

Common settings on digital reverb units include wet/dry, bright/dark, and options for delay time. The wet/dry control adjusts the amount of direct signal (dry) and the amount of reverberated signal (wet). The bright/dark control helps simulate the effects of various surfaces within a natural space. For instance, harder surfaces such as stone reflect high frequencies and create a brighter tone quality, while softer surfaces such as wood reflect lower frequencies and create a darker tone quality. The delay time, which is usually adjustable from milliseconds to seconds, adjusts the amount of time between when the dry signal and wet signals reach the ear. Engineers can transform almost any room into a chamber music hall or concert stadium simply by adjusting these settings.

Delay

Whereas reverb blends multiple wet signals with the dry signal to replicate a natural space, delay purposefully separates a single wet signal from the dry signal to create repetitions of the voice. With delay, you will hear the original note first and then a digitally produced repeat of the note several milliseconds to seconds later. The delayed note may be heard one time or multiple times and the timing of those repeats can be adjusted to match the tempo of the song.

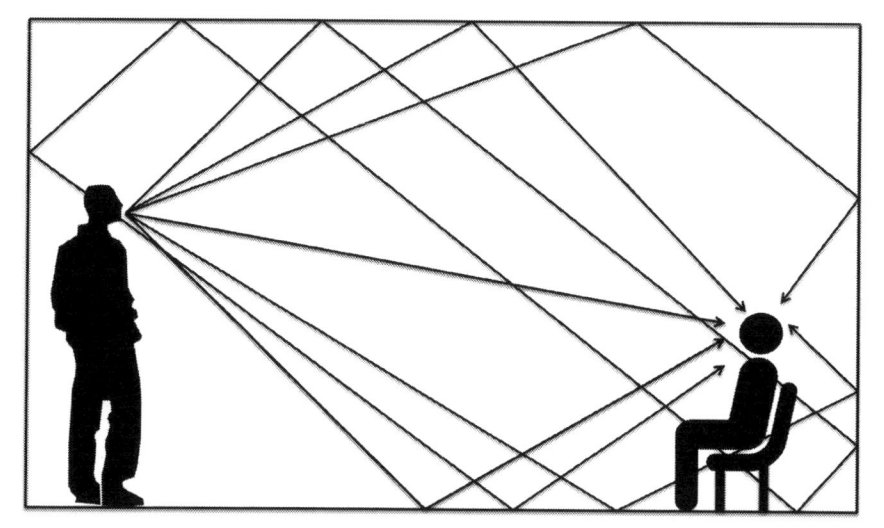

Figure 5.16. This diagram illustrates the multiple lines of reflection that create reverb. *Courtesy of Matthew Edwards*

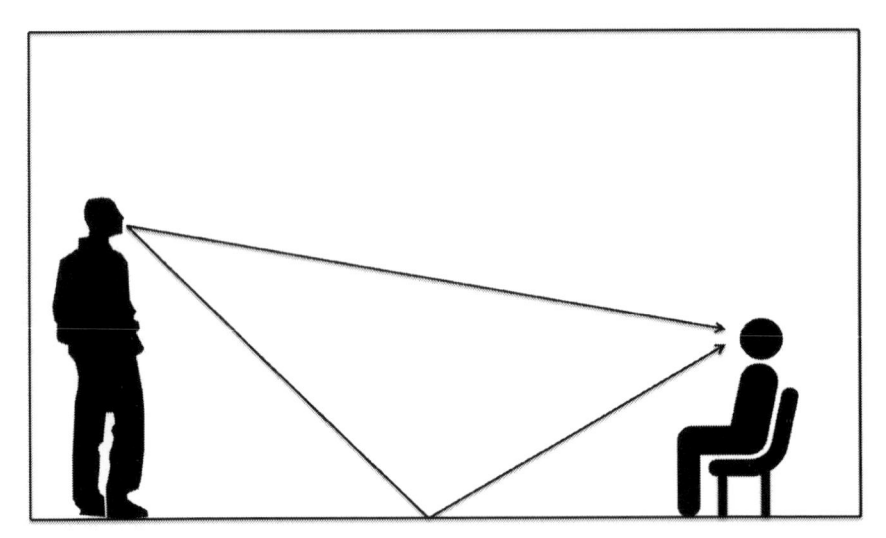

Figure 5.17. This diagram illustrates how a direct line of sound followed by a reflected line of sound creates delay. *Courtesy of Matthew Edwards*

Auto-Tune

Auto-Tune was first used in studios as a useful way to clean up minor imperfections in otherwise perfect performances. Auto-Tune is now an industry standard that many artists use, even if they are not willing to admit it. Auto-Tune has gained a bad reputation in the past few years, and whether or not you agree with its use, it is a reality in today's market. If you do not understand how to use it properly, you could end up sounding like T-Pain.[2]

Both Antares and Melodyne have developed Auto-Tune technology in both "auto" and "graphical" formats. "Auto" Auto-Tune allows the engineer to set specific parameters for pitch correction that are then computer controlled. "Graphical" Auto-Tune tracks the pitch in the selected area of a recording and plots the fundamental frequency on a linear graph. The engineer can then select specific notes for pitch correction. They can also drag selected pitches to a different frequency, add or reduce vibrato, and change formant frequencies above the fundamental. To simplify, the "auto" function makes general corrections while the "graphic" function makes specific corrections. The "auto" setting is usually used to achieve a specific effect (for instance "I Believe" by Cher), while the "graphic" setting is used to correct small imperfections in a recorded performance.

Digital Voice Processors

Digital voice processors are still relatively new to the market and have yet to gain widespread usage among singers. While there are several brands of vocal effects processors available, the industry leader as of this printing is a company called TC-Helicon. TC-Helicon manufactures several different units that span from consumer to professional grade. TC-Helicon's premier performer-controlled unit is called the VoiceLive 3. The VoiceLive 3 incorporates more than twelve vocal effects, eleven guitar effects, and a multi-track looper with 250 factory presets and 250 memory slots for user presets. The VoiceLive 3 puts the effects at the singer's feet in a programmable stomp box that also includes phantom power, MIDI in/out, a USB connection, guitar input, and monitor out. Onboard vocal effects include equalization, compression, reverb, and "auto" Auto-Tune. The unit also offers µMod (an adjustable voice modulator), a doubler (for thickening the lead vocal), echo, delay, reverb, and several other specialized effects.[3]

One of the most impressive features of digital voice processors is the ability to add computer-generated harmonies to the lead vocal. After the user sets the musical key, the processor identifies the fundamental frequency of each sung note. The computer then adds digitized voices at designated intervals above and below the lead singer. The unit also offers the option to program each individual song, with multiple settings for every verse, chorus, and bridge.

THE BASICS OF LIVE SOUND SYSTEMS

Live sound systems come in a variety of sizes from small practice units to state-of-the-art stadium rigs. Most singers only need a basic knowledge of the components commonly found in systems that have one to eight inputs. Units beyond that size usually require an independent sound engineer and are beyond the scope of this chapter.

Following the microphone, the first element in the live signal chain is usually the mixer. Basic portable mixers provide controls for equalization, volume level, auxiliary (usually used for effects such as reverb and compression), and, on some units, controls for built-in digital effects processors. Powered mixers combine an amplifier with a basic mixer, providing a compact solution for those who do not need a complex system. Since unpowered mixers do not provide amplification, you will need to add a separate amplifier to power this system.

The powered mixer or amplifier connects to speaker cabinets, which contain a "woofer" and a "tweeter." The woofer is a large round speaker that handles the bass frequencies while the tweeter is a horn-shaped speaker that handles the treble frequencies. The crossover, a component built into the speaker cabinet, separates high and low frequencies and sends them to the appropriate speaker (woofer or tweeter). Speaker cabinets can be either active or passive. Passive cabinets require a powered mixer or an amplifier in order to operate. Active cabinets have an amplifier built-in and do not require an external amplifier.

If you do not already own a microphone and amplification system, you can purchase a simple setup at relatively low cost through online vendors such as Sweetwater.com and MusiciansFriend.com. A dynamic microphone and a powered monitor are enough to get started. If you would like to add a digital voice processor, Digitech and TC-Helicon both sell entry-level models that will significantly improve the tonal quality of a sound system.

Monitors are arguably the most important element in a live sound system. The monitor is a speaker that faces the performers and allows them to hear themselves and/or the other instruments on stage. On-stage volume levels can vary considerably, with drummers often producing sound levels as high as 120 dB. Those volume levels make it nearly impossible for singers to receive natural acoustic feedback while performing. Monitors can improve aural feedback and help reduce the temptation to oversing. Powered monitors offer the same advantages as powered speaker cabinets and can be a great option for amplification when practicing. They are also good to have around as a backup plan in case you arrive at a venue and discover they do not supply monitors. In-ear monitors offer another option for performers and are especially useful for those who frequently move around the stage.

MICROPHONE TECHNIQUE

The microphone is an inseparable part of the contemporary commercial music singer's instrument. Just as there are techniques that improve singing, there are also techniques that will improve microphone use. Understanding what a microphone does is only the first step to using it successfully. Once you understand how a microphone works, you need hands-on experience.

The best way to learn microphone technique is to experiment. Try the following exercises to gain a better understanding of how to use a microphone when singing:

- Hold a dynamic microphone with a cardioid pattern directly in front of your mouth, no farther than one centimeter away. Sustain a comfortable pitch and slowly move the microphone away from your lips. Listen to how the vocal quality changes. When the microphone is close to the lips, you should notice that the sound is louder and has more bass response. As you move the microphone away from your mouth, there will be a noticeable loss in volume and the tone will become brighter.
- Next, sustain a pitch while rotating the handle down. The sound quality will change in a similar fashion as when you moved the microphone away from your lips.
- Now try singing breathy with the microphone close to your lips. How little effort can you get away with while producing a marketable sound?
- Try singing bright vowels and dark vowels and notice how the microphone affects the tone quality.
- Also experiment with adapting your diction to the microphone. Because the microphone amplifies everything, you may need to underpronounce certain consonants when singing. You will especially want to reduce the power of the consonants [t], [s], [p], and [b].

FINAL THOUGHTS

Since this is primarily an overview, you can greatly improve your comprehension of the material by seeking other resources to deepen your knowledge. There are many great resources available that may help clarify some of these difficult concepts. Most important, you must experiment. The more you play around with sound equipment on your own, the better you will understand it and the more comfortable you will feel when performing or recording with audio technology.

NOTES

1. Paula Lockheart, "A History of Early Microphone Singing, 1925–1939: American Mainstream Popular Singing at the Advent of Electronic Amplification," *Popular Music and Society* 26, no. 3 (2003): 367–85.

2. For example, listen to T-Pain's track "Buy You a Drank (Shawty Snappin')."

3. "VoiceLive 3," TC-Helicon, www.tc-helicon.com/products/voicelive-3/ (accessed May 2, 2016).

PROFILES OF TWELVE CCM PEDAGOGUES

6

KATIE AGRESTA

Born into a family of musicians, Katie Agresta first fell in love with music at the tender age of five when she began taking piano lessons at her parents' music store, the Massapequa Music Center on Long Island. It wasn't long after that she began to sing as well, a talent quickly recognized by family and friends. By age fifteen, this talent had earned her notable distinction as a church soloist within the local community. Ms. Agresta would later go on to college, studying music at Hofstra University, where she earned her BA degree in music. This is also where she first met her teacher of twenty years, Dr. Edward J. Dwyer of Teachers College at Columbia University. She has performed opera throughout the United States and abroad, as well as several solo recitals while on tour in Italy. She has also released a CD of meditational chants, *Inside the Light,* for Aubrey Records and composed the score for Hell, an Off-Broadway show. She has worked as a recording consultant for many years and has assisted at studios in Toronto, Miami, and Paris as well as some of the most notable recording studios in the Tri-State area throughout Long Island, New Jersey, Connecticut, and Manhattan, including places such as Avatar Studios, Mediasound, Record Plant, The Hit Factory, and Sony Studios. ♪

Tell us a little about your background and what led you do become a teacher of contemporary commercial styles.

I come from a very musical family. My mother was a Juilliard graduate and a concert pianist during the 1940s, and my father worked for IBM, hated it, and opened up a music store—the Massapequa Music Center on Long Island. My mother later decided to become a church organist, and she taught lessons at the music store. I got my initial musical training on piano from her before I went on to study with Val McCann, a man who did arrangements for Édith Piaf. I also studied with a guitar teacher, Ray Gogarty, who played with Benny Goodman and many other jazz musicians during the Big Band Era. When I was thirteen, I started voice lessons—also in the music store—and when I was fifteen, my mother invited me to start appearing as a soloist in her church. I sang for a lot of weddings and funerals during this time.

After I graduated from high school, I enrolled at Hofstra University, pursuing a BA in music. My voice teacher at Hofstra was Dr. Edward J. Dwyer, who was also on the doctoral faculty at Columbia University. He wound up being my voice teacher for the next twenty years. I was also studying with a number of different coaches during that time. One of them was Edwin McArthur, who was an accompanist for Rodgers and Hammerstein, and I had the privilege of coaching Broadway repertoire with him for about five years. Mr. McArthur also played for Kristen Flagstad and Florence Foster Jenkins. So I was fortunate to work with some wonderful musicians during my formative years.

After Mr. McArthur passed away, I then studied with a man named Carlo Faria. He was one of the last remaining students of Arturo Toscanini. Carlo Faria coached me in the opera style and was the man who introduced me to Italy. Together we toured Italy and gave concerts in Bellaggio in the Lake Como area and then also gave concerts in other parts of Italy as well. Incidentally, he recently passed away, and some of the friends that I knew at that time got in touch with me through Facebook and last year and also this past spring, I returned to Tuscany where I started singing in Italy again. Last year, my friend Antonio Iannotta and his family hosted a teaching event and celebration for me where I gave a group seminar and also performed for a very large crowd at the Tocano Beach Club along the Italian Riviera in a town called Versillia. This, in turn, led to a return invitation to perform several times in Tuscany this past summer. I look forward to a future that includes many more of these trips to Tuscany and the continuation of a renewal of my singing and performing in a place that had stolen my heart so many years ago.

But backing up, while I was at Hofstra, my brother, who was a guitarist, was playing in a cover band. Their lead singer wound up losing his voice, and my brother asked if I could help him. I realized that I wasn't sure if I could do it. This was in the early 1970s when very few voice teachers were teaching popular styles and no one as yet had focused completely on specializing in the care and training of rock singers. But I was very intrigued by the idea of teaching rock singers and healing the damaged voices of some of the singers who were beginning to come to me asking for help in this style.

I went to Dr. Dwyer and asked for his advice, and he steered me toward all of the medical research that was being done on the voice. I began researching vocal training in the hopes to unlock some of the answers for teaching contemporary commercial styles. I realized that I would have to teach these students differently than classical singers. One of the first things I did differently is reprioritize and reorder the various elements of training. For example, classical singers spend a lot of time working on pure vowels and legato. Rock singers aren't at all interested in that. That was not their problem. Their problem was extreme muscle entanglement and extreme fatigue. In opera, the style is working in harmony with how the muscles optimally function, whereas the rock singer's style bashes up against that ideal muscle function. Once I realized this, I was able to start developing exercises that helped to untangle and release some of that tension. I also developed some warm-ups to help rock singers build the muscle strength they would need to sing in such an intense style, as well as cooldown exercises for after their performances.

These exercises worked with my students, and more people started coming to me wanting to learn how to sing rock styles in a healthy way. At that time in the 1970s, there was a club circuit on Long Island and rock singers were coming from all over the country to play in those venues. My father's music store was located in the middle of all of this, so a lot of business was coming my way. They were all losing their voices and didn't have anyone to turn to for help. Booking agents began to realize that the bands who were working with me were not canceling their shows, and they started sending me their singers. One of these clients was Dee Snider from Twisted Sister.

One day, a girl showed up with very strange hair and a very funny voice. Her name was Cyndi Lauper. She began studying with me, and the year she became an overnight sensation (in 1983 with "Girls Just Want to Have Fun"), I turned down about four hundred singers who all wanted to work with me. A lot of other famous clients came after Cyndi, including Annie Lennox, Phoebe Snow, and Jon Bon Jovi. That's how it all happened. One thing led to another and here we are! My teaching, which was originally supposed to pay for my opera career, wound up going off in an entirely different direction.

What kinds of styles do you currently teach?
Although I am trained to coach all different styles of music, I specialize in teaching technique. The training that I teach can be used by singers for any number of styles because the technique focuses on training muscle function and not on the particular style that you might choose to sing. I have all kinds of students who sing all kinds of different styles. I even have an opera singer or two. Most of my clients, however, are all kinds of rock singers: hard rock singers, blues singers, punk singers, pop singers . . . everything under the sun, really. And for the past fifteen years, I have worked with a lot of Broadway singers as well. I think the reason my Broadway clientele has picked up so dramatically is because of the nature of the way Broadway is going. Music theater singers have to sing all styles nowadays.

I also work as a vocal coach on Broadway. This started for me when my student, John Lloyd Young, won the Tony in 2006 for his leading role in *Jersey Boys*. I wound up being hired as a vocal coach for the production and was eventually asked to coach all of the actors worldwide who were singing the role of Frankie Valli, which is a very difficult role. With everyone, I really focus on their singing technique. I do some coaching, but repertoire and style are not my focus. Another thing that I do is work as a recording consultant. I assist singers with their recording sessions and help them make their albums better and faster.

What, do you believe, are the criteria for teaching these styles well?
The most important first step is that you have to become familiar with all of the styles. You have to listen to the styles carefully and as much as

possible. This is easier than ever now that we have YouTube—there are thousands of examples of rock bands, for example, that we can access instantly. Understanding muscle function is also a must. I also think that you need to be intellectually curious and read voraciously. I own more than six thousand books. I consider myself to be a researcher. Every day I read about things that apply to what I do as a singer teacher.

How do you teach style to students who don't have a strong background in a given genre?
Students need to immerse themselves in the *style*, not just a song. If they are auditioning for a Broadway show that is calling for them to sing in a new style, then they need to familiarize themselves with the entire score, not just the role they're auditioning for. They should also research other shows that might be similar in style. If they are a rock singer, they need to listen to more than just one band. They should also listen carefully to the performers singing the style and—if possible—watch them perform it. Again, YouTube is a wonderful resource.

Understanding the basic history of music is also important. For example, if a student comes to me and wants to work on R&B riffing, I tell them to go back and listen to blues music. Blues music doesn't have a lot of riffing, but that's where they need to start—by understanding the language and the culture out of which the blues arose. The turn of phrase comes out of that original expression, which was then copied in gospel and culminated in Ray Charles. After that, the style goes off in two different directions: soul music and R&B, in which we have riffing. I believe that a singer can't truly understand the style unless he or she knows where it came from.

How did you come up with your method or approach? What does it consist of, and how is it unique?
My approach is really a result of my intensive study with Dr. Dwyer back when I started teaching. He did a lot of research, and he taught what he was learning to me. All of the exercises that I assigned my students were a result of this research. He passed away in 1989, and since then I have continued his research and the development of various modalities that I include in the process of my training of singers. However, I still teach using mainly his concepts, methods, and exercises. I owe him so much.

I think that one thing I have a real knack for is the ability to listen to someone's voice and empathetically tell what's going on in the body. This gives me an advantage in knowing how to fix technical problems with my students. When I listen to them, I try to identify which muscles are being used and fix the ones that are entangled or behaving incorrectly. I then assign exercises that address those muscles or groups of muscles—the goal is to free them up. I enjoy fixing and healing damaged voices, and I believe that everything is fixable. I never give up on a student.

I always tell my students that I have two specialties: one is *building the voice* for performance, and the other is *healing the voice* if it runs into trouble. Physicians and speech-language pathologists will often refer singers to me who have been diagnosed with pathologies such as vocal nodules or polyps. But my approach with both of these specialties is to address the muscle function directly. This approach goes all the way back to my original studies with Dr. Dwyer.

What is your general philosophy of voice teaching?

My general philosophy of voice teaching is that I am there to serve the student. I want the singer to accomplish his or her vocal goals. I don't believe that the teacher should set the agenda for the student—the student's needs should be prioritized. I don't teach the training. I teach the singer the training. To be an effective voice teacher, you have to do that.

I also believe that the teacher needs to respect the music that her or his students are performing. I respect all styles of music, but when I started out, rock music wasn't respected. Most of the singing teachers were very against any kind of rock singing. They thought that it was all screaming and therefore vocally unhealthy. But I never viewed it that way. I never thought that rock music was less worthy than classical singing. When I was a teenager, there was a rock band rehearsing in my basement while I sang Mozart and Puccini upstairs. It was all just music to me. I liked all of it and I still do.

Summarize your core beliefs about vocal technique.

Vocal technique is at the core of everything. It is what a singer needs to be able to sing what they want to with freedom. I have been teaching for almost all my life, and in all that time, I've only met perhaps two or three singers who were so great naturally that they didn't need any technical work. However, virtually all singers need to have a core library of information so that they can accomplish what they are trying to do vocally. Acquiring a steady and reliable vocal technique is the foundation for everything. It is the ground on which a singer stands. Without it, a singer is inconsistent and probably will not have longevity. Technique is profoundly important, which is why I have dedicated my life to studying it and teaching it.

What elements of vocal technique do you think are most important?

Breath is probably the most important thing. It's primary—without it, you're not alive and on this earth! But almost equally important are strength and flexibility. You can be really strong like a football player, but if you can't tie your shoes, your strength won't help you much with singing because the lack of usual flexibility leaves you with a very limited vocal range and can deny you access to your high notes. You also need vocal stamina, which is closely related to strength and flexibility. And you, of course, need to have your health—physical, psychological, and emotional. It is also very useful to a singer to develop their musicianship in as many ways as they can. There are so many elements that are important.

Do you have a favorite vocal exercise that you would like to share with us?

The very first thing that I have a new student do is have them pull their tongue out and hold it while saying "gee-hee-hee." It's very hard to do, and the reason it's so hard to do is that everyone's tongue is too tight for singing. Why? Because we swallow, and the tongue contracts when we swallow. Everyone has a tongue to deal with, and as soon as we get it loose enough to sing, we have lunch, it tenses back up, and we have to start all over again. So I have the singer hold the tongue and then sing "gee-hee-hee" on a single pitch three times in a row. The pitch can be changed each time, and the singer can explore this exercise in different parts of his or her range. Even if someone has been singing for a long time, I still find this to be a useful exercise and a great way for me to "tune in" to where they are at technically and what the muscles are doing.

Have you sung in the past, and if so, which styles? Do you currently sing any of the styles you teach?
My earliest singing experiences were in classical music. I sang in church, studied classically, and sang some opera while studying as a student at Hofstra. I also sang music theater and gave some concerts in Italy. I stopped singing opera when I had some health problems very early in my career. When my health recovered, I tried some blues singing in Chicago. My favorite genre to sing outside of opera might be the American Songbook, Disney songs, and the more melodic pop music. I like all kinds of genres, but I have a big opera voice, and it is hard to put a "size 9 foot" into a smaller shoe, so there are some genres that I can't really sing very well in a stylistically correct way. Nowadays I find myself singing a lot of classic Broadway. A lot of this repertoire fits the kind of instrument that I have.

Who were your strongest influences, pedagogically, vocally, and musically?
Pedagogically, my strongest influence was absolutely my voice teacher of twenty years, Dr. Edward J. Dwyer. I would not be who I am today without him. In addition to Dr. Dwyer, I also studied with forty-four other teachers and coaches. I trained in movement and performance with Wesley Balk, the author of the book *The Singing Actor*. I also studied dance and was coached to sing in seven languages. It is easy for me to name a vocal inspiration. When I was ten years old, I fell in love with Johnny Mathis. I was totally convinced that I was going to marry him! I originally asked for singing lessons because if Johnny ever asked me to sing, I didn't want to be embarrassed. I love his voice to this day and still know all of his songs by heart. When I was a little older, I began listening to a lot of opera singers. I loved Joan Sutherland, Rosa Ponselle, and Maria Callas in particular. I also enjoy listening to baritone singers across all genres. Musically I listen to everything—opera to the Beatles to Gregorian chant to world music to new age and back again. My taste in music is extremely eclectic.

The years I spent during my younger years listening to the radio are also an essential part of my background. I still love to explore all different genres of music, especially music from other cultures and traditions. I have spent my entire life listening to music in order to expand my awareness of all that is in the world to hear. I am now beginning to discover the vast recordings that are available that even include the sounds that are made by the plants and animals of this world.

What is the primary goal when training your students?

My primary goal is to make them happy by teaching them how to sing freely and with confidence. Singing is such an emotional thing. I try to help them sing better, accomplish their goals, and leave the studio happier than when they came in. I try to remain neutral and never judge them. I never ask them if they have practiced when they walk into the room. I just greet them and we get to work. If I can remain a positive force and refrain from judging them, they learn better. I think it's my job to create a space where they feel safe. I want them to feel like they can make mistakes and explore who they are. I also try to be supportive of their goals, no matter how ambitious (or even unrealistic at times) they may seem to be. It doesn't mean that I am not truthful; I always try to be. But I discuss things truthfully in a way that still supports them.

What else is important to you in your work?

I want to make sure that I serve my students and never shortchange them. When I was a younger teacher, there was so much I had to learn about managing the content and flow of the lesson. I had to learn how to manage the intimate experience of a voice lesson and the psychology of the student-teacher relationship. There are so many things that students present to you in a lesson, so I made sure that I continued to study constantly so that I was prepared to help in as many different ways as possible. I also always try to be humble and curious enough to realize when I don't know something so I can either find out the answer or refer a student to someone who already has the answer.

I am also a Naam and Kundalini yoga instructor and Fourth-Degree Reiki Master, so I plan to continue my work with meditative and healing practices, and I have been invited to do seminars with veterans who suffer from post-traumatic stress disorder (PTSD). I am a Biosonic Repatterning Practitioner—healing and directing healing energy with the use of tuning forks—which I studied under the tutelage of Dr. John Beaulieu. I also do "angelic healings" and work with crystals. Some of my students through the years have come to receive private energy healings to help remove some of the blocks that they have in order to be able to perform better.

Over the course of your career, what has been most meaningful?
The most meaningful part of my career has been all the many wonderful relationships that I have had with so many people over the years. The many thousands of people whom I have met and thousands of singers whom I have taught have filled my life to the fullest. Knowing that all over the world, there are people listening to the music of people whom I have trained and helped with their voices fills my heart with such joy. The people with whom I work every day on my staff are the most treasured relationships I have.

Perhaps my long relationships with both Cyndi Lauper and Jon Bon Jovi and the eleven-year relationship with the award-winning Broadway musical *Jersey Boys* also stand out as truly meaningful as well. My long relationship with Cyndi Lauper was my first association with a singer who rose to stardom from obscurity. I began teaching her when she was very young and helped her through some tough times. When she first came to me, numerous doctors had told her that her career was over and that she should give up. But I believed in her and we rebuilt her voice together. When she finally broke through, she was the first solo female artist to break through and have success in that way. It was a major turning point in the history of rock and a landmark for women artists everywhere. It meant so much for me to be a part of that. Our friendship has spanned forty years, and Cyndi still takes three lessons a week with me.

Jon Bon Jovi came into my life in 1988. Little Steven, another great friend and extremely meaningful relationship that I have had the honor to have, sent Jon to me at that time. I am still teaching him to this day, and he is one of the most beloved people in the world to me. I have come to know him and so many people in the Bon Jovi world, and I consider this relationship to be one of the most important relationships I have in my life. Being able to go on tour with Jon all over the world was also a transformative experience. I really got to experience what life is like for these rock singers who are at the top of their profession, and I was able to bring all of that knowledge back to my students.

How has your approach been informed by life experience, and how has it evolved over the years?

As I have gotten older, I hope I have also gotten wiser and smarter. I am also able to get to the bottom of vocal issues and fix them a lot faster. But more generally, when I first started out, I was not focused. During the 1970s and the 1980s, the whole culture was going through a revolution, and partying and doing crazy things was also part of my day-to-day life. It was not until I started to become more famous (as a result of the fame of my students) that my life started to change. I began to realize that the wilder days of my youth needed to morph into a more focused and disciplined time. I had opened my school in 1987, and I had also been singing in Italy, which necessitated a very different lifestyle change for me. And then in my thirties, I started to experience very serious health problems. It was a huge turning point. I had been given medications earlier in my life that had caused serious side effects in my body. I had to be hospitalized and I almost died when I was thirty-seven years old—the doctors gave me three months to live. It was 1987, and back then I was able to get something called "live cell treatment" in Mexico. Lying in the hospital, I had a spiritual awakening. I knew that my lifestyle had everything to do—or at least a lot to do—with my failing health because I shouldn't be thirty-seven and dying. I changed everything about my life: my spiritual approach, my physical approach, my mental, my vocal patterns, my behavior . . . everything! And I didn't die. I am still here. To this day, I am a devoted fan of alternative medicine and holistic practices.

There's a wonderful book called *The Brotherhood of Angels and of Men* by Geoffrey Hodson, and there's an incredible passage that describes the relationship between a teacher and student. He says that a student flies on the teacher's wings until the student is strong enough to fly on his or her own, and then the teacher steps back and watches from afar. It makes me cry every time I think of that passage. That to me is the whole story right there. As a teacher, I have to be the most voracious student of them all because they're all flying on me. It's a sacred relationship. ♪

What are your thoughts on professional organizations? Are you involved with any?

I've never been a club joiner. It's not that I don't think highly of all of the singing teacher organizations that are out there—I think they're wonderful! I've just always been so busy with my private studio. I'm something of a loner in that way. But I have been places to give seminars and talks for organizations like NATS and NYSTA, and I have always enjoyed doing that sort of thing when the opportunity arises.

Do you use technology in any of your teaching?
I use Skype these days for about half of the clients that I teach. Technology has allowed me to have students from all over the globe. In the studio, however, I don't have students singing with the use of equipment. That is reserved for classes. During an actual lesson, I don't like to listen to the muscles and to a client singing with any type of microphone. I find it inhibiting and it gets in the way of what I am trying to hear. A lot of my students are recording artists, and I know quite a bit about the recording process because of all the experiences I have had in that industry. I have done work at all of the major recording venues in New York over the years. Knowing how all that technology works and what singers have to do in that environment is very important. I am often there at the recording session while the singer is in the booth so that they can call on me for advice when something isn't going right. They say, "Katie, what should I do?" and I try to help them. Electronic music is a different animal than acoustic singing, so I need to try to help them sing as freely as possible. But I truly love the recording studio.

What is in your future as a voice pedagogue?
I am developing an app that I am very excited about. It is called "Performance Day," and it is designed for people who are planning a performance and need to engineer their day so that they can best prepare for that performance. There are forty-four warm-up scales and nine warm-down scales. There's also a function within the app that allows you to take a picture of yourself, record yourself, and send me an e-mail for some feedback. I am hopeful that it will be very helpful in addressing someone's vocal needs away from a one-on-one voice lesson. I am donating the proceeds from this app to charity; if you purchase it, you are helping to reforest the ancient sequoias and ancient old-growth

redwood forests. So, by buying the app, you are helping to reforest the earth. This issue is very important to me.

Also, I have recently decided to work on my singing again. I sang in Italy last summer and plan to go back again next summer to give some workshops and sing some concerts. Italian is my favorite language—I love studying it! ♪

7

IRENE BARTLETT

Irene Bartlett has an enduring career as a professional vocalist, a teacher of voice pedagogy and singing voice performance, and a researcher of the contemporary singing voice. Alongside her extensive teaching practice, she works in team collaborations with otolaryngologists and speech-language pathologists in the rehabilitation of injured voices. She is recognized both nationally and internationally as a leader in the field. She is coordinator of contemporary voice and head of jazz vocal studies and voice pedagogy at the Queensland Conservatorium, Griffith University, Australia. To date, she is one of only two pedagogues to have received the prestigious award of Australian Master Teacher from the Australian National Association of Teachers of Singing (ANATS). Dr. Bartlett conducts clinics and master classes at universities and summer programs throughout Australia and New Zealand and in 2017 presented classes at several high-profile music schools in the United States, United Kingdom, and Finland. She has dedicated her teaching career to producing vocally fit, self-motivated, industry-ready, competent, and knowledgeable singing voice performers and singing voice teachers. Reports from performance graduates with profiles of national and international success suggest that her teaching approach has contributed in some part to their outstanding national and international career achievements—most recently, Dami Im (Australian representative to Eurovision 2016; "X-Factor" winner 2014); Katie Noonan and Megan Washington (multi winners at the Australian Recording Industry Association [ARIA] Music Awards); Kristin Berardi (winner of the Montreaux Jazz Festival International Vocal Competition, the Australian National Jazz Award, and the Freedman Fellowship); and Elly Hoyt and Kristin Berardi (Bell Awards, Best Australian Vocal Jazz Album). In addition to their performance successes, her graduate students continue to receive significant academic awards. ♪

Tell us a little about your background. Have you sung in the past, and if so, which styles?
Music has always been at the center of my life. I grew up being told that I could sing before I could speak. As the only daughter and the youngest of five much older siblings, my early music education was greatly influenced by family members' music-listening preferences, and my childhood home was filled with music of every genre. My dad loved to play piano and sing the hits of Bing Crosby, Al Jolson, and Perry Como, but he would also play LPs of Enrico Caruso, Mario Lanza, Joseph Schmidt, and Maria Callas. My mother loved the popular songs of Tin Pan Alley and the classic musicals. My four brothers played and sang along to recording artists of their generation: Frank Sinatra, Sammy Davis Jr., Johnny Ray, Frankie Laine, Elvis Presley, and the Beatles—to name only a few.

When I was sixteen years old, my entire family immigrated to Australia from London. Around three months after we arrived in Brisbane, my dad saw an advertisement calling for singers to audition for a new Australian television teenage music show. I successfully auditioned and became the regular "support act" for all the visiting national pop singers of the time. Moving on from the teenage television appearances, I appeared on prime-time variety shows and, as they say, "the rest is history."

As live performance appearances were organized to promote the shows, so began my full-time singing performance career as a freelance artist in corporate, club, and nightclub venues in both small band (five- to eight-piece) and big band ensembles. Throughout a lifetime as a working "gig" musician, I have been called on to sing across a wide range of CCM styles in just about every possible venue environment including: concert halls (singing repertoire from Broadway shows and the Great American Songbook with audiences of one thousand or more), in the open air on the back of a truck at a rodeo singing country music, fronting rock bands at sports clubs, in intimate restaurant or cabaret settings (singing "torch" jazz songs and classic pop), as a big band "swing" singer. As long as audiences loved the music, I was happy to sing whatever they wanted to hear. I listened and learned all the nuances of a style and happily sang both male and female repertoire in whatever key was presented to me—because no one had ever told me that I couldn't!

What led you to become a teacher of contemporary commercial styles? Who were your strongest influences, pedagogically, vocally, and musically?
About twenty-five years into my performance career, I was approached to teach at a leading national children's performance school. What started as a one-day-per-week appointment quickly turned into five days, teaching one-on-one lessons and group classes to a variety of ages—everyone from age four through adults.

Until this point, although I had worked to refine my television and cabaret performances with the assistance of a *répétiteur*, I had never had a formal singing lesson—there, I've confessed! For many years my performance career was guided primarily by the professional musicians that I worked alongside. These individuals were mature, experienced professional musicians, and as with the master/apprentice practice of the time, I had great respect for their opinions. Their advice was to avoid singing lessons as classical training would change my unique and natural speech-quality voice production. However, on reflection, and in a broader sense, I guess I have had many influences and many teachers. These were great singers and instrumental recording artists, including Ella Fitzgerald, Sarah Vaughan, Carmen McCrae, Jo Stafford, Judy Garland, Connie Francis, Patsy Cline, Dusty Springfield, Dionne Warwick, Shirley Bassey, Barbra Streisand, Frank Sinatra, Tony Bennett, Mel Tormé, Nat King Cole, Thelonious Monk, Charlie Parker, Miles Davis, Coleman Hawkins, Jim Webb—the list goes on and on! I listened and learned, developing a deep sense of musicianship and music appreciation across a range of styles. However, by the time I began teaching, the recording industry had changed dramatically, and it was no longer possible to hear genuine, unaltered, natural human voicing. Now "Auto-Tune" and "digital effects" masked the true singing voice and—for the most part—recordings had become as much about technology as they were about the singing performance of the artist.

In listening to the voices of my young students, I decided that I needed to truly understand how sound is made and not be the performer who teaches others to just "do as I do—sing as I sing." I was on a quest for informing, empowering knowledge to develop my skills as an educated teacher and performer of CCM styles. So began a lifetime of research and exploration into voice science, traditional teaching models, and the world of cultural music styles. In addition to reading everything I could find on voice, I was fortunate to make connections with three speech-language pathologists who were also interested in singing voice. This led to invitations to work in vocology collaborations in voice clinic environments. Seeking further practical experience of voice science and open discussion on voice generally (spoken and sung), I traveled extensively to the United States (for NATS winter workshops and conferences and the annual Voice Foundation Symposium in Philadelphia) and to Canada, the United Kingdom, and Europe to give and to hear conference presentations on singing voice.

As fate would have it, while living with my family in Madison, Wisconsin, in 1995, I had the privilege of studying for one semester with the great jazz bassist Richard Davis. As with every other aspect of my musical journey to that time, although I had been working as a jazz singer, I had never undertaken any formal education in style production. The time spent working with and being guided by Richard was life changing, and his influence prepared me for what happened on my return to Australia when, in July of 1996, I was invited to apply for a teaching position at the Queensland Conservatorium, Griffith University, in the newly established undergraduate degree in jazz voice. My interview/audition was successful, and so began my academic career.

What kinds of styles do you currently teach? How long have you been teaching these styles?
I have been a teacher of singing for the past thirty-six years. I teach across the range of CCM styles—from jazz to pop, rock to country, and

the broad range of music theater repertoire. In my current tertiary work, I teach jazz vocal styles to advanced undergraduates and postgraduate students in one-on-one studio lessons. Within the voice pedagogy program, I teach postgraduate CCM students and "crossover," classically trained students in one-on-one studio lessons covering a range of CCM styles. In addition to my university teaching, I work also with professional CCM performers, refreshing their technique and troubleshooting voice issues as they prepare for auditions and recording sessions. I have been privileged to work with these singers of pop, rock, country, R&B, funk, and music theater (from legit to modern "book" and stand-alone repertoire), many of whom are household names in Australia.

What, do you believe, are the criteria for teaching CCM styles well?
I believe that well-trained teachers who understand the anatomy, physiology, and function of the voice are best equipped to guide their students toward a basic, healthy vocal production. However, if a student wants to develop performance proficiency in a specific music style, I believe that it is incumbent on the teacher to have a strong background knowledge of the specific elements/vocal effects that define the style. I hold a strong view that a genre-based, "one-size-fits-all" voice training approach will not produce efficient, healthy singing in all styles and—in some cases—could cause vocal harm to the singer.

In my view, teachers need to recognize their limitations as far as genre and style are concerned. Using myself as a case in point—as a CCM specialist, I would never propose to train a student in the repertoire of opera. I know and enjoy listening to the great arias, I can analyze and assess the voice production of any singer, and I can assist the establishment of foundational technique regardless of style. However, I have no personal performance experience singing the nuances of operatic musical expression and style, I am not proficient in languages, and I am not trained in—nor am I comfortable singing—with a lower larynx (cricothyroid-dominant) stabilization with an associated wide pharynx setup (other than for creating certain style color dynamics for my CCM performances). Surely then, these same limitations apply to teachers with backgrounds only in classical/operatic styles when the training of CCM singers is involved.

To assist CCM singers to develop a secure and relevant technique, teachers need to respect the singer's style choice and be prepared to develop fundamental appreciation of the music culture and the inherent style-driven vocal effects that define that particular style (many of which are considered faults in classical singing). Most important, there has to be an acceptance that a speech-oriented, neutral-to-higher larynx position and associated shorter, narrower pharyngeal tube is not an option but is foundational to the creation of a genuine CCM sound. Beyond style authenticity, this vocal tract setup is essential for the maintenance of a healthy and sustainable, conversational (thyroarytenoid-dominant) speech quality that—for female singers particularly—has to be sustained far beyond a classical singer's first *passaggio*.

From personal performance experience and my years of observing and training CCM singers, I know that a classical-style vocal tract setup (lower larynx position, wide pharynx) on full breath volumes is unsustainable for CCM singers whose repertoire is produced primarily in lower register settings and delivered through conversational phrasing. While I believe that best practice is achieved by teachers' personal experience of thyroarytenoid-dominant, low-register singing in their own voice, active critical listening to CCM recordings can assist in recognition and analysis of the required resonance patterns, phonation onsets, and vocal effects that may be outside of the teacher's own genre training and performance experiences.

As a final thought—while I believe that all singing voice students should be introduced to a wide range of repertoire both in listening and technical practice, some CCM styles need to be taught only by professional exponents of that style. This is especially important if the singer's goal is professional performance in aural art forms such as jazz and associated improvisational styles—blues, gospel, and R&B—where the essential style elements are strongly experiential and culture based and where free improvisation is an expected and necessary feature of the music. The written notation is set down as a "guide only," and effective teaching necessitates an immersive knowledge and personal performance experience.

How did you come up with your method or approach? What does it consist of, or how is it unique?
I do not subscribe to any particular "method," but rather I have an eclectic approach to voice teaching. I consider myself to be a *voice builder* rather than a singing teacher. While repertoire is important, I believe

that core components of technique cannot be ignored and must be addressed to enable the singer to perform to the best of his or her ability. While not unique, I adhere to an approach where *good singing is good singing* and *bad singing is bad singing*—regardless of the style! In other words, alignment, breath flow, support, and resonance form the foundation for all skilled vocalization *regardless of style or genre of singing*.

How has your approach been informed by life experience, and how has it evolved over the years?
I believe that my life experience as a professional singer, performer, mother, wife, sibling, and friend allows me to be empathetic to the psychological and physical stresses experienced by my students as they dream, build, and/or maintain their CCM gig and touring careers. If they want me to, I can freely discuss performance and life pressures such as performance anxiety, the difficulties of maintaining family and friend relationships, and the financial stresses that come with a career in music. As discussed earlier, I have singing experience of a wide range of CCM styles and have worked in most every performance environment that my students might encounter. They know this, and it seems to engender a sense of connection and trust in the teacher/student relationship. I work to develop singers' awareness that music is a business and therefore requires a strong knowledge of the industry as they develop professional working relationships with employers, audiences, and fellow musicians.

Early on in my CCM career, I learned that I needn't copy but that I could *borrow* ideas from great performers (both singers and instrumentalists). By infusing *borrowed* musical inventions with all the inherent vocal nuances and the deep connections of their life experiences, each singer is able to discover a vocal sound that is unique. In other words, in offering to share my own experiences, I encourage my students to find their own voice—their unique performance identity.

What is your general philosophy of voice teaching? Summarize your core beliefs about vocal technique.
Established, reliable, adaptive, *style-relevant* vocal technique is key to my teaching philosophy where "good singing is good singing" regardless of style or genre. My teaching model is based in voice science: knowledge of anatomy, physiology, and body-mapping constructs. Extensive

research, *insider* experience, and my observations of the progress and longevity of my singing students across thirty-six years of teaching have led me to conclude that *inappropriate or poor technique* (rather than style in itself) is most likely to induce voice damage in singers of CCM styles. The documented longevity of many CCM singers supports the view that CCM style elements can be managed in the long term if employed as *vocal effects* within a healthy, balanced vocal production assisted through style-relevant, effective training.[1] I believe that any technical work must be appropriate to the singer's vocal range, voice weight, stamina, and tessitura while addressing also the specific elements/effects inherent in any given CCM style. To reinforce my own independent and formalized pedagogical training, I learn from and share ideas with my speech pathologist, physiotherapist, performance counselor, and ENT colleagues. I believe in a holistic approach to voice habilitation. That is, to prevent voice injuries in the first instance through evaluation, diagnosis, and intervention to correct inefficient behavioral patterns (habits).[2] If the need arises, I work in collaboration with other voice professionals in the rehabilitation of injured voices.

What elements of vocal technique do you think are most important?

Put simply, *the building blocks of healthy phonation*: alignment, breath flow, support, and resonance. Without an efficient body alignment, the breath flow will be impeded. Without efficient breath flow (exhalation generated and supported through abdominal and torso muscle engagement), the larynx muscles will be over-recruited and vocal fatigue will eventually set in. Similarly, without style-appropriate resonance (ring/ping/*squillo*/twang), the muscles of the larynx, tongue root, and jaw will be unnecessarily recruited with vocal fatigue the direct result of multiple muscular tensions.

What is the primary goal when training your students?

Free open vocal production; healthy, sustainable voice; and performance longevity in whatever genre or style(s) they choose to sing. To achieve this goal, a complex set of physiological interactions has to be set in motion beginning with a balanced and dynamic alignment. I believe this to be the foundation of all free singing.

I teach "body mapping" to enable singers to develop both a proprioceptive and kinesthetic understanding of their instrument particularly in relation to breath.[3] As voice is primarily a wind instrument, breath is the power source for phonation. Instead of describing the "in breath" as *inhalation*, I speak to my students about the alternative word, *inspiration*, which links breathing to the core of artistry.[4] Of course, we breathe from birth as we breathe for life, but as singers we are constantly altering and modifying breath for the task at hand. Therefore, I believe that if the anatomical function of breathing is understood, the singer is better able to apply conscious control.

Of course, breath flow and support are intrinsically linked as all meaningful human sound production (speaking and singing) begins with the pressurization of air in the lungs. I use unvoiced and voiced fricative exercises recruiting abdominal cylinder muscle support as described in the Accent Method system of breath management.[5] These exercises encourage recruitment of the major abdominal muscles and their linkages throughout the torso to create a sustained air flow (intra-abdominal pressure). Through the voiced fricative exercises, the student is able to experience the focused sound produced by the reactive adduction (closure) of the vocal folds in response to the pressurized air flow. At this point, I introduce the concept of resonance to my students. I describe the air flow as the power source that sets the vocal folds into vibration. The kinetic energy (motion) of the vocal folds converts breath flow to acoustic energy (sound), which is resonated and amplified as it passes through the vocal tract (primarily the pharynx and the oral cavity). The sound now has pitch, tone, and quality, and the speaker/singer shapes the sound (articulation), adding rhythm and tone/volume dynamics, thus creating their own unique voice qualities. I believe also that primal sound connections (emotional engagement with the text) enable the singer to work to their full range of expressive capability.

For CCM singers, I focus training on developing a thyroarytenoid (TA)-dominant production with coordinated activity of the cricothyroid (CT) muscles across the vocal range. The CT engagement has to naturally increase activity as the voice ascends in pitch; however, the TA muscles have to maintain a strong antagonistic engagement across the singer's vocal range to produce the consistent speech-quality production that defines CCM style.

How do you teach style to students who don't have a strong background in a given genre?
I believe that *crossover* singing demands a *crossover training regime* that considers all of the genuine and specific style elements of the music, including vocal "effects." I work closely with crossover singers to help them identify appropriate repertoire in relation to their vocal range, voice weight, stamina, and tessitura. For instance, I remind my students that while belting is necessary to some degree in all CCM styles, *all belters are not created equal*. Safe, sustainable "belting" is achievable if the singer learns to love their unique vocal sound rather than mimicking another singer's voice production. To achieve success, they must be willing to work to develop a strong elemental technique while singing within the parameters of their individual instrument.

To assist students in the achievement of their goals, I first need to understand their objectives. I begin by asking them what they want to achieve from crossover lessons. If it is to broaden their own performance practice in a particular style, I ask *how often* they listen to recordings of the style or genre that they want to master. I then ask them to listen *more closely*, taking note of the major elements that they believe define that style. Regardless of the student's background or singing experience, the first lesson is primarily an assessment of his or her natural range in both speaking and singing voice. I listen for any signs of phonation impairment, and if there are indications of voice dysfunction, I arrange a joint consultation with the relevant voice professional in the vocology team before commencing singing voice lessons.

Beyond this first session, lessons begin with general warm-up exercises and the student is asked to sing through a song. This allows me to assess the condition of their singing voice in that space and time as I listen for a style-appropriate vocal tract setup and any habitual voice function inefficiencies. While my teaching focus shifts back and forth from technical work to developing the necessary artistic style elements for the chosen repertoire, I encourage the student to continue to self-monitor their foundational technique: alignment, breath flow, support, and resonance.

When working in crossover lessons with classically trained singers, I focus the technical work in the lower octave of their voice. The intention here is to strengthen the lower-register (thyroarytenoid-dominant) production to support a healthy, resonant speech quality. Conversely, when working with CCM trained students, I use a "top-down" approach, working to strengthen upper-register (cricothyroid-dominant) production. In both instances, my goal is simple—to assist the singer to find a connected core tone across the full range of their voice while purposefully creating specific style elements and effects overlaid on a balanced and healthy vocal production.

Crossover training takes many forms. In my university teaching, I work with established and early-career CCM teachers who want to experience and to be able to teach styles outside of their field of knowledge and zone of performance comfort (most usually these are music theater and jazz styles). I work also with classical voice postgraduate students who want to develop an understanding of the basic elements of CCM styles for teaching in high school and performance school environments. Training for the classical students is focused mostly on achieving and maintaining a conversational speech quality in their lower register appropriate to CCM repertoire. For these university students, crossover teaching lessons are accompanied by lectures in voice physiology/anatomy, the study of student learning modes, teaching models, and critical listening activities.

What else is important to you in your work?
Writing this chapter has caused me to reflect on many aspects of my teaching, and I believe that my pedagogical approach has developed primarily through a love of music and an enduring curiosity about the wonderful *instrument* that is *voice*. Curiosity led me to research the literature of voice science and the writing of the great pedagogues. I unapologetically, and most gratefully, *borrow* and adapt traditional singing voice and instrumental exercises from the Western classical tradition and "world" music cultures to suit the specific vocal and musical demands of CCM styles. I recognize intuition as a powerful tool in my teaching approach; intuition born of life experiences that enable me to address the individual vocal needs of my students. As I listen and experience their voice setup (physical and laryngeal) in my own voice, I hope to inspire a love of music and passion for healthy singing as my students work to create their own unique musical expression and interpretation regardless of style choice.

What are your thoughts on professional organizations? Are you involved with any?

In my opinion, professional organizations are highly important. Although I have more than thirty-six years of teaching experience, I adhere to the philosophy that best practice teachers—even after decades of education and years of experience—know that they should always be students. To this end, I seek continuously to improve my own teaching practice through participation in professional development, peer review, and critical reflection informed by research. More broadly I am interested in established models of learning and pedagogy across a range of disciplines, and this wide knowledge base has been enhanced through my membership in and interactions with a range of professional organizations. Most recently, I have served as a chapter member, national councilor, membership officer, and vice president of the Australian National Association of Teachers of Singing (ANATS); I am a current member, and I have served on the board of the interdisciplinary Australian Voice Association (AVA); and I am an associate member of the Voice Foundation. Through my ongoing engagement with professional development activities offered by these and other professional organizations—such as NATS, PEVOC, Reflective Conservatoire, and Innovative Conservatoire—I maintain currency with advances in voice science, performance practice, and singing voice pedagogy. ♪

Do you use technology in any of your teaching?

Given the extent of engagement that our students have with online technologies, I believe that today's CCM studio teacher has to be conversant with digital platforms such as backing track sites, music writing programs, repertoire sites, recording programs, and the function and application of amplification equipment (live sound reinforcement).

As CCM singers rarely perform in superior acoustic spaces (such as concert halls and cathedrals), they are reliant on live sound reinforcement for both artistic expression (conversational and intimate style interpretation) and performance longevity. As an industry "insider," I can report that rather than being the focus, most CCM performances occur in environments where live music is used primarily to create ambience and atmosphere for a venue. The CCM singer has to produce and maintain their vocal production against a background of white noise (the loud speaking of audiences and the clatter of glasses, plates, etc.) while competing with loud, electronic instruments or recorded backing music. After many years of experience singing in such acoustically inferior venues, and in an effort to reduce vocal loading and associated vocal fatigue, I consider the training of students in the operation and use of live sound reinforcement as a vital component of my teaching practice. This includes advising singers on selection of the most appropriate microphone to voice type and training a basic working knowledge of equalization and mixing of amplified sound for specific performance environments.

I find acoustic analysis programs to be a useful studio tool especially for students with a strong visual learning mode. I have been using VoceVista and Sing&See since they became commercially available. Interactions and communications with students through Internet sites such as YouTube, Skype, and Zoom are commonplace. However, I do not choose to teach using these platforms unless the student has previously studied with me in face-to-face lessons.

What is in your future as a voice pedagogue?

I remain inspired by advances in voice science and intrigued by brain/voice research. I love teaching and I still have a passion for performance, so I will continue to teach and to sing professionally as long as audiences want to listen and singers come to me for training. Globally, the majority of professional, semi-professional, and amateur singers perform in CCM styles, so I continue my lifelong mission to promote the artistic value of CCM performance to the greater community of singing voice teachers. Along with many of my colleagues, I want to further the academic study of CCM performance with the goal of describing and articulating a universally specific CCM singing voice pedagogy. Most of all, I want my students to be *passionate about music* and *passionate in their singing*. I hope to inspire them to be lifelong learners—to share knowledge, to be curious to find out *how*, to question everything they know, and to *never* be afraid to ask *why*.

NOTES

1. Irene Bartlett, "One Size Doesn't Fit All: Tailored Training for Contemporary Commercial Singers," in *Perspectives on Teaching Singing: Australian*

Vocal Pedagogues Sing Their Stories (Brisbane: Australian Academic Press, 2010), 227–43; "Sing Out Loud, Sing Out Long: A Profile of Professional Contemporary Gig Singers in the Australian Context" (DMA dissertation, Griffith University, 2011).

2. Ingo R. Titze and Katherine Verdolini Abbott, *Vocology: The Science and Practice of Voice Habilitation* (Salt Lake City: NCVS, 2012).

3. Barbara Conable, *What Every Musician Needs to Know about the Body: The Practical Application of Body Mapping and the Alexander Technique to Making Music* (Columbus, OH: Andover Press, 2000).

4. Melissa Malde et al., *What Every Singer Needs to Know about the Body*, 2nd ed. (San Diego: Plural Publishing, 2009), 47.

5. Janice L. Chapman, *Singing and Teaching Singing: A Holistic Approach to Classical Voice* (San Diego: Plural Publishing, 2011).

8

ROBERT EDWIN

Robert Edwin has gained international recognition as a singer, songwriter, teacher, and author. He has sung Bach cantatas in church cathedrals and rock songs in Greenwich Village coffeehouses and has recorded four recent albums of his original songs—Robert Edwin: Christian Songs; More to Life: Robert Edwin Sings Songs by Crosby & Edwin; Take Them Along, Our Songs; and Robert Edwin: Legacy—all available at CDBaby.com. His diverse performing career is matched by an equally diverse teaching career: he "preaches what he practices" at his independent studio in Cinnaminson, New Jersey. Mr. Edwin is an associate editor for the Journal of Singing, a chapter author for the Oxford Handbook of Music Education, and a frequent faculty member at the annual Voice Foundation Symposium. He is also co-creator of the child voice training DVD The Kid & The Singing Teacher. In 2001, he was elected to membership in the distinguished American Academy of Teachers of Singing (AATS). ♪

Tell us a little about your background and what led you to become a teacher of contemporary commercial styles.
I got lucky. My parents were both performers and teachers so I grew up "in the business." My mother, the late Helena W. Monbo, was very

comfortable teaching all styles of singing and understood that a variety of repertoire required a variety of vocal techniques. She was a pioneer in challenging and changing the "classical-only" teaching mentality. My father, the late Edwin Robert Steinfort, was a classically trained singer who also got a job singing the song "Yes, We Have No Bananas" in the revue *Barney Google*. Diversity reigned in the Monfort Studio at the fabled Ansonia Hotel on New York City's upper west side. In the mid-1940s, our neighbors on our floor included the Metropolitan Opera heldentenor Lauritz Melchior and soprano Bidu Sayao. I often wondered what they thought of the variety of vocalized sounds emanating from our studio apartment.

You were also one of the great pioneers in changing established culture and establishing CCM as a legitimate pedagogy in its own right. Can you tell us a little bit about your work in this arena?
Here is my take on the origins of CCM voice pedagogy. As late as the 1980s, the mantra for most voice teachers was still "If you learn to sing classically, you can sing anything." I heard this from many well-known pedagogues who truly believed that classical technique would serve all styles and genres of singing because, to them, there was only one voice technique. Our dance colleagues, however, knew differently. They knew that a ballet dancer wanting to tap would have to learn the technique of tapping in order to succeed in that style. Technique always preceded repertoire. Specific genre training always preceded genre performance.

For the singing teacher community, the breakthrough came when the emerging field of voice science proved that different physiological things were happening when singers sang stylistically correct CCM repertoire. The pharynx narrowed, the larynx raised, the mouth spread in a lateral position, the soft palate lowered, and the *chiaro* dominated the *oscuro*. This is completely opposite of what a classically trained singer would be expected to do. Only then did "nonclassical" voice pedagogy (as it was called then) start to gain legitimacy and credibility.

Regarding pivotal moments in CCM pedagogy, the National Association of Teachers of Singing (NATS) was a major player. In the early 1980s, Richard Miller was editor-in-chief of the *NATS Bulletin*, and he asked me to develop the first regular column dedicated to "nonclassical" voice pedagogy and repertoire. The "Bach to Rock Connection" debuted in the last issue of the *NATS Bulletin* in June of 1985, appeared regularly for seventeen years in the *NATS Journal* from 1985 to 1995, and then continued in the *Journal of Singing* from 1995 to 2002. In 2002, I became an associate editor of the *Journal of Singing* and the column was retitled "Popular Song and Music Theater." That column continues to this day and—thanks to my colleague and friend Jeannette LoVetri—we now have a legitimate name for our work: contemporary commercial music (CCM) voice pedagogy rather than the vague and somewhat demeaning "nonclassical."

Acceptance of CCM voice pedagogy has gradually grown over the years as it continues to make more and more appearances at NATS conferences, the Voice Foundation Symposium, and regional and local events throughout the world. I think it is safe to say that CCM voice pedagogy now stands side by side with classical voice pedagogy.

What, in your opinion, is the difference between *style* and *technique*? It is still not uncommon to hear a voice teacher say that one *technique* informs any *style* a singer wishes to sing.
Technique serves style (genre). It is the foundation that enables the style (genre) to exist. Technique is "how" you do something. Style is "what" you do with that technique. For example, if I want to play golf, I will explore and develop golf technique with a golf coach. I will not go to a basketball coach to learn to play golf. If I want to dance ballet, I will seek out a ballet teacher, not a hip-hop teacher, unless it's a hip-hop teacher who also knows ballet.

Therefore, our colleagues who have claimed in the past and still claim today that there is but one vocal technique that is applied to multiple styles totally miss the point. They are saying, in essence, that if one learns to sing with classical technique, one will be able to use that technique in all styles of singing, literally from Bach to rock.

Frankly, about the only thing classical and CCM voice technique have completely in common is perhaps breath management, such as the Italian *appoggio* technique. Breathing can and should be standardized throughout all styles. However, lowering the soft palate, elevating the larynx, narrowing the pharynx, removing the singer's formant, extending mode 1 (TA or "chest voice") in women, diminishing or eliminating the vibrato, and adding noise to phonation fall under the heading of CCM voice technique, *not* classical voice technique.

What kinds of styles do you currently teach? How long have you been teaching these styles?

I teach alternative to zydeco and everything in between and have been doing so since 1975. Since most current CCM styles owe their birth to early Southern blues, I have many of my students do basic twelve-bar blues exercises where they improvise over a classic pattern: four bars (measures) of the I chord, two bars of the IV chord, two bars of the I chord, one bar of the V chord, one bar of the IV chord, one bar of the I chord, and finally one bar of the turnaround V chord. This pattern can be repeated for as long as one wants to do it. My professional blues and R&B singers could do it for the entire lesson and never repeat their riffs and runs (CCM talk for melismas). My beginners, however, usually greet this exercise with a blank stare and a "What should I sing?" response.

I even have my classical students do this exercise. Since they are taught to respect the lyricist's and composer's wishes and sing what is written on the music page, they often struggle to improvise their own melody and lyrics. For them, it serves as a dramatic cross-training exercise.

We do major and minor keys in a variety of tempos. Lyrics can be scat syllables ("do wah, do wah"), vowels, random words and phrases, or full stories. I think my favorite was an extended political rant against uncaring politicians by one of my rock singers.

The twelve-bar blues can stretch range and enhance register coordination as well as challenge students to step out of their comfort zone. Beginners usually focus on the tonic and stay there like a person standing on a high ledge until encouraged to jump off into more melodic options. It's an exercise that's fun and one that covers a lot of pedagogic bases.

What, do you believe, are the criteria for teaching these styles well?

As they say in the Broadway show *The Music Man*, "You gotta know the territory." I believe teachers have to have singing styles "in their throats" in order to teach them well. That is to say, they have to know what they are asking their students to do from both a technical as well as an experiential perspective. Efficient and stylistically appropriate technique varies greatly from style to style. I may not be able to riff as well as some of my professional blues singers, but I can riff and know what it should feel like and how it should sound.

Regarding a teacher who doesn't have the requisite background in a given genre . . . well, that's like asking the school tennis coach who has only played tennis to take over coaching the basketball team. I would hope teachers who are unfamiliar with a specific style would swallow their pride and "learn the territory" or refer students to a teacher who has some expertise in that genre.

How do you teach style to students who don't have a strong background in a given genre?
If a student comes in to my studio and says, "I'd like to be a rock singer, but I don't know much about it," my first response is this: "Listen to singers who are good at the style you want to sing and then copy, within your own vocal limitations, what you hear." Imitation and repetition can eventually lead one to finding his or her own voice and individuality. I have no problems with stylistic novices playing a musical game of "follow the leader" to get them started in a new genre, be it Bach or rock or whatever.

How did you come up with your method or approach? What does it consist of, or how is it unique?
My method and approach evolved from years of study, research, and experience. My primary source was my mother, the aforementioned Helena W. Monbo. I taught in her New York City independent studio for ten years. I got to hear and work with opera and oratorio singers; Broadway singers; pop, rock, and folk singers; cantors; voice-over artists; and jazz vocalists.

Regarding a method, I have taken my cue from my mentor and my first editor-in-chief at the then *NATS Bulletin*, Richard Miller, who never branded or certified his approach. Richard was a fine teacher who developed his fact-based pedagogy from a multitude of sources—the collective wisdom of the ages, so to speak. I have tried to emulate both his humility and his expertise in my work.

Regarding uniqueness, I treat the human voice as an extension of the total person. My teaching integrates the actor and singer throughout the whole training process, not just in repertoire development. I believe mechanical, emotionally disconnected, and robotic voice exercises can doom a student to uninspired singing. My students tell stories in their vocalises, which allows them to segue seamlessly into repertoire. I also encourage my students to sing to their vocal extremes. How low can you go? How high? Three-octave ranges are not rare in my studio. My singers use their whole voices and stretch the limits.

What is your general philosophy of voice teaching? Summarize your core beliefs about vocal technique.

My teaching is fact-based, gender-neutral, and style-specific. A lot of voice pedagogy still wallows in pre-science beliefs, practices, and terminology. Diaphragms don't sing, sound can't be placed, and the voice doesn't come out of a hole in the top of the head. Even my seven-year-old students know they don't "fill their tummies up with air." Also, male and female larynges are functionally quite similar. Therefore, all my singers use all of their voices from bottom to top. I like to say that I have "Ms. Tenors" and "Mr. Sopranos" in my studio. We now know so much more about the singing system than we did centuries ago. Pedagogy is improving, but it still has a long way to go to reach twenty-first-century standards.

My goal with all of my students is to help them get to the next level above where they are at the moment. For a talent- and technique-challenged singer, that can mean improving audiation so she can sing on pitch and in rhythm. For another student, it might be gaining greater voice range in order for him to do a certain role. For yet another singer, it could be developing confidence so that student can compete at the professional level. It's all about levels. I feel teaching starts with where the student is. I use the image of the shopping mall entrance sign that says, "You Are Here." That's where we begin our journey around the "voice mall," finding technique and repertoire stores to shop in. For many, that first store needs to be a belief in self.

What elements of vocal technique do you think are most important?

I like to work with the "-*tions*" (pronounced "shuns") to isolate and integrate all aspects of voice technique. I start with body posi*tion* (posture), then respira*tion* (breath management), audia*tion* (hearing and reproducing pitch), phona*tion* (vocal fold activity), registra*tion* (the "gears" of the vocal folds), reson*ation* (amplifying and filtering the sound source with our three flexible resonators), articul*ation* (shaping sound into understandable language), and emo*tion* (the feelings that connect us to our stories and songs).

You mention audiation, which brings up an important point. A lot of times beginning voice students have not had formal training in piano and music theory. Do you have any strategies for teaching ear training, sight reading, and basic musicianship in a lesson?
I often center my voice exercises around music theory. With musically illiterate beginners, I start them off with learning the musical alphabet: the seven letters A through G. If they have audiation issues and are pitch-challenged, they sing just the individual notes using the alphabet letter as the lyric. As they learn to listen more critically, they move to three-note scales, again using the letter as their lyric. Five-note and eight-note scales follow when appropriate.

Then they'll attach those seven letters to the treble clef to learn the lines and spaces by singing their names. Once they are comfortable with the basic musical alphabet, they need to learn the other fourteen notes, the flats and sharps. This gets tricky because of enharmonic issues. I find that those students with good math skills do much better in this kind of training than math-challenged students. The latter group are happy to learn that some of our finest and most famous singers were musically illiterate. However, that still doesn't get them off the hook with my exercises.

Gradually, most of my students start to have fun singing music theory and anticipate moving forward in technical difficulty. Solfège is then introduced. Eventually, they'll sing the circle of fifths with relative minors; chord patterns with root, first inversion, and second inversion; and diatonic, chromatic, and pentatonic scales.

Exercises in sight singing are preceded by intervallic work. They sing, literally, "unison, a minor second, a major second, a minor third, a major third," and so on up and down the scale. Their ears are then matched up with their eyes as they learn to see and hear intervals.

Have you sung in the past, and if so, which styles? Do you currently sing any of the styles you teach?

I have been a professional singer for more than fifty years literally embracing all styles from Bach to rock. I signed my first recording and publishing contracts in the late 1960s. My "street cred" is fairly high in my studio because my students know I've been there and done that in many venues. In fact, my latest album of original music, *Take Them Along, Our Songs* got a rave review in the September 2016 issue of the *Journal of Singing* "Listeners Gallery." The album includes rock, pop, classic music theater, jazz, folk, country, and some hybrids. I'm pleased and grateful to still be singing in *my* seventies rather than in *the* seventies.

Who were your strongest influences, pedagogically, vocally, and musically?
Musically and vocally, fellow baritone Robert Merrill covered my "Bach-ish" side while Gordon MacRae exemplified—for me—classic music theater singing. The Beatles and the Rolling Stones influenced my "rock-ish" singing and listening worlds. In terms of folk music, I listened to Josh White, Bob Gibson, and a lot of the Kingston Trio. Pedagogically, after my mother and father, Richard Miller has had the strongest influence on my teaching.

What is the primary goal when training your students?
My primary goal is to respect and treat all who come into my studio as the unique individuals they are. I need to know how they think and feel, their hopes and dreams, their present voice technique and repertoire, their talent potential and their "teachability." Only then can I attempt to develop a healthy and efficient voice technique that can bring repertoire to life.

What else is important to you in your work?
The philosophical umbrella that covers my studio is ethical behavior modeled by me that hopefully has a positive influence on my students, some of whom are in single digits, age-wise. For example, many of my newer students ask to take pictures of my music with their smartphones. I tell them that is the equivalent of walking into a local convenience store and walking out with an item without paying for it. They are so accustomed to getting things free on the Internet that they have lost all sense of obligation and responsibility to performers, composers,

lyricists, arrangers, publishers, and the music community in general. In my small way, I am trying to reverse that trend. I have gotten a lot of help with that mission since our organization, the American Academy of Teachers of Singing (AATS), published a paper in 2016 called "Accessible Publication: Copyright and Integration of 21st Century Means of Publishing for Academic, Personal, and Professional Use of Printed Music." ♪

Also, I give each student my full attention during the lesson by minimizing distractions such as e-mail, phone calls, and the telling of personal stories not germane to their training and education. At $120 an hour, talk is not cheap!

How has your approach been informed by life experience, and how has it evolved over the years?
Life experience creates a mental library of situations and responses, especially those that continually repeat themselves in the teaching studio. The veteran teacher's library usually has more material from which to choose than that of the beginning teacher. I use my personal library to address my students' individual needs, whether they be technique-related, repertoire-based, or attitudinal. More important, my library is not a museum. It is continually expanding with new experiences and material that help me in my work.

What are your thoughts on professional organizations? Are you involved with any?
I am actively involved with NATS, AATS, ASCAP, the Songwriters Guild, and the American Federation of Musicians (AFM). Unfortunately, "divide and conquer" seems to be the motto for much of corporate America when it comes to unions and professional organizations. There is tremendous strength, enlightenment, and support in numbers. Going it alone makes one much more vulnerable to manipulation and threats as a professional as well as a person. ♪

Do you use technology in any of your teaching?
My studio is a living music technology history lesson. I have a 1960s TEAC reel-to-reel tape recorder, a 1970s HK T45 turntable, a 1980s Sony dual cassette deck, a 1990s Sony CD player, a 2010 Superscope

PSD450 digital recorder, and a 2015 HP laptop computer (I misplaced my eight-track player many years ago). I have records—everything from breakable 78s to the latest vinyl; tapes—big reels to mini-cassettes; and, of course, CDs. I have Shure microphones from my gigging days of the 1960s as well as new high-end Sennheisers. I have guitar amplifiers, three guitars, and the Bose Personalized Amplification System. I have VoceVista, Skype, YouTube, and a plethora of other resources at my fingertips. Also, my students' headshots, past to present and black-and-white to living color, line my studio walls. All in all, my independent studio is armed and ready for almost anything (except eight-tracks).

What is in your future as a voice pedagogue?
I have scaled down my studio teaching load so I have more time to write a book about my life in music as a singer, songwriter, teacher, and author. After authoring more than thirty years of columns for the *Journal of Singing*, much of that body of work as well as other material can coalesce into a book. I also hope to keep active in my professional organizations and continue to do master classes, workshops, lectures, and consulting worldwide. Or I may retire and play more golf. I turned seventy in June of 2016 and I can hear the clock ticking . . . louder! ♪

9

ELISABETH HOWARD

Elisabeth Howard *holds undergraduate and graduate degrees in classical voice from the Juilliard School. She is known as a pioneer in teaching contemporary commercial singing and is the originator of the Vocal Power Method. She is the author of the* Vocal Power Method Toolkit, *which includes the* SING! *e-book and audio, the* Born to Sing *video, and the* ABCs of Vocal Harmony *e-book and audio. After twenty years teaching Broadway performers in New York, she established the Elisabeth Howard's Vocal Power Academy in Los Angeles, training more than one hundred Vocal Power voice trainers. Ms. Howard is past president of the Los Angeles Chapter of NATS, was an adjunct professor at Pepperdine University for fifteen years, and has given workshops and master classes for singing conferences in eleven countries. There are more than fifty certified Vocal Power trainers throughout Italy alone. Ms. Howard is the voice teacher of Paige O'Hara—the voice of Belle in the 1991 Disney film* Beauty and the Beast—*Lionel Richie, and Priscilla Presley and coached Sting in preparation for the Grammy Awards. Elisabeth maintains studios in both Los Angeles and Chicago.* ♪

Tell us a little about your background and what led you to become a teacher of contemporary commercial styles.

I grew up in Brooklyn, and as far back as I can remember, I always enjoyed listening to pop, jazz, R&B, and rock 'n' roll, as well as opera, chamber music, music for solo instruments—such as the piano, flute, violin, or cello—and orchestral symphonic music. My father was a violinist and an opera lover. Our Saturday afternoons were filled with the beautiful sounds of the Metropolitan Opera broadcasts on WQXR. However, I also listened to the top rock 'n' roll station, WINS, with the famous DJ Alan Freed.

I began classical piano lessons at the age of five and cello at the age of ten. At my first piano recital, my teacher had me sit at the piano and improvise in the style of Bach, and I became hooked on Bach! I continued with my piano lessons for many years and also played cello in the orchestra beginning in elementary school and throughout high school. In fact, while I was a voice major at Juilliard, I was also secondary major in piano. You could do that back in those days. At twelve years old, I was practicing Bach and Mozart and also writing pop songs. My uncle, who was in the entertainment business, had me play and sing three of my songs for a record company. The record company told me the songs were great and offered me a contract, but I turned it down because they said the songs needed a few changes, and I was reluctant to do that. Ha!

I began studying ballet at the age of five at my uncle's ballet school, and when I was eleven, I was offered a full scholarship at Ballet Arts Studio in Carnegie Hall. At the age of fifteen, I received a vocal scholarship in voice at the Williamsburg Settlement House in Brooklyn. I was also performing quite a bit as soloist in my high school chorus and as a member of the All-City High School Chorus. My mother owned a neighborhood dance and music studio called the Lanza School of Dance and Music on Flatbush Avenue in Brooklyn. It was a family affair with my mother teaching dance, my father teaching violin and piano, my uncles teaching piano and guitar, and me teaching piano and ballet. I guess my mother thought I was singing well enough, and so she asked me to teach not only piano and ballet but voice too. I was really scared, but it was a way of paying for my own voice and piano lessons. So, with great trepidation, I reluctantly accepted the challenge.

My very first lesson was on a Saturday morning, and this sweet seven-year-old little girl with long blonde curls came in for a half-hour lesson. I looked at her and she looked at me and we started in. I enjoyed every minute of it. She wanted to sing a popular song and so we did. Why not? That was the beginning of a sixty-year-long romance teaching contemporary commercial music. Subsequently, my mother sent me many students over the years in every genre from classical to pop . . . and let me tell you—I loved it!

I enjoyed exploring the myriad colors and variety of sounds that the human voice was capable of producing. I enjoyed dissecting with the students the pronunciation, phrasing, and use of vibrato from style to style. I was absolutely fascinated. Analyzing, understanding, and teaching the components of the various genres of music became the very fiber of my being.

My income from teaching voice and piano paid for my voice lessons through high school and Juilliard. Upon graduating from Juilliard, I was awarded a graduate assistantship to Indiana University, and during that first year, I applied to Hunter College in New York City to teach voice on their music faculty. Hunter College invited me to be their Artist in Residence and to teach their voice classes, provided I go back to Juilliard to get my master's degree. And I still had ten private students. It was a very heavy load, but I was happy and grateful for this opportunity.

During the time that I taught at Hunter (from 1965 to 1967), some of the students asked if they could sing music theater and the pop songs of Barbra Streisand. Walking by my classroom door at the time, one was likely to hear one student singing "People," another singing Schubert's "Heidenröslein," and yet another singing "Caro mio ben." We had great fun! Everyone learned from each other. The classical students were fascinated by the belt voice exercises, while the pop and Broadway singers were fascinated by the high, sustained soprano notes. My classes were from time to time audited by staff members of the music department. Administration and staff didn't know what to make of me but told me there were long lines at registration to sign up for my classes. The head of the music department increased my hours and had me teach also at the uptown campus. Those were very interesting and formative days.

After two years at Hunter and after receiving my master's degree from Juilliard, I got married to my high school chorus buddy. We rented an apartment on the upper west side of Manhattan, and I continued to teach my private students in every conceivable style from classical to pop and jazz. During this time, I taught many students who were performers on Broadway.

During that period, I also obtained an agent and was cast in more than fifteen musicals in New York City, on tour and in summer stock, both as a belter and as a legit soprano. It was during a workshop production of *Blood*—a contemporary musical at Joe Papp's Public Theater—that I rediscovered a talent from my youth: songwriting. The cast of *Blood* was composed of singer-songwriter-actors, and in a six-day-a-week, six-hours-a-day, six-month-long workshop, we wrote the music and script to *Blood*. We wrote and rehearsed every day, even on Christmas and New Year's! After the show opened and closed, I found myself with an obsession to continue writing and performing original songs. I quit my music theater career to spend the next few years writing contemporary commercial songs. My husband at that time, Howard Austin, was an awesome singer and wrote wonderful poetry. We combined our talents and within a year were offered a contract with MCA Music for our pop songwriting. He quit his day job and joined me, and we made a full-time go at being singer-songwriters. We formed a duo, Kane and Glory, and we performed our original songs on two keyboards with our band up and down the Eastern Seaboard. Even though I had left my opera voice on the back burner as a performer, I still maintained a full studio of voice students, which included classical singers as well as music theater and pop students. This studio variety has continued to the present day. I currently teach pop, jazz, rock, R&B, country, music theater, classical, and opera.

After teaching Broadway performers for twenty years in New York City, I relocated to Los Angeles in 1978 and set up my private studio. I then trained several of my own students to teach the Vocal Power Method™ and founded the Vocal Power Academy. Subsequently, Dr. Henry Price, head of the voice department at Pepperdine University, invited me to be an adjunct professor at Pepperdine to teach music theater majors. I taught there for fifteen years. I also maintained my full schedule of private students, performance workshops, and Vocal Power Showcases. ♪

What do you believe are the criteria for teaching these styles well?

I believe a voice teacher should, above all, *appreciate* the musical style she or he is teaching. A teacher should be able to demonstrate in his or her own voice a variety of registrations: upper register/head voice/falsetto; lower register/chest voice/modal; the mix for higher singing; and safe belting in both male and female voices. Vibrato control is a major issue in most singing styles. The ability to blend registers is also very important. A singer also needs to be able to create a variety of vocal colors. Color is an important part of my pedagogy—I teach chest color, mouth color, mask color, and head color. To achieve some of my desired effects for emotional expression, I use terminology such as *back L*, *throat cry*, *throat laugh*, *creaky door*, *glottal attack*, and *breathy*, to name only a few. I teach singing on the pure vowels and using consonants for drama.

A voice teacher in contemporary commercial music as well as classical singing should be able to teach and demonstrate how to control vibrato. For jazz ballads, a slower "throat" vibrato is needed and, for scatting, a faster and narrower "shimmery" vibrato. In R&B ballads, a slow and wide vibrato is desirable. In most styles, a diaphragmatic vibrato—for long, sustained tones—is typical. In jazz style, delayed vibrato is typical, and in rock style, little or no vibrato is common. A teacher of contemporary commercial music should be able to teach rhythms and phrasing such as syncopation, back phrasing, and anticipation. Pronunciation varies greatly from style to style, and the teacher should make sure the student sings with the pronunciation appropriate to the style.

I also believe that teacher of contemporary commercial music should teach improvisation. Exercises using the blues and pentatonic scales are beneficial in teaching the runs and licks that are built on these scales. For example, in blues, jazz, and R&B styles, the blues scale is used for melody lines as well as for licks. In R&B style, the notes of the pentatonic are used for runs and licks as well as melody lines. In rock style, the notes of the pentatonic scale are prevalent in melody lines. I teach my coloratura techniques from classical style and transfer them over to pop style for runs and licks.

How do you teach style to students who don't have a strong background in a given genre?
The musical *Hair* opened the door to the modern musical. Since then, singers have been required to be able to audition and sing with authenticity songs in the style of shows such as *Godspell, Jesus Christ Superstar, Rent, Spring Awakening, Aida, The Lion King, Mamma Mia, The Book of Mormon,* and *Jersey Boys*. In music theater, there is no longer the typical "legit" soprano, mezzo, tenor, and baritone leads like we had

in musicals such as *Carousel, The Most Happy Fella, Brigadoon,* and *Oklahoma.* To be able to compete in today's music theater industry, you have to be able to sing like Pavarotti one day and Mötley Crüe the next. It is quite a challenge!

My pedagogical approach is very simple. I give the student vocal exercises that are appropriate to the new style. We choose a song in the desired style—either on a CD from my library or on YouTube—sung by a recognized recording artist. We listen to the entire song first to absorb the overall feel of the style. Then I take them phrase by phrase, methodically and in slow motion, carefully copying every nuance. The ear guides the voice. The voice experiences muscle memory, and the ear and voice work together and are being trained to listen and copy—yes, *copy*—every nuance in that new style. *Being authentic is in the details.* I have a system in place for elements of style, which I touched on earlier:

1. vibrato type: slow, fast, wide, narrow, straight tone, or delayed
2. register: head, chest, or mix
3. vocal colors: chest, mouth, mask, head
4. special effects: *back L, throat cry, throat laugh, creaky door, glottal attack,* and *breathy*
5. pronunciation: pure vowel sounds, consonants, regional diction (Southern, British, East Coast, etc.)
6. licks and runs: how to execute them with accuracy and authenticity

If we are preparing for an audition for *Dreamgirls,* for example, we will work on a song closest to that style. In other words, a song that could have easily been in the show—such as a Whitney Houston song or a Jennifer Hudson song—would be appropriate.

When a student desires to explore "classical style" and is unfamiliar with classical singing, I play an excerpt or two of a classical piece for the student. I point out stylistic characteristics, such as vibrato on every note: a shimmery vibrato on faster, moving notes and diaphragmatic vibrato on high, sustained notes. We also discuss other elements of technique and style, such as raising the soft palate to obtain the appropriate color needed for that style of singing, classical diction, and precise rhythm. In the end, we must honor the composer. I give the student a list of several singers they can listen to on YouTube that are close to their own voice type because a singer of their own voice type is much easier to relate to than, for example, if I sing a phrase to a baritone in my own voice. (Although I have been known to sing "Bella siccome un angelo" pretty well!)

There are so many styles out there, and they really can't be grouped into broad categories anymore. When you say "classical singing," do you mean Puccini or Mozart? Or "nonclassical singing," do you mean Ella Fitzgerald or Eric Clapton? You can't even say "music theater style" anymore—are you speaking of *Rent* or *The Phantom of the Opera*? I remember when I had a new student come into my studio and I asked him, "What kind of music do you listen to?" He said, "I listen to the classics." I was so surprised because he looked so "hip." I remarked, "Really, like who?" He said, "Yeah, like the Who, Led Zeppelin, and the Grateful Dead." It made me laugh!

How did you come up with your method or approach? What does it consist of, and how is it unique?
The Elisabeth Howard Vocal Power Method is a simple, step-by-step approach to vocal technique, and my intention is to take the *mystery* out of singing. My journey began when I had vocal problems right after I graduated from Juilliard: throat and tongue tension, the inability to begin a note on the breath (onset), releasing a note at the end of a phrase, and so on. I was also losing the ability to sustain my high notes (devastating for a coloratura soprano), the ability to sing a legato line, and other issues. I was still young (in my early twenties) and was totally perplexed by this dilemma. I went to a total of fifteen different voice teachers within one year to try to find answers, but no solutions were found. My then husband, Howard Austin, was an excellent singer and self-taught. He demonstrated to me how he learned to sing with an even, diaphragmatic "vibrato on the breath" by listening to singers like Mario Lanza and copying the sound. This was a revelation to me, and as I worked with Howard in just a little while, I found that I could release a lot of the tongue and throat tension just by singing with what we called a "diaphragmatic vibrato on the breath." My high notes above high C gradually returned, and I could once again sustain them without becoming vocally fatigued.

There was another young voice teacher, Eric Thorendahl, who had been an accompanist for Madam Novikova, one of the major opera voice teachers in New York at the time. He showed me how to balance my air pressure with my vocal folds for a clear and healthy tone. He showed me a new way to approach breathing and support—"lean out and down"—which was the exact opposite from what I had been taught: "pull up and in." He also showed me a "tongue release" exercise where you sing a simple two- to five-note scale while stretching and holding your tongue out as far as you can: first, with a paper towel; second, without the paper towel; and then again the third time, at which time your tongue is released back into normal position. I also used this method for sustaining notes with vibrato. I have heard that these days this technique is more widely used, but in the early seventies, this was a revelation—and it saved my life!

I studied the techniques of many singers in various styles and created a simple, step-by-step method called the Vocal Power Method. The method teaches breathing, support, power, projection, vibrato, dynamics, vocal colors, the mix voice, and special effects. The two most innovative and unique techniques associated with the Vocal Power Method are what I call "diaphragmatic vibrato on the breath" and "the mix," which I learned from listening to the phenomenal Broadway/pop singer Melba Moore in the early 1970s. She had the most fantastic high notes that sounded like they were still in her chest, and when I repeated what she did, I couldn't believe it. They were in head register without strain using a predominance of "mask" with the soft palate down. I labeled this "the mix" because it felt like a "mixture" of head and chest registers. After hearing the constant pleading of my students to write a book on my method, in 1980 I finally published these concepts in *SING!* I believe I was the first to write a book on contemporary commercial singing that included an audio cassette with exercises and singing examples. Subsequently, I expanded the book and added more audio files, which are now in e-book form. The Elisabeth Howard Vocal Power Method is unique because it is a step-by-step, clear system with scientifically based techniques. It teaches anyone who wants to sing how to sing, and I believe anyone can sing!

What is your general philosophy of voice teaching? Summarize your core beliefs about vocal technique.
A teacher must have high standards, trust their technique, and instill confidence in their students. A teacher should provide a safe place in

which to learn, improve, and make mistakes. Even though we strive for perfection, there should never be undue stress put on the student to achieve more than what is realistic. Singing in the church choir, participating in community theater, singing karaoke, and just simply singing for one's own enjoyment should be encouraged and embraced.

A teacher should appreciate the style the student wishes to study. A teacher should know how to teach the vocal techniques required for singing in that style. A teacher should always be honest with themselves and with the student in terms of what he or she is capable of giving the student. If a teacher feels that another teacher is more qualified teaching opera, then the teacher has an obligation to communicate this to the student and refer the student to someone who is an expert in that area. Students pay a lot of money to take voice lessons. In the opera world, time is of the essence. Opera houses book years in advance based upon auditions that occur now. There is a step-by-step progression from an undergraduate degree to graduate school, young artist programs, and a career. It is important to get to the right coaches, agent, and manager; learn the appropriate roles; enter competitions; and so on. There is no time to waste, and the window of opportunity is narrow.

Time is also of the essence in the pop world, where being "young and talented" is the name of the game. A teacher should always be honest but not ever demeaning, degrading, or insulting. Singers in general are very (*very*) sensitive. One wrong word can stop them from ever wanting to sing again. Seriously. No one was born on the operating table with a natural singing voice. The first vocal tone is always a big "wah" as a baby! We all started somewhere, but we all started at the beginning. Some of us were fortunate to grow up in a musical family, and our ears were trained even before we sang a note.

The voice is an instrument, and you need the tools to play it. A good teacher can provide those tools. Every once in a while, someone would say to me, "I don't know if I should waste my time and money on lessons if I can't sing." My response was always, "If you went to a piano teacher, would you say, 'I don't know if I should take lessons; I can't play the piano'?" Of course not!

A successful voice teacher should be knowledgeable in the techniques needed for the style he or she is teaching. A successful voice teacher should love people and should take pleasure and delight in seeing a student leave their studio happier than when they came in because that student made progress. A successful teacher should embrace the idea of making a person's life better through the love of singing. We make a contribution to the world when our students succeed. It's like throwing a rock into a lake and the circles get wider and wider until the circles fill the lake. A great voice teacher loves the idea of helping a singer achieve their dream.

To summarize my core beliefs about vocal technique:

1. A solid vocal technique enables us to freely express our emotions and, above all, honor the music, composer, and lyricist—not merely sing notes.
2. Breathing and support must be consistent, correct, and automatic. To paraphrase Pavarotti in Jerome Hines's famous book *Great Singers on Great Singing*: "Support is like being in the bathroom and staying in that position until the end of the phrase." Dynamic resistance between the inner and outer intercostal muscles and resistance with the lower subcostals should be taught on the first lesson and reinforced at every lesson: "out and down," not "up and in." Use the same set of muscles as one uses for coughing, (gently) sneezing, blowing up a balloon, and going to the bathroom (sorry, but that's the sensation).
3. Control of vibrato, and even the ability to sing with no vibrato, is essential in today's market. It is required in the recording studio as well in choral groups and vocal ensembles—basically anytime a singer is required to blend with other voices.
4. Control of dynamics: the ability to balance breath pressure with the vocal folds for all dynamics from *piano* to *forte* as well as the ability to *crescendo* and *decrescendo*.
5. Control of vocal coloration: for expressive singing, one must have the ability to alter the configuration of the vocal tract to enhance the emotion of the word or phrase.

In conclusion, a solid vocal technique allows a singer to: (a) get through long rehearsals; (b) sing in spite of illness; (c) sing eight shows a week; (d) sing on demanding tours; (e) sing over a band or orchestra; (f) sing to serve the music; (g) sing well into the "golden years" with an untarnished "golden" voice! This is what every singer dreams of—longevity!

Have you sung in the recent past, and if so, which styles?
I have never really stopped singing; I have sung and performed all my life up to the present time. I performed a one-woman show called *Op'ra to Pop'ra* in which I sang opera arias, music theater, jazz, rock, and country songs. The presentation was designed to prove that the human voice was capable of singing in any style. I have sung opera roles such as Violetta in *La traviata* as well as music theater belt roles such as Amy in *Company*. I have also performed my own original pop songs as a singer-songwriter. One of my proudest achievements as a singer was to win the title of "Ms. Senior America 2012," a pageant in which—at the age of seventy-one—I sang the opera aria "Sempre Libera" from *La traviata*, which included high D♭ at the end of the cadenza!

Who were your strongest influences—pedagogically, vocally, and musically?
The strongest pedagogical influences in my life were Howard Austin, a wonderful self-taught singer, along with my close friend from Juilliard, John DeMain. They together helped me understand and use the "diaphragmatic vibrato" I have described previously. Howard is actually the one singing on all my *SING!* CDs and on our *Born to Sing* DVD. John DeMain went on to conduct all over the world and has even conducted Placido Domingo in performance. He is now artistic director for Madison Opera. Eric Thorendahl, who I knew from Juilliard days, helped me understand the balance between the vocal cords (as we called the vocal folds in those days) and breath pressure.

My strongest influences vocally were opera singers: Roberta Peters, Rita Streich, Maria Callas, Joan Sutherland, Beverly Sills, Eleanor Steber, Elizabeth Schwarzkopf, and Anna Moffo. I also love and admire the male voices of Mario Lanza, Dietrich Fischer-Dieskau, Luciano Pavarotti, Placido Domingo, and Roberto Alagna. My favorite music theater singers are John Raitt, Barbara Cook, Ethel Merman, Paige O'Hara, Susan Watson, Alfred Drake, Julie Andrews, Barbra Streisand, Sutton Foster, Kelli O'Hara, Idina Menzel, Kristin Chenoweth, Patti Lupone, Jerry Orbach, Mandy Patinkin, Michael Crawford, Joel Grey, Rex Harrison, Brian Stokes Mitchell, and Florence Henderson. In the realm of popular music, I learned a lot by listening to Frank Sinatra, Tony Bennett, Melba Moore, Judy Garland, Linda Ronstadt, Laura Nyro, Carly

Simon, Mariah Carey, Whitney Houston, and Christina Aguilera. In R&B, Aretha Franklin, Etta James, Patti Labelle, Mary J. Blige, Luther Vandross, and Teddy Pendergrass are my favorites. In jazz, there is of course the great Ella Fitzgerald, Billie Holiday, Cleo Laine, Billy Eckstein, Nat King Cole, and Eva Cassidy. In rock, I liked Janis Joplin, Pat Benatar, Heart, Bonnie Raitt, Sheryl Crow, Steven Tyler, Steve Perry, and the Who. In country, I loved Patsy Cline, Reba McEntire, Trisha Yearwood, Tammy Wynette, Johnny Cash, Randy Travis, George Jones, and Mel Tillis—just to name a few!

My strongest musical influences are Johann Sebastian Bach, Wolfgang Amadeus Mozart, Johannes Brahms, Richard Strauss, Giuseppe Verdi, Giacomo Puccini, Stephen Sondheim, Andrew Lloyd Webber, Lionel Hampton, Dave Brubeck, Benny Goodman, and many more. I encourage my students to listen to all genres of music, to broaden their tastes. I believe that one should embrace *all* styles of music. You can specialize, but *never* be a snob or you will be left behind.

What is the primary goal when training your students?

I always aim for perfection and a professional level of singing with all my students. My standards are high, and the students know this coming in. My primary goal is—first and foremost—to give them a solid foundation in vocal technique. We then work on applying the technique to the songs that they will perform for auditions and shows.

Music theater covers genres from opera to rock. I think it's nearly impossible to be a first-rate professional singer in every genre. I believe one has to specialize on what they do best. If you are a belter, then be a belter and be the best you can be. If you are a soprano, then be a soprano and be the best you can be. If you are a baritone, then be a baritone. Don't try to be a tenor. If you are a tenor, then be a tenor and don't try to be a baritone. It's important to know your type both vocally and physically in music theater. In pop, it's important to find personal vocal style as well as to create a visual stage image.

My approach to teaching singing besides the technical aspects has to do with being positive and encouraging. Singers are sensitive individuals and often quite insecure. We are exposing who we are every time we sing. We take to heart everything everyone and anyone says to us. One negative comment from someone we don't even know or respect can cancel out one thousand positive comments. That's just the way we are, and I make it a point to be encouraging at every lesson with every student. I am always honest with my students and believe strongly that with hard work and belief in oneself we can achieve our dreams.

What else is important to you in your work?
I believe it's important to prepare students for auditions and shows. I give separate eight-week workshops—with piano accompanist and sound system—culminating in Vocal Power Singer Showcases about four times a year. The showcase performances are accompanied by a live three-piece band and present all styles from rock to music theater, jazz, country, and opera. The showcases include my own students and the students of the other Vocal Power Trainers. This is a great way of sharing and enjoying the experience of seeing our students grow and achieve their goals. In these workshops, I teach additional performance techniques, including choreography; I was a professional dancer before I was a singer. Having studied four years at HB Studios with Uta Hagen in New York City, I also teach treating the song as if it were an acting monologue. We also address personal image—having "a look." Since 1980, our Vocal Power Academy has presented 154 Singer Showcases starting in New York City and subsequently in Los Angeles.

Preparing for a showcase encourages the student to be laser focused, come to lessons consistently, and make an extra effort to stay healthy. Students get to share their talents with family and friends, and—if they are ready—they can invite agents. Performing in showcases affords a safe environment to experiment and take risks. It's a great place to prepare for auditions. As their teacher, I watch each student and I take mental notes and I can see what we need to work on next. Perfection is in the details!

How has your approach been informed by life experience, and how has it evolved over the years?
My life path is surprising if you consider where I was in elementary school. My parents divorced during World War II when I was only three years old. My mother was a single working parent, and the going was rough in those years. She remarried when I was five, and we all struggled making ends meet. My second father was an interior designer

but also an excellent professional violinist who played in various local orchestras. He made sure I had piano lessons as well as cello in school and always had the classical music station WQXR playing on the radio. As I mentioned before, Saturday broadcasts of the Metropolitan Opera Live were a ritual in our family.

Perhaps the insecurity I felt during those years contributed to my being a vulnerable and passionate performer. I watched my parents work shoulder to shoulder in the interior design business, and then later my mother, a terrific entrepreneur, opened a dance and music studio where I began my first voice teaching. I learned from my parents that hard work and discipline achieve goals and that if you work hard enough, the impossible becomes possible. Being accepted to Juilliard, working with Kim Hunter in *The Prime of Miss Jean Brodie*, performing Violetta with orchestra, obtaining a singer-songwriting contract with MCA Music, and winning the title "Ms. Senior America 2012" were a few of the life experiences that helped me not only to grow but to help my students achieve their goals.

These experiences made me even stronger in my resolve to help my students through obstacles, to work hard, to pay attention to details, and to keep on keeping on, no matter what life throws at them. I know that everything that has happened to me was for the purpose of sharing these experiences with my students to help them achieve their dreams. I have always believed that we are all on this earth to make contributions to others.

What are your thoughts on professional organizations? Are you involved with any?
I first joined NATS in the mid-1980s. I loved the teachers, the students, the events, and I never missed a meeting. I was thrilled to be invited to be on the board of directors of my local chapter and started out as the publicity director for two years, then vice president (in charge of workshops) for another two years, and finally president in 2000. I am so grateful to NATS because I was given the opportunity to conduct my Vocal Power workshops and master classes for NATS chapters in California, a NATS regional convention, and for the NATS "Music Theater III" winter workshop in Seattle. In 2000, I was invited to do a three-hour workshop and master class for the NATS national convention in

Philadelphia. From that workshop and master class, I was subsequently invited to conduct Vocal Power workshops and master classes at national conventions in Italy, France, Australia, Switzerland, Canada, Brazil, the Mozarteum in Austria, ICVT in Helsinki, and EVTA in Oslo. In recent years, I have also conducted workshops and master classes for the regional and national voice teacher conferences in the United Kingdom.

NATS truly helped me launch my international teaching career. Because of the exposure at the NATS conference in Philadelphia, I met and bonded with Anna Gotti, who was then vice president of AICI (Associazione Insegnanti di Canto Italiana)—the Italian professional organization for voice teachers—and she invited me to Italy! Anna became director of Accademia Vocal Power Italia, and together we have coordinated Vocal Power workshops, master classes, and Vocal Power teacher certification exams every year since 2001. We have trained many Vocal Power Trainers throughout Italy, and my books *SING!* and *The ABCs of Vocal Harmony* have been translated into Italian. I owe so much to NATS and am so grateful that I became involved with the organization.

Do you use technology in any of your teaching?
I use a microphone for the pop singers when we work on a song. I use a mic on a boom stand for myself at the piano. A pop singer will most always perform with a mic. There are exceptions, however; for example, in the case of auditioning in a pop style for a Broadway show. Casting people do not usually provide a mic, so you have to just do the best you can. For a pop singer in the recording studio, there are head sets, and reverb (echo effect) is used in the cans (earphones) so that the singer can hear his or her voice the way it will sound in the actual recording.

For pop singers, amplification is used on stage in a live performance. Therefore, I believe that the singer needs to practice with a mic in a lesson because the mic is not merely for amplification; it is also used for intimate sound effects that one can't achieve without a mic. Soft, sensual, breathy singing is an example. Reverb creates an entirely other feel. Reverb is an effect we definitely don't want in classical singing, particularly in the singing of coloratura phrases. For this reason, I do not use a mic for classical singers or for music theater singers, unless we are practicing for a special outdoor amphitheater performance where an entire sound system will be provided.

The use of YouTube is a must in my studio. I believe it is a great learning tool. As discussed in detail earlier, I use YouTube for the study of personal style. I can literally lay my hands on any song in any genre and listen to any artist that ever recorded that song. We can even listen to multiple artists sing the same song and choose which artist we prefer.

Personal style is developed by listening to and emulating the artists we admire. It's automatic and is absorbed naturally. The ear is the most powerful tool we singers have, especially when learning a new style. If you ever are curious to know who the vocal influences were on a particular artist, just go back to when they were teenagers and look up the popular singers on the pop charts. You will say, "Aha!" A good example is Professor Longhair, who was on the pop charts when Elvis Presley was a teenager. All the great instrumentalists learned by listening and emulating instrumentalists whom they admired and who came before them. Why should singers be any different?

What is in your future as a voice pedagogue?

Teaching is my life, and I plan to do it for as long as I can. I am looking forward to continuing to conduct Vocal Power workshops and master classes and, in particular, working with voice teachers who are interested in teaching contemporary commercial music.

10

JOAN LADER

Joan Lader's more than thirty years of providing vocal training and rehabilitation for professional voice users was commemorated last June when she was presented with the American theater's highest honor, a Tony Award for "Excellence in the Theater." Ms. Lader received a BFA from Penn State University in theatre arts with a minor in music. Trained as a speech-language pathologist in graduate school, she specializes in working with singers and actors and—in collaboration with New York's top otolaryngologists—rehabilitation of injured voices. Her extensive practice includes leading actors and singers from Broadway, film, opera, R&B, rap, rock, and pop. Ms. Lader is a certified master teacher of the Estill Voice Training (EVT) system and also has extensive training in the Alexander Technique, Fitzmaurice Voicework, and the work of Arthur Lessac. She has given master classes at universities and summer programs throughout the country, is a consultant at NYU's New Studio, and serves on the advisory boards of the Voice Foundation and Manhattan School of Music. She is particularly proud to be involved with the National Young Arts Foundation (YoungArts), whose participants so often become the stars of tomorrow. ♪

Tell us a little about your background and what led you to become a teacher of contemporary commercial styles.

I have been a music theater geek since I was two years old! When I was young, there was a radio station called WVNJ (The Best of Broadway) that played an entire show at 8:00 p.m. every night. I saw my first Broadway show (*The King and I*) when I was four years old and *South Pacific* shortly thereafter. I grew up in New York City, studied dance and piano, and ended up at the High School of Music and Art (La Guardia) as a voice major. I was a theater major at Penn State, performed in summer stock productions and regional theater, and ended up in a repertory company Off-Broadway singing Gilbert and Sullivan.

My most memorable bad audition was my last audition. It was for a role in the Broadway production of *Annie*. I was asked to sing for Martin Charnin, the composer and director. I sang a song from *70, Girls, 70* entitled "Where Do the Elephants Go?" He was not amused but consented to call me back if I would sing "I Got Rhythm." Intuitively, I completely understood why he wanted me to sing that song. He wanted to know if I could belt, and I couldn't. So I transposed the song down and sang it like a baritone. The whole experience was embarrassing, and I thought to myself, "I can't do this anymore." I knew I needed to find someone who could help me sing in this style, but in those days, you either could do it or you couldn't. I searched for teachers who could explain the process but to no avail. As a character actress, I knew I was doomed if I couldn't figure this out.

In the early 1980s, I happened to be at the Voice Foundation Symposium at Juilliard where I met Jo Estill. She was teaching a group of doctors how to belt. I sat in the back of the room and stayed to talk to her after the session. I had never heard anyone explain belting before and I was fascinated. She invited me to join a group of teachers and singers to study with her. We met every Saturday in her apartment on 57th Street for two years. It was a vocal playground. She began with extensive work in anatomy and physiology, acoustics, and voice science. We experimented with producing various qualities. She felt that all voices were beautiful, so there was no judgment and we were able to work in an extremely safe environment. I was able to do things with my voice that I had never dreamed I'd be able to do. She was doing research at that time that no one else was doing. She brought scientific understanding and technical innovation to the teaching and rehabilitation of voice.

Out of all the teachers we are interviewing in this book, you had the closest relationship with Jo Estill. Can you tell us a little bit more about her?
Jo was an incredibly dynamic person. Although she was a trained opera singer, she could sing in a variety of styles, such as folk, opera, country, and belting. But most important, she was curious. She wanted to know *how* she was able to do this. She was interested in getting singers to be able to do three things: (1) to *feel* what they were doing, (2) to *hear* what they were doing, and (3) to *see* what they were doing. She earned a master's degree in music education, but it was through the speech and hearing departments that she began to arrive at some answers. Jo continued this work at the Upstate Medical Center in Syracuse. Her studies included anatomy and physiology of the larynx and the entire vocal tract, acoustics, voice science, instrumentation, and audiology. She even made X-rays of her vocal tract while she sang! This investigation led to what she initially labeled vocal modes or qualities (*speech, sob, opera,* and *twang*). This eventually led to the exploration and explanation of six vocal qualities: *speech, falsetto, sob, twang, opera,* and *belt*. Jo wanted to systematize what singers do so that they would sing with confidence and awareness. Most of all, she was simply inquisitive. It was this insatiable curiosity that made Jo who she was, and this quality is what allowed her to accomplish what she did. Basically, she demystified singing! ♪

You were also trained as a speech-language pathologist. Can you tell us a little bit about your clinical experience? Did you work with any prominent otolaryngologists?
Oh yes, many. One in particular comes to mind: Dr. Friedrich Brodnitz. There were three very famous doctors at that time: Dr. Leo Reckford, Dr. Eugen Grabscheid, and Dr. Brodnitz. The three of them worked almost exclusively with singers. Dr. Brodnitz wrote a book called *Keep Your Voice Healthy: A Guide to the Intelligent Use and Care of the Speaking and Singing Voice*. It was a very important book back then. I worked with him extensively while I was in graduate school and wrote my master's thesis under his guidance (on the Vienna Boys Choir, of all

topics). He would make 78 recordings of all kinds of singers with various pathologies and developed a therapeutic "chewing" technique that was revolutionary in its day. It was designed as a natural method for developing good speech and voice. The goal of this therapeutic technique was to prevent vocal hyperfunction. I was also privileged to work with the magnificent Dr. Wilbur James Gould. Dr. Gould was one of the founders of the Voice Foundation. He was the first doctor to promote an interdisciplinary approach, bringing together otolaryngologists, voice teachers, speech-language pathologists, acousticians, and speaking voice trainers. I currently work with Dr. Gwen Korovin, Dr. Peak Woo, and Dr. Lucian Sulica. Oren Brown was not a physician, but he was a superb voice teacher with an interest in the juxtaposition of art and science. I heard him lecture on many occasions and admired the diligent work he did as both a researcher and a teacher. ♪

What kinds of styles do you currently teach? How long have you been teaching these styles?

I have been teaching for more than thirty-five years. I do a lot of cross-training, which basically means getting students to sing in many voice qualities, including styles of music that are not in their wheelhouse. Although music theater is my most concentrated genre, I enjoy giving master classes to singer-songwriters, jazz artists, opera singers, and pop/rock performers as well.

What, do you believe, are the criteria for teaching these styles well?

I think it's essential that you become familiar with the music and artists who perform in these styles. It's important that you understand and are able to communicate how these sounds can be produced in a healthy manner. In other words, as Jo (Estill) believed, it is possible to isolate and control the individual anatomical structures in preparation for producing different vocal qualities.

How do you teach style to students who don't have a strong background in a given genre?

This happens all the time! First, I need to know what it is that they do regularly and where their normal comfort zone is. We then try to make it playful so that they feel comfortable stepping out of their box. We also discuss anatomical differences between what they usually do versus what they need to do to sing the new style successfully; the shape of the vocal tract, the position of the larynx and tongue, and so forth might be different. Basically, we just play! Sometimes I'll have them imitate animals or different types of sounds so that they can experience new ideas. It's really an individual thing since every student is different. However, it's rare that a singer will refuse to work in an unfamiliar genre. I cross-train with all of my students. It's fun to hear opera singers belt and to hear rockers singing Italian art songs.

How did you come up with your method or approach? What does it consist of, or how is it unique?
I'm not sure if I would call what I do a specific "method." Since my training has been as a speech pathologist as well as a performer and singing voice teacher, my approach is fairly eclectic. I have stolen techniques from so many sources. I'm not sure if it's unique, but it is certainly a holistic approach that focuses on the whole body and mind connection in addition to what's happening at the level of the larynx. I've also studied Alexander Technique, Feldenkrais, yoga, Fitzmaurice Voicework, Lessac Kinesthetic Training, Linklater, Pilates, Gyrotonic, and of course the Estill Voice Training™ system. I have taken additional courses in myofascial release techniques and worked with osteopaths, shiatsu practitioners, and massage therapists. All of these methods have informed my teaching, and I try to give each of my students what they need to be successful.

What is your general philosophy of voice teaching? Summarize your core beliefs about vocal technique.
That's an interesting question. My general philosophy about teaching voice is not to feel that you need to convince the student how smart you are but rather to empower them with the tools to work on their own. Good technique involves "getting the most bang for the buck." In other words, a singer must have the technique to produce a variety of sounds throughout the range of the voice with the least amount of vocal effort. If you can get a student to sing on their interest rather than on their principal, you have done a good job. I have chanted this mantra for years!

As I mentioned above, I am not sure if there is anything about my technique that is particularly unique because I am honestly not sure how others teach. There are so many teachers specializing in contemporary commercial music. I do think that often the differences from teacher to teacher have more to do with how something is communicated than the technique itself. For example, I consider myself to be a very committed teacher. I am literally on call 24/7. I am also a very strict teacher—sometimes I tell my students that it's against my better judgment for them to go on, and I expect them to listen to me. This is why trust between the teacher and the student is so important. I am not sure how other teachers work in terms of protocol and this sort of thing, but this is very much my style and approach. It's a close relationship. However, I don't want my students to be so dependent on me that they can't work on their own. After all, they are on tour half the time.

What elements of vocal technique do you think are most important?

I think it's important to understand the basic anatomy and physiology of the instrument and the relationship between all of the subsystems: the respiratory system, the phonatory system, and the resonating and articulatory system; in other words, the power, source, and filter. If you have a larynx that's been compromised, you are going to have problems at the filter level. But if you have a normal larynx, you can make many adjustments to produce many different types of sounds. Isolating these various components and understanding how they work with one another is essential.

Do you have a favorite vocal exercise that you would like to share with us?

Not really. I use many types of exercises depending on the student's needs and degree of competence. I use a variety of semi-occluded vocal tract (SOVT) exercises, *messa di voce*, and *staccati* as well as introducing Estill figures and qualities. Every student is so different. I do, however, try to integrate various aspects of body work (alignment and airflow) with every vocal exercise that I give my students. Whenever someone sings, I am evaluating the entire body and how it moves through space—not just the voice. Every exercise I assign is designed with this "whole picture" in mind. It's a very holistic way of working.

Have you sung in the past? And if so, which styles? Do you currently sing any of the styles you teach?
I sang for many years. I studied classically (and sang pretty poorly as a classical singer), but I later sang folk music and music theater both in college and professionally. I also played guitar and piano when I was younger. I don't sing very much anymore due to my busy teaching schedule. Most recently, however, I did sing four lines of "Getting to Know You" at my Tony honoree acceptance speech!

Who were your strongest influences pedagogically, vocally, and musically?
My strongest influences pedagogically were my clinical teachers in graduate school in vocal therapy, my work with Jo Estill, and my own curiosity and exploration of the body in relationship to sound. However, my most important influence has been my students. As I have said before, they are all so different in their talents and temperaments, so there is never a "one size fits all" approach.

What is the primary goal when training your students?
The primary goal is to help them achieve with confidence and repetition the skill set to perform eight shows a week. In a nutshell, there is nothing new under the sun. In essence, what I am trying to do is synthesize the available theories, techniques, and research with the ultimate goal of providing singers with the necessary skills to sing with confidence and beauty of sound and to promote longevity.

What else is important to you in your work?
Trust, mutual respect, and the willingness to experiment and play. Without this kinship, the work will be compromised and less effective. This is why I also think that lessons should be private. Occasionally a student may ask if it is all right for a third party to observe, and I will sometimes agree to that, but the dynamic is certainly different. That being said, the most important part of my work is to promote and assure vocal health and longevity.

How has your approach been informed by life experience, and how has it evolved over the years?

I think it is really important that I worked for so many years as a professional actress, singer, and voice-over artist. As a result, I am able to understand the anxiety and frustration as well as the disappointment that is often part of the artistic process. I also understand the exhaustion as well as the ups and downs with which these artists are confronted. These experiences have made me a better listener, and hopefully, I am able to provide a safe haven for my students. Many of my students say that my studio is the "room of secrets." I really do think that this feeling of freedom and trust is essential when guiding young artists.

What are your thoughts on professional organizations? Are you involved with any? Why or why not?
I'm a member of both NATS and NYSTA and have participated in NYSTA's professional development program. I have participated as a lecturer, panelist, and master teacher for both of these organizations, as well as for the Voice Foundation's annual symposium in Philadelphia. There is much to be said in favor of collegiality. I think these organizations do a lot of good for our profession: they provide current information, offer helpful courses, sponsor competitions, and discuss topics that may be of interest to teachers from areas where professional theaters and other resources don't exist.

Do you use technology in any of your teaching?
I do teach occasional Skype lessons, but only if I have worked with the student before. It's not really the same as working with someone live. The delay factor alone is really problematic. I am also a very "hands-on" teacher. I do so much with my hands, and that's obviously not possible with Skype. I never Skype big groups of people. I just use it for occasional one-on-one instruction. Estill has a wonderful program called Voiceprint that I use as a biofeedback tool since there are some students who are visual learners and enjoy seeing the sound they are producing spectographically. I also instruct students and teachers with supplemental videos of normal vocal folds as well as pathological conditions. Blue Tree Publishing has some wonderful new software with videos of the larynx, the vocal tract, respiration, vowel and consonant production, and swallowing, to name only a few resources.

As I mentioned earlier, I do a lot of work with YoungArts. I usually work with kids between the ages of fifteen and eighteen who are singer-songwriters, pop singers, and jazz artists. Most of them use microphones. Obviously, you have to work with them while on mic, but it's extremely beneficial to hear them sing unamplified. So we do it both ways: I work with them on mic and off. Lack of technique is certainly more apparent when they have to sing without a microphone. I never work with someone who insists on being "on mic" 100 percent of the time.

What is your future as a voice pedagogue?
Wow . . . I've never thought about that, but maybe there's an opportunity in the afterlife! However, it's such an exciting time to be teaching now. There is so much more information and collaboration between otolaryngologists, speech pathologists, and voice teachers than ever before. We can actually explore and quantify different vocal qualities as a result of research and exploration. When I first started teaching, people didn't strobe singers—that was not necessarily part of an ENT's examination. The laryngeal mirror was the key device. Also, vocal technique teachers have finally embraced the fact that there are some excellent singers who have been trained in techniques that do not come under the heading of "classical" or *bel canto*. This was unheard of forty years ago. I'd love to share some of this information with some of my former teachers, who certainly never believed that!

One last thing: congratulations on your honorary Tony Award! That is such an accomplishment and so great for our profession that they awarded one to a voice teacher.
Thank you so much. It was shocking to say the least. I don't think that's ever been done before. It was a big surprise and the whole experience was just so lovely.

11

JEANNETTE LOVETRI

Jeannette LoVetri began teaching in 1971. She has had an extensive career and is a well-recognized vocal expert in contemporary commercial music (CCM). She travels extensively presenting lectures, workshops, classes, and seminars on CCM and on her own method, Somatic Voicework. She has received the Van L. Lawrence Fellowship from the Voice Foundation and the National Association of Teachers of Singing (NATS), a lifetime achievement award from the New York Singing Teachers Association (NYSTA), and a citation from Centro de Estudos da Voz in Sao Paulo, Brazil, from speech-language pathologist Dr. Mara Behlau. Her students have appeared on and off Broadway, on television, in national tours, on recordings, and in concert halls throughout the world and have been nominated for or won Grammys, Tonys, and other music industry awards. She works with international celebrities and nonprofessionals referred by laryngologists and speech-language pathologists. She has authored numerous research and pedagogy articles and has been interviewed for academic and music industry publications. ♪

Tell us a little about your background and what led you to become a teacher of contemporary commercial styles.
I grew up in Connecticut in the 1950s and 1960s. I sang in public school, took piano lessons, and played music from Broadway shows and sang

as I played. I started voice lessons at the age of fourteen or fifteen and in high school was very active in music studies, chorus, madrigals, and music literature. In 1966 I got the leading role in *The Music Man* in a local youth production guided by Broadway professionals and in 1967 landed the leading role in *Show Boat*. Then in 1968 I played Ella Peterson in *Bells Are Ringing*, which was a belt role. As a lyric soprano, I taught myself to belt.

After that, I got into Manhattan School of Music to study classical singing. I was totally miserable. I would have been happy in a music theater degree program, but back then there were none. Degrees generally available were in classical voice, drama, or speech-language pathology. I did not want to go into any of those professions, so after the first year, I quit college and got a job taking classified ads in the local newspaper. From then to now, everything I have learned has been as a "private student" in lessons, classes, workshops, seminars, and courses of all kinds and by voracious reading, personal mentoring by others, and lots of trial and error.

My training then was strictly classical, but much of my experience was not. I had to make sense of that on my own, and I was really interested in seeing that younger singers did not have to go down that same convoluted path with no guidance or support.

What kinds of styles do you currently teach? How long have you been teaching these styles?
I do not teach style; I teach technique, or what we now call vocal function, for singing. I work with vocalists in all styles of CCM including music theater, jazz, folk, rock, pop, gospel, R&B, alternative and experimental music, and—sometimes—classical music. Most of my students are working professionals; some are quite famous; others come from speech-language pathologists or medical doctors and are amateur singers. I have worked with professional Broadway children and average kids for more than twenty-five years. My first adult Broadway vocalists arrived in 1980, and some of my students now have leading roles on Broadway. I am quite capable of working in either a classical or a music theater style, but I don't generally work with the music itself in the other styles, just the vocal production.

What, do you believe, are the criteria for teaching these styles well?

One of my strongest beliefs is that those who teach should sing well and sing in the sounds appropriate to the style. I don't mean vocalize well; I mean be able to stand up in front of an audience and deliver an entire song effectively. I have no fear of making any sounds. If a human being makes it, I will make it. I also believe that teachers who are not willing to attempt to make the sounds the students will need in music are doing the students a tremendous disservice. Singing is an applied skill, and we learn a lot by listening to the teacher's example. The teachers also limit themselves unnecessarily by making only those sounds they are personally comfortable making. This is not helpful to the student who may need a different aural example. It allows the teacher to hide within his or her own safety zone and asks the student to do something the teacher is not willing to learn. In my opinion, that is not only unfair to the student, but it is also based on the teacher's fear, and fear is never a good basis upon which to base any kind of instruction.

I believe you need to have the sound of various styles "in your ear" by listening to many singers in that style from many eras and to many artists. You need to know about vocal health, voice science/acoustics, and physical coordination. As a teacher, it is imperative that one can hear healthy function in belting or in "mixy" pop singing and that all sounds, *all sounds*, be made freely, without any direct movement of structures within the throat. I am *opposed* to manipulating the throat to get to a preconceived result. I am *against* moving the larynx, the area above or around the larynx, the palate, or any area from the back of the mouth to the vocal folds on purpose.

I do not rely upon "resonance" and "breath support" as primary teaching tools. I am well aware of vocal acoustics (harmonic/formant relationships), but I don't pay much attention to them. Instead, I work from register balance (chest/head/mix) and from vowel sound purity or accuracy, paying particular attention to the middle range of each singer. I believe in the old principles of strengthening the head and chest registers independently and allowing the "mix" of both to arise on its own. I do address breathing coordination in the body through intercostal/abdominal isolation and strengthening and work on postural alignment.

In almost all cases, CCM styles are "chest register driven," meaning that they come out of speech and are carried up into high pitches without modification. My work is about cultivating greater aural and kinesthetic awareness while singing and helping singers extend beyond the confines of conversational speech into highly developed vocal responses, over time, that suit the needs of the music and satisfy the heart of the singer. The sound has to feel like it belongs to the singer, or they won't sound unique and authentic or be able to communicate honestly.

We all know that an "operatic sound" is ridiculous in a rock song, but the idea that "classical training" somehow prepares you to sing in any style refuses to die. Clearly, if this were true, every opera singer would sound great in any music, no matter what the style. Rockers could go up onto the stage at the Metropolitan Opera, and singers from that house could go to Madison Square Garden and give a rock concert. That doesn't happen because the two styles are worlds apart, although there are some people who have the kind of vocal instrument that could probably have gone either way—Audra McDonald, Marilyn Horne, Jonas Kaufman, and Tony Bennett come to mind. The training for these styles is also very different, particularly as the level of the singer becomes more elite.

My work seeks to combine science and art, vocal health and vocal expression, freedom and strength, reliable vocal production with spontaneous expression, and consistent sound with great variability of vocal quality. It takes time, but it is easy to learn and allows for progress in every session. I consider that the work should be a healing experience (with the word "healing" taken in the broadest possible sense) for both the singer and the teacher.

How do you teach style to students who don't have a strong background in a given genre?
"Style" is a combination of musical acuity, emotional sensitivity, and technical facility. It's possible to be a master of a style—jazz, for instance—and have no technical ability whatsoever, singing only with limited vocal output. Billie Holiday was someone who didn't have much vocal technique or remarkable natural vocal resources (the voice itself was modest) who was an incredible singer who left a significant mark on the jazz world. Her style was her own, as is true for every great

CCM artist, and arose as much from her inner response to the music as anything else. We have all heard opera singers try their hands at jazz. They may have a good sense of the style, of the feeling for the music, but without singing from an "unpolished place," the music always suffers from being oversung and overproduced or stilted—what the jazz singers call "square."

A student who wishes to learn how to be comfortable in a style has to spend a lot of time listening to great singers from all eras in that style. There is no substitute for educated ears. The student needs to immerse herself in the style, read about it, attend live performances of it, and, when that has been done for quite some time, find a teacher who deeply understands the style. The student needs to know, however, that someone who understands it may or may not know anything whatsoever about vocal function or production and may not be able to help the singer overcome any vocal limitations that will impact the style. If you can barely sing, it is futile to ask for "a legato line" or "more consistent tone" in a song. How is the student going to provide those things when she can barely control a vocal exercise?

If you are asking someone to learn to phrase uniquely, you must look at all the ingredients of the song. That would include the lyric and how the words are set into the vocal line, the chord structure, the rhythm, the tempo, the key, the overall volume level, and the tessitura. It would include any arrangement of the song (if one exists) or the context (such as a musical production) and, for those who are performing, the venue (large, small, acoustic space, or one with sound equipment). The inflection of the words, the glides of both pitches and consonants, the stops and starts of entrances, the rhythmic base underneath the vocal line—all of these have an effect on the overall contour of the song, and each vocalist must have conscious control over them if she is going to find a way to own both the sound of her voice and the style of the music in an authentic, satisfying way.

How did you come up with your method or approach? What does it consist of, and how is it unique?
I came up with my approach first through my own explorations of singing, attempting to do multiple styles while studying "classically" with various teachers and coaches. I was repeatedly told that I couldn't sing

any CCM style without "ruining" my voice and my technique, but I did not find that to be the case. I simply could not understand why that would automatically be true. We only have one larynx and one set of vocal folds, but we are all capable of making almost unlimited sounds. Why wasn't there a way to make the sounds you were seeking without doing any harm?

I crashed my voice into several walls, working on my own, knowing absolutely nothing about vocal health, and having zero guidance from my singing teachers about anything outside classical repertoire. They were trained as musicians, linguists, and perhaps actors. They could not give me information they did not have. As far as I remember, there were no degrees or even studies in voice pedagogy in 1967.

When I arrived in New York City in 1975, I auditioned for anything I could find. Even then, the shows that were being done were "pop/rock" so I sang in them. I worked out for myself how to make the sounds the music needed, and I was never told that I was "too classical" even though I continued to take classical voice lessons up until 1978. My teacher had sung at New York City Opera and at the Metropolitan Opera, had a degree from Manhattan School of Music, and had studied at the Mozarteum in Austria. He was at that time a student of Cornelius Reid, who turned out to be a big influence on my work in subsequent years. I also sang at Riverside Church and at Marble Collegiate Church as a soprano and continued to do weddings as a classical vocalist. I sang with many Broadway artists in gospel/R&B concerts throughout the city for more than five years. I also did some small operatic roles at the same time.

I began to have vocal problems at about twenty-eight. My voice would get hoarse and raspy, my high notes were hard, and my voice was struggling. I continued to teach myself to belt and sing in a heavier operatic quality at my lessons. My teacher told me that my voice was "growing" and that these unhappy vocal symptoms would go away on their own in good time. They did not. I was frequently hoarse, but I never lost my voice completely. I was teaching (starting in 1971) and still managed to help my students, but at no time did anyone suggest that I see a "throat doctor." In hindsight, I am sure I had nodules caused by pushing my chest register to "grow" my voice into a louder, fuller place. Finally, I had to stop auditioning because singing got so very hard. I was very discouraged, but my teacher still did not think anything was wrong. I ceased my lessons. By then I had had eight teachers and six coaches and had been studying singing for almost fourteen years. I was dreadfully confused and quite lost and had no resources regarding where to turn. Finally, I stopped performing. I was twenty-nine.

It was suggested that I attend a course at Juilliard called "The Voice Foundation Symposium: Care of the Professional Voice." I knew nothing about it and it was expensive, but I was desperate to understand what was going on with my singing, so I saved up my money and went. *It changed my life.* It was there that I understood for the very first time how we make sound and what the larynx is. I learned how it worked. I heard what vocal nodules sound like in a singer's voice. I had sounded exactly the same. Fortunately for me, when I stopped auditioning, I also stopped practicing, and whatever was in my throat went away on its own.

I have returned for the Voice Foundation Symposium in the first week of June every year since then (that is, since 1978). Through the Voice Foundation, my entire vocal world opened up and I began to find what I had been seeking: accurate, helpful, and objective information about how the voice works. These days there are many more conferences and all of them include voice science, voice medicine, vocal hygiene, and pedagogy, but back then, the symposium was just about the only place such information was easily available. It is still the senior congress of voice professionals from multidisciplines in the world. My enthusiasm is undiminished, so I look forward to going every year. I consider myself very lucky to have found the symposium at a time when many singing teachers were still dismissive of voice science as being necessary for singing teachers. They were wrong and I knew it. Now, things are very different. There are currently many resources for singers and teachers of singing to learn about vocal function, understand vocal health, comprehend vocal hygiene, and grasp the physical parameters of breathing and of vocal acoustics. This is good news for everyone.

My approach is holistic. It is grounded in voice science but also in compassion and kind-heartedness. It teaches vocal function through balancing all the ingredients in making a voiced sound, and at the same time, it encourages exploration, experimentation, and patience with the process. It incorporates awareness of the goals of the singer and of the needs and requirements of the marketplace, but it honors the individuality of each singer. It encourages a sense of vocal empowerment, freedom, and highly responsive control all done through patient repetition of pitches, vowels, and various levels of volume.

I am writing this at the age of sixty-eight. I still sing classical repertoire and can also do a jazz tune and a rock song, and although I was diagnosed with a left vocal fold paresis in 2013, I am happy with how I am singing, although it certainly isn't the same as it was twenty years ago. I believe how I sing is a testament to how and what I teach. I am blessed to have many high-level vocal performers in multiple styles who have studied with me for as long as thirty-five years using my exercises to stay in excellent shape for elite venues all over the world.

What elements of vocal technique do you think are most important?

I think everything is important. (Bad answer, I know.) The voice is a hologram. It reflects the entire body and person. Anything in any part of the body, the throat, or the mind can impact how we sing. What is "no big deal" for some singers might be a mountain for others. The only way to look at a singer is at the entire human being who sings. Voice is an extension of the person, of the mind, of the heart. I don't want to teach a larynx, a second tenor, or a time slot. I want to teach people who come in with a life.

I get to know my students. I want to know about their families, their aspirations, the things that matter to them. How else can I support them being the artists they want to be? Within the lesson, I create a safe space where anything can happen (and often does) and singers can become emotional with or without reason with no shame or embarrassment. What happens in a lesson is private unless the student gives permission for someone to observe. That happens often, as I frequently have students from various universities or colleagues from out of town come to the studio to watch me teach. What happens in the studio, however, stays in the studio.

Posture matters, coordination matters, breathing matters, vocal production is important, freedom is important. Stamina, strength, flexibility, ease, beauty or not as the student chooses, style—all of these are important. How do we leave any of them out? As is true with any complex physical skill that also has an element of creative spontaneity integrated in it, it takes time to do well and many factors are influences. All of them are important. None can be glossed over or left out.

Have you sung in the past, and if so, which styles? Do you currently sing any of the styles you teach?

I sang classical music and then music theater. After I got to New York City, I sang pop/rock, jazz, gospel-style R&B, and more classical music. I sing rarely now, but occasionally I perform at a friend's choral concert as both a classical soloist and a pop singer. I have also done vocal improvisation for his chorus. I still sing at parties and weddings, and so far, no one is throwing tomatoes! I also sing at every course of Somatic Voicework™, my method that I teach, in a short recital typically with other people who are on my faculty. People need to trust me, and if I sing for them, they can draw their own conclusions. Insofar as teaching goes, I work with all styles helping the vocalists get to the sounds they want in whatever music they choose to sing. If it is more than one style, then we work on more than one way to vocalize so that all styles are available and comfortable. ♪

Who were your strongest influences, pedagogically, vocally, and musically?

I was influenced first by the pedagogy books of Cornelius Reid, although I never studied with him. I like William Vennard's book, *Singing: The Mechanism and the Technic* (1967), better than any other and read my first copy so many times it fell apart. I have read Richard Miller, Oren Brown, Janice Chapman, Meribeth Bunch Dayme, and many, many other books of traditional classical voice pedagogy as well as books by contemporary commercial writers—some of whose ideas strike me as being very odd. I have read many books on vocal health including those by Robert T. Sataloff and books on multidisciplinary vocal production by Alison Behrman and John Haskell, Ingo Titze, Johan Sundberg, Michael Benninger and Tom Murry, and—more recently—Wendy LeBorgne and Marci Rosenberg, and Leda Scearce. I had the amazing opportunity of observing Dr. Sataloff and his professional staff many times and of working with Peak Woo alongside the fellows at Mount Sinai Hospital, who guided me to understand voice medicine from a much broader perspective. I was able to spend a full week with Johan Sundberg, staying in his home, to learn about vocal acoustics and vocal anatomy and physiology with him and the late Patricia Gramming and Ninni Elliott. I had the opportunity to spend four days with Ingo Titze while he studied vocal vibrato and had electrodes inserted into my larynx. That was an *interesting* experience. I also worked with Daniel R. Boone (SLP) in two workshops given in New York City on vocal and speaking voice health. These great experts in vocal medicine, vocal production, speech hygiene, voice research, and pedagogy were generous mentors, teachers, and guides to me in my early days. I am deeply grateful to every one of them, and to many others along the way, for sharing their expertise with me without hesitation. It has been a great gift.

Musically, I was influenced by my early childhood. My mother was a professional dancer, and her sister was a singer. They worked in the posh nightclubs on Bourbon Street in New Orleans in the 1930s. Music was part of my life from an early age, as we sang at home—both my parents had pleasant singing voices. I learned about music in public school, and I was very responsive to all styles. It moved me, and that was without any conscious effort on my part. Music was living, breathing, and powerful from my earliest memory, and it remains so now.

I was also influenced by my early acting training in Connecticut and in New York. I had several different kinds of training, and they were all useful to me. I have also been strongly influenced by my spiritual studies, which began at the age of twenty-two, when I withdrew from formal participation in the Catholic Church and struck out on my own to study various spiritual and philosophical teachings from all over the world. Humanistic psychology was and is a strong influence upon my life. I have clear ideas about what it means to be an artist; an open, loving human being; and a contributing member of society. They are part of my philosophy of how we need to serve the needs of our students and of the music simultaneously.

What is the primary goal when training your students?
My primary goal is vocal balance. When the voice is "balanced," all the ingredients in vocal sound are homogenized. The voice works freely and easily. It can be loud or soft. It can go high or low (over at least two octaves). It can be warm or bright, intense or gentle. It can move

through music quickly or glide smoothly over slow phrases. It is clear and consistent but not machine-like. It can sing in a variety of styles as needed. The singer is instantly recognizable and feels satisfied with the sound and the feeling of singing. The singer understands how to stay vocally healthy and can hold up to moderate stress without losing vocal function and knows when to seek help from a speech-language pathologist or laryngologist.

What else is important to you in your work?
I care a lot about the profession at large. I care that we are still a profession that has no licensure; we have no official codification. If you get ten of the top teachers of singing in a room and ask them about what they think singing is, they will give you ten totally different answers. That leads to teachers feeling unsupported and, in recent years, a heavy reliance on formal education leading to terminal degrees, when, in fact, holding such a degree is no guarantee at all that the person can sing well or teach anything to anyone. I think that can lead to a lot of contentiousness between teachers over things that have been well-established as being factual and warrant no argument. It wastes time. We can place too much emphasis on mechanical production and not enough on emotional communication and artistic finesse; or we can place too much on communication of the meaning of the lyrics without taking into consideration the way the sound is being produced. Both are out of balance.

There are few opportunities for older, more experienced teachers to mentor younger ones even though we know this is beneficial on both sides. Conversely, the older teachers with a solid track record of success can be maligned rather than revered by younger or new teachers, in a wrong-headed approach that allows them to trash rather than heed their senior colleagues while attempting to establish their own legitimacy. That's awful.

I care that contemporary commercial music be respected. Period. I never saw any style as being "lesser." I created the term to eliminate the word "nonclassical," which means "nothing, not important, negated." Most of the styles of CCM are American born and need to be honored for their folk roots. They are also far more popular and more financially successful than any classical style—including opera—was, is, or will ever be. They and the artists that sing them should never have been denigrated by anyone, most especially academic scholars who do not bother to delve into the rich history and tradition of each style.

How has your approach been informed by life experience, and how has it evolved over the years?

I love to sing. It is a high experience for me. It gives me great joy, and it fuels me to continue teaching every day after forty-five years of sitting in my studio. This passion keeps me fresh and allows me to teach every lesson as if it were the first and to regard every singer as being the most important vocalist I have ever worked with. Singing is the wind beneath my wings, and it has supported me in striving to be of service, to lift up others in song and singing, and to shed light on the path of becoming a better vocalist in whatever way I can every day. It soothes my soul to hear a great voice, a great vocalist, and a memorable song or performance. How amazing that we have the thing called singing!

Singing has been my companion in times of great sorrow or stress. It has been my friend when my voice was not at its best. It has accompanied me on my life's journey. It is deeply connected to and is a part of the reason why I am alive on the planet. My singing continues to evolve and change and this, in turn, changes my teaching. I am still reliant on the same basic tools I started with in 1971, but they are now more accurate and more efficient and I have a faster and greater rate of success in helping singers reach their goals.

I am saddened that so much of what we hear is adulterated by electronic manipulation. We rarely hear a CCM singer who is not passing his or her sound through a complex collection of electronic equipment and the hands and ears of a sound engineer and that's a loss. Very few people have an experience of being in close proximity to a well-trained voice in a conditioned body and of hearing a glorious sound coming into their ears without any help except that which comes from the singer's own lungs. While I understand that electronic amplification is necessary in CCM styles and a good sound system and engineer are crucial to vocal health and success, it is important for young audiences to have a chance to be impressed by the sheer glory of one human being making vocal music relying only on their natural assets.

What are your thoughts on professional organizations? Are you involved with any? Why or why not?

I am a member since 1978 (now emerita) of the New York Singing Teachers Association (NYSTA) and a past president of that organization. I am, since 1980, a member of the local chapter of the National Association of Teachers of Singing (NATS). Since 1999, I have been a member and am now secretary of the American Academy of Teachers of Singing (AATS) and have recently joined the Pan-American Vocology Association (PAVA). I belong to the Voice Foundation and am on their advisory board. I think all of these organizations are very important, as there are many things that we can do and share together that we cannot possibly do as individual teachers or members of a voice faculty at a university. The organizations hold us together in an informal identity that is all we have until and unless we ever find a way to codify our expectations about teaching and teachers. They serve as conduits for information and for providing opportunities to gather together socially. They allow us to maintain awareness of the newest and most important developments in the profession. Voice science is expanding exponentially, and we need keep abreast of what is being discovered. Our professional organizations serve a very important function in seeing that all of this continues to develop. We need them all.

Do you use technology in any of your teaching?

The only technology I use in the studio is Skype or other Internet video services. I teach people in Brazil, Canada, Australia, and on the West Coast. It's not totally reliable, but it serves its purpose. I have a microphone and an amplifier, but I really do not use them. I started in the "old way" with nothing external to help and I stick to that. I expect others to deal with the electronic side of performance, but I do ask questions about the audio situation in a performance. I need to know if the vocalist is using an "in-ear" or a stage monitor. I need to know if there is someone on the sound board or if there is no one running things and the singer is doing his own sound. I want singers to understand how to speak to the sound engineer about the acoustic feedback so they get what they need to hear in order to sing well. Mostly, I leave technology (which is very important) to others who are more comfortable giving advice and guidance.

What is in your future as a voice pedagogue?
As long as I can sing, I will teach. As long as I can write, I will share what I know in the written word. As long as I am physically able to help others learn to sing, I will strive to be a better teacher and to learn and grow. I hope that I can share what I have learned in a long and very unusual path, gathering information from many sources and amalgamating it into a form that I can share with others who would be interested to know about it. I will do my best to continue to give back within the profession and to keep promoting respect for contemporary commercial music and artists within academia and in scholarly or scientific research. I hope to leave behind something that will be helpful to others. That would be more than enough.

⑫

MARK MEYLAN

Mark Meylan is internationally recognized as one of London's top singing teachers, specializing in music theater. He also teaches clients from all areas of contemporary commercial music, particularly jazz, pop, rock, folk, and world music. He works with actors from film and television as well as those recommended by agents, casting agents, producers, the BBC, the Royal Shakespeare Company, and the Royal National Theatre. He also retrains injured voices, working in association with laryngologists, speech and language therapists, and manual voice therapists. He is one of the founders of VoxOp, a support group for singers with vocal issues, particularly post-op. He spent fifteen years as an active member of the British Voice Association (BVA), chairing the education committee and serving as conference director for the first Pan-European Voice Conference (PEVOC). Mr. Meylan spent six years on the council of the Association of Teachers of Singing (AOTOS). He has been on the faculty of Voice Foundation Symposium in Philadelphia and has given a master class for the New York Singing Teachers Association (NYSTA). He has presented papers and workshops in Athens, Frankfurt, Hamburg, Salzburg, Stockholm, and throughout the United Kingdom. He has been the official vocal coach for many West End shows, including Starlight Express, Saturday Night Fever *(London and Cologne)*, Thoroughly Modern Millie, Sister Act, Flashdance *(London and UK tour)*, Bombay

Dreams, I Can't Sing (The X Factor Musical), Mamma Mia! *(London and international tour)*, Memphis, Book of Mormon, Sunny Afternoon *(London and UK tour)*, The Last Five Years, An American in Paris, Beautiful, The Girls, Dreamgirls, Annie, *and for nine years with* Jersey Boys *(London)*. Mr. Meylan *was one of the vocal coaches on the film of* Les Misérables, *working with Eddie Redmayne, Anne Hathaway, and Hugh Jackman. He prepared Daniel Radcliffe for his role in* How to Succeed in Business without Really Trying *on Broadway, and he prepared and maintained Emma Thompson for the role of Mrs. Lovett in* Sweeney Todd *in New York and London. He has also prepared and maintained several prominent actors for Olivier Award–winning roles, including Imelda Staunton* (Gypsy), *Katie Brayben* (Beautiful), *Amber Riley* (Dreamgirls), *and Adam J. Bernard* (Dreamgirls). ♪

Tell us a little about your background and what led you to become a teacher of contemporary commercial styles.
I initially went to a conservatoire as a classical singer where I was poorly taught, so I ended up not achieving the singing career I had originally hoped for. I therefore moved into teaching singing, piano, and some class music in mainstream education and teaching singing in drama schools here in London. After a few years, I decided that if I was going to teach, I should have better teaching qualifications, and so I took a music education degree at Kingston Polytechnic. As I was now self-funding my own education, I carried on teaching singing in drama schools to pay my way. When I finished the coursework, I started teaching five days a week in drama schools. Eventually I had enough requests for private tuition, and I cut back to four days. And so it went until I left drama school teaching altogether to have my own private practice as a singing teacher.

What kinds of styles do you currently teach? How long have you been teaching these styles?
From the start, I have had to teach all kinds of styles, and thankfully between home and school I grew up listening to music ranging from Sibelius to Dusty Springfield to Purcell to the Beatles. This meant that I've never been afraid to examine the nuts and bolts of a song to try and understand what makes it tick or what makes it great. As I am based in

London, the majority of my clients—about 65 percent—are music theater performers. The remainder includes pop, rock, jazz, soul, folk, and world music singers. One of the joys of working in music theater is that this genre covers so many styles, and much of this is happening because of the way music theater is developing. Some of my singers have to sing in a classical vocal quality while others have to sound like a rock singer.

What to you are some of the differences between music theater and CCM styles?
These days I think that's a very difficult question. There is a lot to unpack here—how long have you got?! All the non-music-theater clients I teach are being themselves, either creating their own material or creating their version of something that already exists. This means that for them there is freedom in their creativity—from keys and notes of the melody to speeds, the general vibe and style, and instrumentation of the track—until ultimately it works for them.

In music theater, the actor is telling a story and the songs have a varied use in the show. One of the main issues crossing both areas is when an actor is portraying a real singer, something that is quite common at present. I was the official vocal coach for *Jersey Boys* here in London for the nine years that it played in the West End. I was also the official vocal coach for *Beautiful* and *Sunny Afternoon*. With great respect, I doubt that Frankie Valli, Carole King, or Ray Davies would sing eight shows a week for a year—and that's with them being themselves! Even if the actors are sharing the role and only performing six shows a week, we still have to find somebody to portray these singers in quite an unreal environment and with big vocal demands, as the audience want to hear all the hits and hear them as they know them. All these actors have to find a version of that singer that is acceptable to the audience and the musical supervisor and sustainable for the length of their contract.

What, do you believe, are the criteria for teaching these styles well?
My clients who are solo artists invariably have the stylistic elements of what they want in place and are usually looking for vocal help to develop or maintain their instrument. I may get asked by a manager to help strengthen a singer's voice as they have a tour with more shows than

usual in some weeks or increasing numbers of shows toward the end of the tour and they want to get the singer to be "match fit."

A jazz singer may be looking for vocal maintenance or for help to explore new colors or a new sound or to strengthen a particular area of their voice. In the past two years, I worked with an emerging soul singer who had various needs: he wanted to maintain his instrument and find a way to be able to sing his whole album at a gig. He had hitherto only been able to record one or two songs a day. Each artist has very specific personal needs and comes to me for different reasons.

Many singing teachers of my generation were trained classically, and so they really have to expand their toolbox in order to effectively teach and understand CCM styles. As I said, I heard so many different singers in the course of my own journey. It's ultimately about understanding the final product and what the performer wants that to be and then back-tracking through the vocal system in order to achieve this: examining the style in terms of resonance, phonation, airflow, and air pressure and then deciding what this sound needs and how to enable the performer to produce it.

How do you teach style to students who don't have a strong background in a given genre?
Listening first, then describing and discussing. I usually start off by listening to a recording with my client in my studio and asking them to identify (a) what they think they're hearing, and (b) how different it is from the way they normally sing in both vocal quality and style. I will also ask them if they have any ideas as to how they might achieve this new genre, so they can start to understand the nuances of the musical style and the vocal colors that are required.

If they are an established client who has a working knowledge of my work and language, we may well discuss and explore some ideas straight away. Otherwise, I will look at the areas of their voice that may need to be developed or refined, and I am there to guide and help them reorganize the vocal tract or whatever other aspect of their singing that needs work for them to access the sounds and style that they seek.

It all depends on the needs of the individual. Most of my solo artists are seeking vocal technique, whereas the music theater performers have to be able to access the sounds and style as set by the existing show or by the needs of the musical supervisor on a new work. The final decision about style is never mine. For my solo artists, it rests with them and their management, and for the music theater singers, it rests with the musical director and musical supervisor.

The phrase that you used, "reorganize the vocal tract," is a unique one that isn't heard or used very often. What do you mean by that?
I mean reorganize the vocal tract! I'm looking at all the options—laryngeal height, tongue position, tongue tension, jaw position, mouth shape, soft palate position, soft palate tension, and anything else above the vocal folds. To have the pliability to reorganize the vocal tract and to enable the singer to create the sound they desire and with optimal vocal efficiency is the name of the game.

How did you come up with your method or approach? What does it consist of, and how is it unique?
I'm not sure that it is unique. I have experienced and witnessed a lot of good and bad teaching, so I guess I've done what most teachers do—I've cherry-picked the things that I like, the things that I understand, and the things that I can make work in my studio. By "things" I mean not only exercises but also ideas, concepts, and research. I don't think I do anything clever—I've just put it together in a way that I can understand and in a way that I know that I can pass it on to my clients. I believe that my job is understanding how to enable my clients to have access to the various elements of vocal technique and making sure that they can do this.

A major focus of my work with all my clients is ensuring that they have access to efficient, pliable air flow and air pressure. I teach all my clients Accent Method breathing, a technique that I find to be invaluable. Accent Method is a speech and language therapy technique developed by the Danish phonetician Svend Smith, and in a simple explanation, it is based on relaxation and allowing the body to do what it already knows. A colleague of mine here in London once said that "it bores your body into getting it right," and I guess that that's probably quite true as the technique is very repetitive.

The reason that I feel that this is so important is that different vocal qualities require different breathing strategies and breath management regarding air flow and air pressure, and for many of my clients, this flexibility between flow and pressure is key. A book has recently been published by Ron Morris and Linda Hutchison based on the Accent Method that is entitled *If in Doubt, Breathe Out*! This reminds me that I have taken my Accent Method learning from Ingrid Rugheimer, Sara Harris, Dinah Harris, and Kirsten Thyme-Frokjaer and made it my own—to work for me in my studio with my clients—which means that I suspect that I do not teach the method in its pure form. ♪

What is your general philosophy of voice teaching?
I can trace my philosophy of singing teaching to a specific event. At the very start of my teaching career, I was approached by a woman who ran a children's theater workshop to take over the musical direction of a production of *Oliver* she was mounting. The outgoing musical director was holding the auditions that I was asked to observe, which was slightly awkward as I was about to assume his job. I spent the afternoon listening to lots of children and teenagers screaming their heads off, quite inarticulate and mostly out of tune, producing sounds that wouldn't last two performances—let alone the seven that were required. From that day forth, I wanted to ensure that all the singers I worked with approached making sounds in a healthy way. Singers' voices should last as long as they want to sing. I strive to give my clients a vocal technique that will last a lifetime, whomever I am working with.

Summarize your core beliefs about vocal technique.
I can do this in a single sentence: *Vocal technique is a refined and detailed understanding of the balance between airflow, breath support, posture, efficient phonation, and how to realistically and healthfully access vocal qualities.*

What elements of vocal technique do you think are most important?
For me it always has to be a balance. Whether that be a balance within the instrument to keep the top and bottom accessible and pliable, or whether that is making sure that Elphaba sings something "legit," light, or classical during her contract, balance is key. My clients are singing eight shows a week in a musical or many gigs on a tour, and so the laryn-

geal musculature can easily think that the way it sings now is the way to sing forever and it is easy to lose a previous vocal quality. People's voices change after singing the same thing nightly for a year.

I encourage my clients to know and have easy access back to their "home neutral." This is what I casually refer to as the voice they wake up with in the morning. When I coached *Jersey Boys*, none of my Frankie Vallis woke up sounding like him, although three of the thirteen I coached came pretty close. The rest had to move from their "home neutral" to sing the show, and over the course of a year, their "home neutral" got much closer to Frankie Valli. This is great for that job but not so useful when they have to audition for their next job, which could be *The Phantom of the Opera*! Also, knowing "home neutral" can really aid a rock, folk, or jazz singer as they determine how far away some of the sounds they are exploring are from their natural setup, and therefore whether this is something they want or need to explore. In London, many music theater actors are young, so it is important that they make realistic choices about what their voice can do. They have all the enthusiasm and energy of youth, so I try to make them aware of what their facility is at their stage of development.

I've already mentioned Accent Method breathing, which is key to my work. The other area of technique that I feel must be prioritized when teaching CCM is vocal registers. Music theater encourages a voice to be chest dominant and many of the other styles like this weight—it seems only the contemporary pop boys want to explore middle register and falsetto. I require all of my singers to have access to their full range, working seamlessly throughout all their registers. Sadly, I hear too many pop/rock men and badly trained music theater men who have not sorted out middle register and struggle to sing healthily and consistently at the top of their voice, thereby struggling with mix and falsetto.

Interestingly, a lot of exercises I use and my concepts come from classical pedagogy. I really like Richard Miller's work on registration as set out in *The Structure of Singing*. However, his breath management work with the held ribs for *appoggio* doesn't work for me in CCM—I can't adhere to "rib-holding" as part of a support strategy and much prefer the excellent work on breathing outlined in Janice Chapman's book, *Singing and Teaching Singing*. When I want a client to have a classical singing support, this really works as my clients can move freely and—where appropriate—stay in character. For physical underpinning in a rock voice or belter, I find the "upper body anchoring" taught to me by Jo Estill to be invaluable. ♪

During the hour I have with my clients, I will often carry out some postural adjustments and suggestions. I encourage them to undertake one of the many postural journeys that are available, finding one that they enjoy, as this is a long commitment. While I really value Feldenkrais and Alexander Technique, I will suggest that the fit gym-going and dance clients explore yoga, tai chi, qigong, and sometimes Pilates. Through any of these approaches they can get a sense of what their habitual posture is as opposed to their natural posture and make subsequent changes.

Have you sung in the past, and if so, which styles? Do you currently sing any of the styles you teach?
I sang classically professionally in my early twenties, but I don't perform anymore. I never really had good experiences as a performer, and subsequently performing did not excite me. Teaching does excite and energize me, however. I am a teacher—it is my skill, my identity, and my vocation. If there is any skill that I know better than you, I can find a way to break it down so that you can learn it.

Do you ever model for your students? Do you sing in your studio?
I tend to model phrases to show how I would sing them, but I don't want to be copied. I model sounds both good and bad! Sometimes I might sing a verse or chorus of a song if I'm looking at acting through the song. I may do this several times with the same part of the music so that the client can hear the different sounds that different thoughts can produce. I think it is important that, as I'm expecting my clients to be able to sing in various vocal qualities, I can have a good go at them as well. Thankfully my voice is still flexible, although I wouldn't pay to hear me sing heavy metal!

Who were your strongest influences, pedagogically, vocally, and musically?
Vocally and musically, I always wanted to be Dietrich Fischer-Dieskau! As a teacher, Janice Chapman. She is a colleague of mine who teaches

classical singing. In some ways, our journey has been similar since the late 1980s. We attended the same lectures, conferences, and courses and even arranged some of those events ourselves, so we had many of the same influences. Janice has proceeded to undertake much more research than I and has produced an excellent book called *Singing and Teaching Singing*. While many of the concepts from the book are the same as mine, she is primarily a classical pedagogue, whereas I am working with singers who are amplified, sing eight shows a week, and have to produce a range of vocal sounds to match the music and tell the story. Janice is certainly someone I respect and admire as a fellow pedagogue. While there are some fine teachers out there in the UK, there was no one else who put together the technical work necessary for CCM teaching.

My other influences come from other fields, particularly speech and language therapy. Both Lesley Mathieson and Christina Shewell have influenced and shaped my thinking, particularly on rehabilitating a damaged voice. In recent years, two Australian speech and language therapists, Deb Phyland and Ron Morris, have fueled my work and taken me forward. The (sadly) now retired otolaryngologist Tom Harris was also influential in my professional life. He was always accessible, and I could call him whenever I was unsure about something and had a question. He and his wife, the speech and language therapist Sara Harris, would always find the time to talk, and it was invaluable bouncing ideas off them over the years. On my first trip to the Voice Foundation in the early 1990s, it was wonderful to meet Jeanie LoVetri and sit with her and talk about our work. Knowing that there was a like-minded colleague out there who was facing similar questions and problems was wonderful and reaffirming.

What is the primary goal when training your students?
To earn a lot of money! Just kidding. To make sure that they can achieve as much as they can with their voice and that they can use their voice to fulfill as many of their dreams as is realistically possible. Also, even though they are singing for professional reasons, it is also important that they get some joy out of their singing. When a new client has their initial assessment with me, I finish my history taking by asking, "And what do you want to get from me?" It is important for them to have

sight of their goals and aims as they are spending hard-earned money to study singing. I have to be realistic within the profession and make them understand that there are other factors apart from singing that allow people to get work or bring them success. I am careful to point out the journey that has to be undertaken to acquire their vocal technique needs. I'm not the right person to work with if you want a quick fix for an audition—I get no satisfaction from just tinkering round the edges of repertoire. I try to aim to facilitate my clients in a way that works for them, giving them the skills they need now and helping them to achieve vocal longevity.

What else is important to you in your work?
It is important that I am available for the whole person. For many of my clients, their singing lesson is the only time in the week when they are privately one-on-one in a professional environment. For some, they equate this time with a talking therapy session, and for others, they are young and away from home for the first time. In both cases, this can encourage people to divulge things to me that are not related to their singing.

I feel it is important that my clients feel safe enough in my studio to explore making new sounds, and with this, some gain the security to share personal information. It is important to acknowledge their emotional needs, and if they want, I am happy to offer advice and guidance, but this is on the strict understanding that I am not a therapist or counselor—I am their singing teacher.

How has your approach been informed by life experience, and how has it evolved over the years?
Having had such poor tuition at college and afterward—which stopped the possibility of me having a performing career—I want to make sure that I do my best to help my clients achieve their goals and dreams. I think that in trying to enable my singers, it also encourages me to improve. I always see a client who is stuck as someone I am failing, and I look at my approach and my information to see how and what I can change to take them forward. What goes on in the studio is my responsibility—I am the teacher. I can't be the right match for everyone, and so after ten sessions, I have an appraisal with each client to see how they

feel and examine the progress from both sides. If I feel things are not correct and I am really unable to help someone, I discuss this and suggest teachers to whom they might be better suited.

Over the course of many years, I have gained a reputation with conductors, laryngologists, producers, and managers as being the person who can "fix" issues or "create" a voice that can sing a particular role. The many years of being asked to achieve all manner of vocal wonders in various arenas have always taken me back to the mechanism, the anatomy, the process, trawling all manner of things so that I can find a way for the singer to not only get there, but also to stay there healthily and efficiently. I am often asked to perform magic, but I always maintain and try to get everyone to understand that there are no shortcuts to sustainable vocal technique. With the growing awareness of manual voice therapy here in London, I encourage all my clients who have a heavy vocal load to explore and embrace this, and I work in conjunction with several manual voice therapists.

What are your thoughts on professional organizations? Are you involved with any?

In the United Kingdom, we have two main organizations of interest to singing teachers: the British Voice Association (BVA) and the Association of Teachers of Singing (AOTOS), the latter being our equivalent of NATS. I think that—in their different ways—they both do some excellent work in disseminating information, giving people a way of sharing information and experiencing new ideas. In the past, I was heavily involved at the committee level with both organizations. When I resigned from AOTOS, I was chairman elect, and for many years, I was chair of the education committee for the BVA. I was also one of the conveners of the first Pan-European Voice Conference (PEVOC) in London in 1995. Also in the 1990s, I attended the Voice Foundation Symposium in Philadelphia regularly and gave several workshops there. ♪

As an only child who works on his own in a one-on-one setting, committees are not really my forte! I find all the bureaucracy distasteful—it moves too slowly and sometimes the self-seeking agendas of fellow committee members can be overwhelming. I like to attend things so that I can learn and be inspired, but as I have developed and grown with my own work, I begrudge giving up a Sunday to hear the "same old, same old," dressed up as a new discovery by an eager but inexperienced twenty-something. When I first started out, the Voice Research Society (the predecessor of the BVA) was a young organization with a strong sense of being multidisciplinary. It had members who shared and discussed in a generous and open manner, and this was exactly what I needed and when I needed it. It feels now that the world of singing and voice research has become a more hardened industry.

Do you use technology in any of your teaching?
Not really. I'm old school—all I need is a piano and something to record on. I work in one-hour sessions with my clients, and this hour is already filled with topics like Accent Method breathing, technical development, and then putting that into a song—it often feels that I am battling with time management. I record all my clients' vocal exercises cleanly so that they have a specific practice regime, and I always encourage them to record their lesson. Usually lessons are recorded on their phones or computers, but I still have two clients who use cassettes and even one who uses MiniDisc—that little device that came and went quickly!

I'm not a fan of Skype for teaching—I think it is limited and the singers who use it regularly are often not sounding very good. How do you know what you're really hearing? It is so condensed! How can you monitor posture? You can only run material if the singer has some access to an accompaniment at their end, and don't get me started on poor Skype connections! I would only use it as a last resort, such as with a client who is away on tour who is stuck and needs my help.

What is in your future as a voice pedagogue?
I currently have three clients whom I now mentor in a study group, and they have become "associates" of mine. My aim in the process is to help them become the best teachers they can be. While they are obviously supporters of my work, I am not looking for them to teach my way or my "method." Rather, I am enjoying guiding them through the various aspects that I feel it is important to know to be a good singing teacher of CCM. I find it meaningful to make time to pass on what I have learned to the next generation.

⓭

LISA POPEIL

Lisa Popeil *is one of LA's top voice coaches, with more than forty years of professional teaching experience. She is the creator of the Voiceworks Method,* Total Singer *DVD, and the Total Singer Workshop. Lisa is an international lecturer, researcher, and vocal health consultant. She serves on the advisory board of the Voice Foundation and is a voting member of NARAS—the Grammy organization—in addition to ASCAP, SAG-AFTRA, and the National Association of Teachers of Singing (NATS). She has contributed to both the* Oxford Handbook of Singing *and the* Oxford Handbook of Music Education *on the subject of commercial vocal genres and has been published in the* Journal of Singing *and the* Journal of Voice. *Ms. Popeil is the co-author of the book* Sing Anything: Mastering Vocal Styles *and creator of the* Daily Vocal Workout for Pop Singers *CD. She holds a BFA and MFA in voice from California Institute of the Arts.* ♪

Tell us a little about your background and what led you to become a teacher of contemporary commercial styles.
I grew up in downtown Chicago and at the age of six attended a children's music theater program called Jack and Jill Players. I remember

belting out "Seventy-Six Trombones" from *The Music Man* with two little boys on either side of me. The only vocal advice I remember receiving was "Louder, Lisa, louder!" As much as I enjoyed the program, it became obvious that my voice was becoming hoarse, so my mother found a classical voice teacher for me, the wonderful Gisela Goettling. I began studying with Mrs. Goettling at age seven and continued taking lessons until I moved to California when I was fifteen. Prior to moving, I performed the roles of Aldonza in *Man of La Mancha* and the title role in *Little Mary Sunshine* at my high school. For the Aldonza role, I sang all the high notes in head voice, I'm sure!

Around the age of eleven, I began writing my own pop songs and asked my teacher to show me how to sing like the vocalists on the radio. That did not go over well at all! She equated pop singing with vocal demise and warned me that I might lose everything we had worked for. This was a typical attitude that many voice teachers had back then. Every time I sang higher notes, I automatically sang in my head voice and couldn't figure out how to sound like Aretha Franklin or Barbra Streisand without discomfort.

I knew that many pop and soul singers sang wonderfully with nary a lesson, so how hard could it be? That was the beginning of my journey. Once in California, I continued with classical voice and eventually got my MFA in voice from California Institute of the Arts, all the while continuing to write my little songs and studying piano and composition.

In the 1980s, I took a stab at the record business, making records and working with producers, managers, public relation experts, and radio promotion guys. I even did some session work and performed and recorded with Frank Zappa and "Weird Al" Yankovic. It was at this time that I began experimenting with various vocal styles and studying what made one style different from another.

All along, my goal has been to become the best singer I could be and understand what I was doing so that I could feel confident and consistent with my voice. The thing that eluded me still was singing in high chest voice. After much experimentation and, strangely enough, "feeling" my vocal folds as I was singing, I discovered several actions that allowed me to raise my chest voice higher, but it took another decade to codify these ideas into a simple, teachable model.

What kinds of styles do you currently teach? How long have you been teaching these styles?

When I first started teaching (at age eighteen), I didn't really have a clear concept on how to teach. Like many young teachers, I simply passed on a few exercises that I knew from my training. Over the years, I taught on and off, and fortunately—as a pianist and musician—I was able to accompany and teach music theory, which helped increase the services I could offer.

I began teaching pop and classical singing more earnestly in the late 1980s, both privately and at a community college for ten years. Since I have an interest in all vocal styles—I have sung everything from medieval to avant-garde and also in Bulgarian and East Indian for television and film—I have always taught whichever style I could research, replicate, and then pass on to a student.

What, do you believe, are the criteria for teaching these styles well?

If I had to pick one criterion for effective teaching, it would have to be the ability of the teacher to make the vocal sound and produce it well, with stylistic authenticity. Although imitation has historically been the main way musicians learn to play and sing, many of my teachers could not demonstrate what they were requesting from me. It was frustrating since I so much wanted to please my teachers and give them the sound they wanted, but mostly it was a guessing game. I would sing and then ask, "Is that what you want?"

In order to master a vocal style, a singer has to put in the time to listen to the acknowledged greats in that genre and model their vocal production, resonator shape, phrasing, expressive stylisms, and even their dialect. That is a lot to ask of one person. But I think that mastering vocal styles prior to teaching them is still a reasonable goal.

How do you teach style to students who don't have a strong background in a given genre?

When it comes to honing style authenticity, I usually begin with resonator shaping, which I call "mouth shapes" for short. For instance, when I teach R&B, I demonstrate a mouth shape I call "water in the mouth," and for sultry jazz, I use "fish lips." Each mouth shape helps create a basic resonance that can then be made precise by changing laryngeal height (lower or higher) or altering pharyngeal width (neutral, constricted, or wide).

Also, each style requires varying degrees of nasality, ring, or brightness, so I offer simple suggestions on how to achieve the appropriate resonance by consciously controlling these three "colors." Even finding the correct vocal fold closure can affect style accuracy.

Sometimes allowing more "air" in the sound—meaning less adduction in the vocal folds—is exactly what the song requires. In commercial singing, varying one's vocal fold closure can really make the difference in whether the singer sounds expressive. In pop singing, for example, a singer might choose to be airier in the verses and strive for cleaner and firmer closure in the choruses.

Phrasing differences, singing in the correct dialect, even being more "mumbly" (or more crisp) in one's enunciation can signal authenticity. Also, assuming a certain posture, using established gestures, and understanding the historical basis of a style can all be vital tools in creating a memorable performance that feels "real."

How did you come up with your method or approach? What does it consist of, and how is it unique?

While in my thirties, I received a call from an acquaintance who recently had been hired to head a community college music program. The school's vocal teacher had just passed away, and I was asked to replace him and teach two group classes. They were three hours each: one was for classical singers and the other was a pop/karaoke class.

My first night of teaching was absolute magic, which I liken to the feeling of a lightning bolt when you finally meet "the right one." I opened my mouth and all this stuff about singing, acting, dancing, psychology, and performing just came rolling out. I knew I had found my true calling and committed that night to spend the rest of my life teaching.

Around the third year of teaching my college class, a student mentioned to me privately that I had a system. I replied skeptically, "I do?" "Yes, you do, and you should make a video." That comment definitely gave me pause. My intention was not to create a method. Rather, my approach is based on the idea that there are certain basic concepts that all singers should know about and be able to do. These include posture, support, breathing, precise control of vocal registers, finding one's highest and lowest note, fixing vibrato problems, controlling vocal fold closures, understanding vertical laryngeal heights and pharyngeal widths, explaining the meaning of resonance, and showing "three bands": *ring*, *nasality*, and *brightness*. For singers interested in changing styles or mastering a style, I have broken down many elements of style including dialect, stance, emotions, and stylisms (e.g., cry, fry, yodel, riffs, etc.) unique to each style.

What *does* seem to be unique in my approach is my ever-growing understanding of vocal registers and how to fix register problems quickly. This is based on a fairly radical model that allows singers to sing any (or nearly any) note of their vocal range in *either* chest or head and also is based on sensation in and around the vocal folds. It's definitely a different but effective way to take registers from where you feel vibration to what you actually can feel at the vocal fold level.

I also have found, by touching my neck with my fingers (and now through MRI research), that a missing ingredient in raising chest voice higher in a comfortable and attractive way is the action of the hyoid bone. It seems to pull forward as pitch ascends in chest voice and may be a missing ingredient in the pedagogy of belting. I have theories about the action of the thyroid and cricoid cartilage relationship as a result of this pulling forward of the hyoid bone and am continuing to research this phenomenon.

What is your general philosophy of voice teaching? Summarize your core beliefs about vocal technique.
I believe that voice teaching is a sacred art form and that teachers have a moral obligation to care deeply for the unique people who put themselves in our hands. Each student should receive what they came for, and that can of course vary. Too many teachers give the same vocal exercises to every student, no matter their level, ability, style, or goals, and call it a voice lesson. I have also seen LA teachers who flatter wildly every new student who walks in the door. This might be good for the singer's ego in the short term, but this practice strikes me as immoral and eventually harmful.

In private teaching, many students who come to me have emotional baggage that they drag to their lessons. Taking the journey to vocal improvement can provide people with healing and inspiration, which can permeate other areas of their lives. I studied psychology in college, and it has been extremely helpful to me in dealing with the insecurities and negative self-talk that is so prevalent in singers, especially beginning singers.

My core beliefs about vocal technique are few and can be summed up in a single statement: *Singers who desire vocal mastery should be provided with a clear and concise approach to the skills and tasks of confident singing in whatever style most interests them and that allows them to sing with minimal harm and maximum thrill.*

What elements of vocal technique do you think are most important?

Ever since I was very young, I suspected that "support" was a key ingredient in being a good singer. My experience, however, was that there was no agreement between my teachers on how to teach me support, and I was mightily confused by the whole topic. I strongly believe that much of the tension singers experience in their necks, jaws, and tongues is simply compensatory tension for inadequate or incorrect abdominal breath support.

I also find that a surprising number of singers do not know their absolute vocal range, which is all the stranger since it is quite easy to determine. Every musician knows the range of their instruments, so why not singers?

Vibrato also confused me. In my training, I was always told that "you either have it or you don't" or my teacher would say "don't try to make a vibrato." I happened to have vibrato problems and did not know what to do to improve my vibrato speed and pitch. Once I began to think of vibrato as a volitional ornament that's a mechanism I could feel and control, it was a revelation and my confidence improved dramatically. As a result, I now teach vibrato (and straight tone control) as mechanisms and show people how to speed up, slow down, or eliminate straight tone without vocal fold pressing, which I consider the most dangerous vocal technique problem.

I am well aware that the topic of vocal registers is a thorny basket. Having said that, I think too many otherwise excellent singers unfortunately do not have the necessary control to sing a variety of styles easily and reliably. Smoothing register transitions is not as big a problem, in my opinion, as some pedagogues think; and learning to sing in either chest or head on any note with some measure of volume control is an achievable and worthy technical goal, especially if a singer wants to be able to "do anything" with their singing voice. Mastery of multiple register permutations is one of my favorite vocal technique topics.

Do you have a favorite vocal exercise you would like to share with us?

Yes, there is an exercise I call "pressure lips" and use it as my first choice when teaching belting. When done correctly, the sound is at medium volume and staccato. The lip closure (for the "b" consonant) should be held a tad longer than in speech, with a feeling I call "sticky lips." This helps create increased subglottal pressure with less airflow. Also, the vocal folds "square up" prior to making sound. That means that the vocal folds (and even the false folds) pre-shape themselves into a taller-edge, "squarish" shape and are more approximated (closer together) in preparation for a modal (chest) register sound. When done correctly with the support method I teach (upper belly "magic spot" *out*, lower belly *in*), the vocal folds can more easily maintain the modal register shape and vibrational pattern as the pitch rises.

Figure 13.1. Bee Pressure Lips Exercise.

It's important to feel like you're "holding your breath" during the exercise. Of course, air is coming through, but the sense is that you're holding your breath quite intensely. To summarize, this exercise helps the vocal folds stay in a "talking" sound comfortably to an F5 (for females), resulting in a psychological breakthrough of "That didn't hurt and I went how high?!"

Have you sung in the past, and if so, which styles? Do you currently sing any of the styles you teach?
Though I sang classically as a child, in my teens, I enjoyed singing music theater and writing pop songs in the style of Joni Mitchell and Elton John. In college, I expanded into early music and some contemporary classical works. Later I explored rock and R&B, and now I prefer to perform jazz standards. I have sung on almost all of "Weird Al" Yankovic's records and was on my first number one album in 2014—*that* was unexpected! Recently, I've reprised my Frank Zappa performances at European festivals. That style has been called "weird opera" and consists of jazz phrasing and much improvisational silliness.

Who were your strongest influences, pedagogically, vocally, and musically?
I fondly remember singing jazz standards with my father at the piano, as well as opera. My mother got us season tickets to the Chicago Lyric Opera when I was seven years old; I remember being propped up on a velvet pillow as we watched these wonderful productions. I also sang and played along with pop records and—later—auditioned for music theater productions at school. Each of these styles felt like four legs to the table.

In pop, I was influenced by Elton John, Joni Mitchell, Barbra Streisand, Aretha Franklin, and the many Motown artists I heard on the radio. In elementary school, I played Glinda in *Wizard of Oz* and Oliver in *Oliver* (at an all-girls school), which I loved. In my voice lessons, we sang in French, German, and Italian from the beginning, and I loved how classical singing was akin to a time machine, like stepping into the life of a character from a painting. It was wonderful.

My approach to teaching is different than my experience as a student. Most of my teachers focused on vocal exercises as the basis for learning to sing. And although I am not against exercises for warming up or training, my approach is more song oriented. There are so many hundreds of wonderful songs to be experienced, and—in my opinion—a weekly drudge of exercises can keep one from attaining excellence as an actual singer. I often try to fix technical problems while working on songs. This process gets to the good stuff sooner and students seem happier.

What is the primary goal when training your students?

As a teacher and mentor, I feel committed to providing clear answers to questions. Hopefully, if I do that successfully, my students will experience noticeable improvement in vocal ability and control at every lesson. My happiest moment is when a student says, "I can't believe how much I learned in just half an hour!" That really warms my heart.

What else is important to you in your work?

Based on my own experience of learning about music, art, languages, accent reduction, composition, gesture, composition, psychology, songwriting, record production, and pop artist development, I love to help singers expand their interests and skills so that they are well-rounded creative artists, not just singers who sound good. One never knows which endeavor or direction might be thrilling (or lucrative) until one tries something a little outside the box!

How has your approach been informed by life experience, and how has it evolved over the years?

As much as I loved my lessons with many interesting teachers (and I'm so thankful for them), for many years I felt an underlying thread of frustration. I would ask questions that could not be answered. Or it seemed like my ability to *guess* was an integral part of my voice training. I would beg them: "Please, just tell me what to do to be a better singer." So I'd have to say that my teaching approach is an attempt to take the mystery out of singing, to be task-oriented, to solve vocal problems quickly, and to share a system that explains any vocal style and breaks down the tasks of singing into small, understandable bits.

What are your thoughts on professional organizations? Are you involved with any? Why or why not?

I've enjoyed being a member of organizations, particularly the Voice Foundation, since I have a big interest in voice research and medicine. Each year I learn something new at the Voice Foundation meetings in Philadelphia—in fact, I think of it as my ongoing college experience. I've been a member of NATS for many years and am glad to see how much more open to new ideas and vocal styles they've become. I encourage young teachers to join both organizations at minimum.

One issue has always intrigued me and it's this: among the most expensive voice coaches in Los Angeles ($400 per hour and up), not a one is an active member of a professional organization. Does that mean that they don't believe they need to learn something new? Or perhaps they feel intimidated surrounded by teachers who have put a lot of time into their own educations? I really don't know.

My most favorite professional activity is to attend international voice conferences, and I wish more of my colleagues would consider participating. PEVOC (Pan-European Voice Conference) is particularly wonderful, and ICVT (International Congress of Voice Teachers) is also very good, especially for classical voice teachers enlarging their scope.

Do you use technology in any of your teaching?
I love my Korg transposing keyboard—I couldn't live without that lovely piece of equipment. I also have a recording studio composed of a Rode N2 microphone and use Logic Pro X on an iMac. My students love singing into the mic with headphones; whether I record them or not, the ability to really hear themselves increases their pitch-matching and singing skills quickly and dramatically.

More and more, I have been cowriting songs with students. We then create arrangements and professional quality recordings. For live work training, I have a separate room with a stage, lights, and sound system. In that space, we work on microphone technique, how to move like a professional, how to create a musical set, how to enhance charisma, and how to invent patter to create an audience/performer interaction.

Since I believe that learning to sing well is primarily an auditory experience, I purposefully do not use visual acoustic analysis aids on a regular basis for training purposes. I have been offering Skype lessons since it became available and have been so grateful for its availability. I have had very few problems with it and love that I can share my screen with a student and can easily upload links and PDFs. Though I do use FaceTime, it has not provided some of the extra features that I appreciate having on Skype.

What is in your future as a voice pedagogue?
As I head into "Act III" of my life, my main focus will be to increase my international traveling and lecturing. I adore flying and presenting

workshops and would love to share my work, particularly on the topics of commercial voice, belting voice production, and sharing the Voiceworks Method™ with teachers around the world. I have always been interested in voice research and have been fortunate to have had the opportunity to work with some awesome technology and researchers. Armed with my long list of research topics, I'm looking forward to continuing to experiment and explore new technologies as they come along. Recently I have had numerous requests to sing and perform, so I am opening my mind to these possibilities as well. ♪

14

DAVID SABELLA

David Sabella is a NYC-based voice teacher, internationally recognized as a master teacher in music theater and contemporary commercial music vocal techniques. He is currently on the music theater voice faculty at Montclair State University, Fordham University, and the Open Jar Institute. Previous faculty appointments include NYU's Tisch School of the Arts, CAP21, the New School's Mannes College Preparatory Division, SUNY Purchase, and SUNY New Paltz. He has also been a faculty member and workshop presenter at the Voice Foundation Symposium in Philadelphia and throughout the contiguous United States, Alaska, and South America. Mr. Sabella is a member of the National Association of Teachers of Singing (NATS) and was president of the New York Singing Teachers Association (NYSTA) from 2008 to 2014. As a performer, Mr. Sabella enjoys a very successful and varied career. He has performed on Broadway in Chicago for ten years (1996–2006) and Off-Broadway in Jules, Kiss and Make Up, Hexed in the City, Foxy, Watch Your Step, and So Long 174th Street. His voice-over work is featured in Peter Pan and the Pirates (Fox) and Teacher's Pet (Disney). Prior to his career in music theater, Mr. Sabella had a highly successful career as a classical countertenor and was the winner of the Luciano Pavarotti International Voice Competition in 1995. Operatic credits include Orlofsky in Die

Fledermaus *(Lincoln Center)*, *Ottone* in L'incoronazione di Poppea *(Utah Opera)*, and the title role in Giulio Cesare *(Virginia Opera)*. *He has appeared as a principal soloist at Carnegie Hall and Lincoln Center in Bach's* B Minor Mass, *Handel's* Messiah, *and Peter Schickele's* Three Bargain-Counter Tenors. *His discography includes* Giulio Cesare *on the Koch International label and the original cast recordings of* Chicago, Foxy, Watch Your Step, A Special Place, *and* Everybody's Getting into the Act. ♪

Tell us a little about your background and what led you to become a teacher of contemporary commercial styles.
My young life (before college) was spent in pursuit of a music theater career. I graduated high school early, moved into my first NYC apartment at age sixteen, and began auditioning and taking classes. My brother was having a successful career on Broadway, and my mother was a big band singer, so it was almost expected that I would have a career on stage.

After two years in NYC, I realized I needed a "real" education. So I applied to SUNY Purchase and was immediately accepted. This was at a time when there were no music theater schools. You either studied "music" or "theater" but not "music theater." Being just a little more confident in my singing (at the time), I chose the music school, where I met my first (and only) voice teacher, Marie Traficante. The curriculum was exclusively classical music, and being a tenor, I enjoyed many operatic leading roles throughout my college career. But it was in my senior year that I discovered a completely different part of my voice: my countertenor. Of course, at that time, I didn't call it that. It was a party trick, singing high soprano arias to the amazement of my friends.

Right after college a friend of mine suggested that I audition for La Gran Scena Opera Company (a company of male sopranos and mezzos, parodying great opera arias and scenes). I was accepted into the company and toured with them for more than five years. With LGS I sang duets and arias from *Madama Butterfly*, *Lakme*, *Aida*, *Die Walküre*, *Der Rosenkavalier*, and many others. It was a fantastic way to learn the operas. In order to lovingly "spoof" them, you had to know the works inside out and really get into the psyche of the character. Turning the motivation on its side ("spoofing" it) while staying true to the story—and the character's real feelings—was a great challenge. These early years of my career consisted of touring all over Europe with La Gran Scena while also performing in regional music theater and summer stock. It was heaven.

Then, in the early 1990s, countertenors became very "mainstream." Brian Asawa won the Metropolitan Opera National Council Auditions. I was in the audience and was just amazed at the velvet, supple quality of his voice. I sat there thinking, "Oh, my gosh, I can do that!" I then took two years off from performance and voraciously studied anything about baroque-era singing that I could get my hands on. I redirected my training with Marie to focus on my countertenor voice and coached with baroque specialists and conductors at the Met. By 1995, I began to enter the competition circuit as a countertenor and won several prestigious competitions, including the Luciano Pavarotti International Voice Competition. From there I received contracts to sing different operas all over the United States. My career seemed to be taking flight in the direction of classical music. And then *Chicago* happened.

Kander and Ebb's *Chicago* was being presented as part of the City Center "Encores!" series. *Chicago* is the only music theater piece in history to use a countertenor (male soprano) in one of the roles. My connections to Broadway landed me an audition for the role and ultimately the job. That show then moved to Broadway, and I happily went with it. From 1996 to 2006, I performed in *Chicago*, both on Broadway and on the national tour. In addition to these performances, I also maintained a classical career, singing oratorios and concertizing.

All this was concurrent to my private (and institutional) teaching. I had always been able to model both male and female sounds for my students. And with the debut of the musicals *Brooklyn* and *Wicked*, young girls were coming in to the studio and trying to sing F5 and A♭5 in a belt sound. Most of them were way too heavy, trying to "chest" the sound in that range. I could do it, but for me it was a kind of beefed-up, "witchy" falsetto. And that's when the light went on in my brain. I realized that, in my study of countertenor, I had learned to manipulate the registration and resonance of my voice in such a way to sound feminine. And—with a few more minor adjustments—I could get to this female high contemporary belt. And if I could do it, I could teach others to do it. These experiences inaugurated another period of intense study, this time in voice pedagogy—specifically, vocal anatomy and acoustic resonance. Hearing *through* the sound and being able to make the sound is what allows me to communicate this very different resonance strategy to both male and female singers. So, in a very roundabout way, through the study of classical countertenor, I have become a leading teacher in contemporary voice techniques. Go figure!

What kinds of styles do you currently teach? How long have you been teaching these styles?
I have been teaching for more than twenty years, and I teach most styles of CCM, all music theater, and some classical styles. And I also work a lot with singer-songwriters who write their own material.

In classical music, I prefer to stay in the baroque and *bel canto* era (the repertoire that I performed most often). And in CCM, I usually stick to the more lyrical forms of that music. However, the current craze for *Hamilton* has a lot of people coming in to try their hand at rap. And this takes a very specific skill set, massive support and breath control, extremely precise articulation, and a spoken resonance all the way up the scale. It's a fantastic development in our field, to be able to help these artists who beforehand would never have stepped into a voice studio.

Singer-songwriters are among my favorite clients. They have a vision for their music and a clear vocal identity. They are not looking to "build" a sound. They know how they want to sound. My job is to help them get there safely and easily. Interestingly enough, these songwriters don't always key their songs in the best key for their own voice, and their articulation sometimes hinders their storytelling. So there is a lot to do. The sound of their voice may not change all that much, but the level of their performance and ease of singing (and sometimes their range) increases greatly.

What, do you believe, are the criteria for teaching these styles well?
First, be able to make the sounds yourself. You must be able to model the registration and resonance qualities you want the student to replicate. All of us come to this career by first imitating the sounds we want to produce: as young children, in our bedrooms with a hairbrush, or as high schoolers (and college-age young adults) imitating pop/rock and

Broadway cast albums. We imitate first before we learn to create. Having a teacher who can clearly and *healthfully* model the right sounds is extremely important. I'm not saying that the teacher has to be a master at every resonance strategy known in music. But he or she should at least have some sensation of feeling these resonance options within his or her own voice, even on a minimal, nonperformance level.

Secondly, understand and *respect* the unique stylistic requirements of each genre and resonance strategy you teach. I have often said, to many teachers around the country, during various workshops that I have given, "You don't have to like the sounds you are called upon to teach. You just have to respect that the sound is a valid choice for the genre." For example, jazz singers should not sound like opera singers. And by all means, *keep it healthy*. A CCM technique is not the absence of proper technique. It is as specific as Western classical music—very different but just as specific. There is nothing missing or "less than" in a CCM technique.

How do you teach style to students who don't have a strong background in a given genre?
This is a great question, and it is indeed very hard. My short answer is YouTube! But within that statement is the need for a study of vocal history. It amazes me that many students come to college to study music theater without *any* knowledge of music theater history and no knowledge of performers or shows more than twenty years old. It is so disheartening to be in a music theater institution and have students give me a blank stare when I mention names like Betty Buckley and Patti Lupone. Students today do not have any personal or historical recollection before the year 2000. Think about that—2000! And a lesson hour is not necessarily the time for a history lesson. But, at some point, you can't really move forward until a real historical perspective is gained. At the very least, students need to have a good understanding of what the tonal target might be. What can (and should) the human voice sound like within the given genre? YouTube to the rescue!

How did you come up with your method or approach? What does it consist of, or how is it unique?
As I mentioned above, my "method" grew out of an understanding of *bel canto* and baroque principles and specifically the application of the *voce*

faringea to more contemporary styles, which allows the singer to sew up the gap between the head voice and chest voice through manipulation of the resonance strategy.[1] What started out as conjecture on my part soon turned into factual evidence, using the voice visualization software VoceVista. I began a three-year study—often working with VoceVista's creator, Donald Miller—to examine the objective vocal characteristics of my young female belters, using the methods I had devised and taught them. This study proved conclusively that it was possible to have a raised closed quotient (CQ) and a lowered subglottal pressure through manipulation of the *resonance tract* (*not* the registration directly). In other words, you could get a "chest voice" sound without thinking deliberately about going into chest voice. Did the registration change? Yes! But the singer did not willfully apply greater subglottal pressure to make it happen. Instead the registration was altered by resonance factors above the vocal source.

This was about the same time that Ingo Titze had published his theories of "non-linear" vocal tract resonance/reactance. Learning of Dr. Titze's hypothesis and findings encouraged me to continue with my own research in this area, which led to my presenting my initial findings at the 2010 NATS convention in Salt Lake City, where Dr. Titze was present at my lecture. Although my research at the time was somewhat controversial, Dr. Titze, Dr. Miller, and Scott McCoy all encouraged me to continue with this work. Each of them (together and separately) greatly enhanced my understanding of the anatomy and acoustics of the voice and allowed me to further this study and method with some modicum of confidence.

Now, I must also say that there were many respected teachers across the country all working on these issues and techniques simultaneously and unbeknownst to one another. Through open discussions and sharing of information, many of my colleagues contributed to my understanding and ability to teach these techniques, whether they knew it or not. To each of them I am indebted, and together we have created a twenty-first-century pedagogy that we all can be very proud of.

If there is a uniqueness to my approach, it may lie in the fact that my first investigations into this research came about as a result of my questioning my own ability to manipulate the register and resonance of my own voice, to sound more like a female. It occurred to me that if I could do this and approximate a high contemporary female belt, then why couldn't a real female do the same thing? In this way, my work as a countertenor greatly informed my pedagogy and methodology.

Application of these techniques comes in various technical exercises for breathing, registration, resonance, and articulation. These are the four "legs" of the technique. I give all my students many various exercises in these "legs" to keep the voice from becoming used to any one set of exercises. Just like going to the gym, you've got to vary the exercise to continue to reap the benefits of the workout. Some of the exercises I use include straw phonation (thank you, Dr. Titze), the consonant orchestra and articulation series (thank you, Arthur Lessac), and specific pharyngeal ("cry") voice exercises that I have both learned from others and developed myself. ♪

What is your general philosophy of voice teaching? Summarize your core beliefs about vocal technique.
I have a few core beliefs. Above all, do no harm! I know that sounds more like a doctor than a voice teacher, but it's really true. I don't believe that *any* singing should be difficult. Yes, you must learn certain techniques that may require a diligence of study. But nothing should hurt or feel uncomfortable—the singer should never have the sensation to cough or gag or have a tickle in their throat. And at the end of performance, the singer should feel like they could turn right around and do it again because on Wednesday and Saturday they will! Currently on Broadway there is a trend toward eliminating the Wednesday shows altogether (they are historically the least well attended), making Wednesday the day off, thus changing the schedule to a very difficult five-show weekend. The current schedule for these shows is: Thursday, Friday, Saturday (matinee), Saturday (evening), Sunday (matinee), Sunday (evening), Monday, and Tuesday. That means from Friday night to Sunday night (forty-eight hours), you do the show five times. *Five times* in forty-eight hours! If any aspect of your singing in the show is difficult for you to manage, you will not get through the week, let alone a long run. Health, safety, and ease are goals that must be attained.

Another new philosophy (and mantra) of mine is this:

Registration = the way the voice is made.
Resonance = the way the voice sounds.

There are *many* ways to belt, and not all belters are created equal. Sopranos can certainly belt, but they do it much differently than mezzos. And with that in mind, we can't expect all belting to be done in the same way, taking into account their given vocal range. Yes, it all must *sound* like belting. But the mechanics of how each singer makes that sound will vary. So, personally, I'm not so concerned with what to call "the way it's made." I'm most interested in "the way it sounds." Does it sound like a belt? Then it's a belt. After applying the techniques I've showed them, many singers report that it "feels too easy" or "doesn't feel like I'm working." These reports stem from a lack of pressure that the singer was previously used to using in order to achieve the sound. Now, in the absence of that pressure, they doubt what they feel. My response is twofold: "How does it sound?" and "Does it hurt?" If it sounds like a belt and feels easier than you thought it would be, then bravo! After all, it's called belting, not bleeding.

Respect the world you are in. For instance, if you're singing in a pop/rock style, sound like a pop/rock singer, not a music theater singer singing pop. This is actually a huge issue right now, with many casting directors complaining that singers sound "too trained" or "not raw enough" for the rock-style shows they are casting. Many music directors and coaches will instruct singers to "put a little stank on it." Well, how do you teach "stank"? My answer: carefully and authentically.

There is no one "right" sound for CCM singers. Even a vocal pathology can be used to great advantage if used wisely and safely. Take for instance the obviously damaged voices of Rod Stewart or Michael Bolton. The rasp in these men's sounds is completely acceptable within the genres they perform. And, even with an obvious vocal deficit, a CCM singer can have a substantial and lucrative career.

This contrasts with a classical model, where a very certain (and very clear) vocal tone is required. If a student doesn't acquire a certain tone, resonance strategy, or vocal gesture (like "turn over"), then you know you have got work to do to master those necessary techniques. However, the same is not true for CCM singers. The "turn over" in a CCM sound is much different than its classical counterpart and is very rarely necessary at all. Additionally, these singers rely upon a microphone. It is an industry standard, and there is no circumstance where they will be performing without one. This lack of self-amplification allows for a more intimate vocal production, which can dramatically offset a singer's sense of support. So again, support, articulation, registration, and resonance are key issues in a CCM technique. Does this sound familiar? Classical and CCM teachers really do have a lot in common. Where we differ is in the resonance strategy we choose to employ to achieve the aesthetic of the genre.

What elements of vocal technique do you think are most important?
I named several in the question above, and honestly, I do believe that *all* elements of vocal technique are important. However, the application of technique in each genre is very different and varies with the style one is singing. A music theater director, or music director, will constantly ask the song for "more text" or to "tell the story," whereas a classical conductor may ask for more legato line. What they are *both* asking for is the connection and support of the consonants. So, in a CCM technique, there is not much discussion about legato line, but we work consonant action and support diligently.

Another element of vocal technique I find indispensable is the discussion of resonance strategy. What is the sound you are aiming for, and how can we make that sound *safely*? This also takes a good amount of ear training, which allows the student to adjust their concept of the sound for which they are aiming. We all know that singers are misguided by the sounds they hear in their own head. In a CCM technique, there is an additional challenge: higher resonances that are present in contemporary belting are often interpreted by the inner ear as an unpleasant buzzing sound, like an annoying bee in the very center of your head or nails on a chalkboard. When young singers first experience this, they pull away from it and bring the sound back into their lofted resonance, where it sounds much better to them. Only over time can they embrace the buzzing bee, which then allows the contemporary sound to come out. I often say, "I can teach you how to sing a belted high F in about fifteen minutes, but it will take your body eighteen to twenty-four months to trust it."

Have you sung in the past, and if so, which styles? Do you currently sing any of the styles you teach?
Yes, I have sung professionally in all the styles I teach. I have sung on Broadway, on national tours, and in Off-Broadway productions. I have

sung leading roles in operas and as an oratorio soloist at both Carnegie Hall and Lincoln Center. And I have performed in both cabaret and concert venues across the United States. As I said earlier, if I am not comfortable modeling the sound, then I don't feel I am the best teacher for the job. That being said, there are days in which I have one belter after another all day, and I can't model a female belt for six to eight hours straight. But the fact still remains that I have made (or know how to make) the sound I am wanting the student to emulate.

Who were your strongest influences, pedagogically, vocally, and musically?

Pedagogically, I am indebted to Scott McCoy, who opened my eyes to vocal anatomy and voice acoustics, as well as Donald Miller and the VoceVista visualization software. Ken Bozeman's book *Practical Vocal Acoustics* has also been very helpful. However, the largest debt of thanks I have is for my first and only voice teacher, Marie Traficante. She was an active member of NATS and NYSTA and very well versed in vocal anatomy and acoustics. She taught me in a methodical way using these tools, and when I need to touch back into my healthiest technique, I always refer back to her original exercises. Tradition looms large in vocal excellence regardless of the genre you are singing. The trick is applying the traditions to new and various styles of voice. ♪

Vocally, I have many idols that range from Luciano Pavarotti to Bruno Mars. And, of course, growing up my vocal goddesses were Maria Callas, Judy Garland, and Barbra Streisand. As an adult, that list has grown to include Renée Fleming, Lorna Luft (who is a client of mine), and a host of Broadway and cabaret singers who are currently working.

Musically, I have a few teachers in particular to thank, including Leyna Gabrielle, Peter Schlosser, and Ira Siff. These are all people who taught me to justify (earn) every musical notation in the score. Everything that happens in the music—dynamics, keys, time signatures, accidentals, and so on—happens because your character said, felt, thought, or did something to make it happen. And, if the music is a reaction to your inner life, then you need to have that inner life before it appears in the music. This concept of "earning" everything that appears in the music is a guiding principle toward creating an authentic performance that is unique to each performer. This work leads me into the realm of "vocal coach" rather than "technique teacher," but for me, they go hand in hand.

What is the primary goal when training your students?
Guiding them to their authentic performance. This is so much harder than it should be. In an era of instant gratification (think YouTube and other social media), it is *extremely* hard to get students to turn inward and cultivate their own sense of self within the music. No copying, no imitation. Each singer needs to make the song their own in a very personal way.

When I give a student a new piece of music that they do not know, I forbid them to listen to it. First, they must memorize it as a monologue, doing all of the necessary "actor's" work for the song:

What is the *point of view*? (To whom are you talking?)
What is the *objective*? (What do you want?)
What is the *conflict*? (Why don't you get it right away?)

If this work is done first, then they will come to the song as the composer did, starting with only the words (in most cases). The words (and the cadence of language) inspire the rhythm. So, by the time they are done with this step, they are always, and unwittingly, very close to the actual rhythm of the song.

Next, we go through a three-step process of *recite, excite*, and *contour*. The reciting has actually been done in their monologue work, so it's time to "excite." In this technique, the student speaks the words in a very high, "excited" speaking voice. Often, they speak it higher than the pitches require without even knowing it. Finally, we "contour," which is approximating the contour of the vocal line. I don't give them pitches. I only play the first chord, and then they go up and down with their voice, as indicated by the music. This often leads to a greater understanding of the inflection of speech the composer is indicating, which—in turn—leads to greater understanding of the character's (or songwriter's) motivation.

After all that we start to sing it, and the result is a very authentically thought-out interpretation of the song, as if it were written for them. The more we do this work, the faster it gets. Eventually the student is almost able to do it unconsciously, and their personal craft has grown.

What else is important to you in your work?
Having a unique and recognizable voice is essential to a career in CCM. We must be able to recognize the singer within two or three measures (preferably less). The same of course is true for elite classical singers. It is widely believed that the sound of Maria Callas's voice in the opening phrases of "Casta diva" actually changed the timbre of the strings behind her. Whether you subscribe to that belief or not, it is the singularity and instantly recognizable quality of a voice that distinguishes it from all others. And in music theater, the speaking and singing voice need to match throughout the evening. In a contemporary market, the actor cannot speak with one resonance strategy and then sing in another. The result would be off-putting and "take us out of the story."

This has always been the goal in music theater, even though we do perceive that the golden age of music theater had more to do with lofted sounds. If one carefully studies the acoustic sound spectrum of such great music theater singers like Julie Andrews, Mary Martin, or Barbara Cook, you will hear without a doubt a conscious effort to retain a spoken value sound all the way up to the second *passaggio*, and—in some cases—through it. Accordingly, the articulation of these singers is also a credit to their profession. In both "Till There Was You" from *The Music Man* and "In Buddy's Eyes" from *Follies*, one can hear Barbara Cook consciously closing her vowels to maintain a speechlike sound through the top of the treble staff. And Julie Andrews always did a lot more speaking than lofting, although the impression was that she was a very "legit" singer. And, of course, male singers have always had to maintain a spoken voice sound. Think of the inimitable sounds of Frank Sinatra or Tony Bennett (still singing high As at age ninety).

I stress this as an important component of the work because so many institutions and private teachers are mistakenly striving to enhance their student's lofted sounds. And while this may be a necessary component of a healthy technique—yes, everyone needs to learn how to lift the soft palate in a yawning gesture—it will not facilitate the student being able to work in the profession right out of school. I cannot tell you how many hundreds of singers I have worked with, both male and female, who have gone through a four-year program only to hit a wall in professional auditions because they do not sing how they speak. This may be the single most important thing to address in the CCM technique.

How has your approach been informed by life experience, and how has it evolved over the years?
Life (and age) have affected my teaching. In my youth, I felt a responsibility to share the knowledge that I had with the student (whether they asked for it or not). And to that end, I actively used both anatomical and acoustical terms within the lesson. My lessons almost became mini voice science lessons. It was a valiant effort, filled with good intentions, but didn't leave much time in the lesson for the subjective, the expressive, and communicative: the *art* of it. I've come to realize that with youth came zeal and determination. But with maturity comes patience and understanding. I realize now that although *I* need to know all the anatomical and acoustical information (because that is my job), the student doesn't necessarily need (or want) to know any of it. Most students are only looking for the *how*, not the *why*. So, after all those years of research and developing my techniques and strategies, I'm really the only one who needs to know them. Giving my students the tools for the *how* and then turning my attention to the more subjective and artistic concepts proves to be a better plan of attack for both of us.

What are your thoughts on professional organizations? Are you involved with any?
I am a member of NATS, NYSTA, and the Voice Foundation. I do believe in being part of a larger community of teachers. That's one of the reasons I have enjoyed being on faculty at various institutions. I also feel that it is important to maintain connections to the people and organizations that are doing the cutting-edge research in our field of voice teaching and voice science. In the past twenty years, there have been great strides made in understanding very complex acoustical concepts. The emergence of the non-linear vocal tract resonance model really revolutionized the way many voice teachers work. The information is out there, published by all three of the organizations I listed above. If you are a serious vocal professional, it is incumbent upon you to stay current with the latest research papers and articles that can and will enhance your pedagogy and craft.

As president of NYSTA (the New York Singing Teachers Association), I worked very hard to make sure that all of their core curriculum courses—Vocal Anatomy and Physiology, Voice Acoustics and Resonance, Vocal Health for Voice Professionals, Singer's Developmental Repertoire, and Comparative Pedagogy—were available as on-demand, online courses so that that *any* teacher or singer in the world could take them 24/7. The resources are out there—use them! ♪

Do you use technology in any of your teaching?
Many readers of this book think of me as the "tech guru" of voice teachers. In my younger days, I was very infatuated with the use of various technologies within the studio, such as voice visualization software, electroglottograph (EGG), video broadcasting, and online lessons. My research hours unintentionally bled into my teaching hours, and I was so focused on the objective data of resonance and registration that somewhere along the way the communication of the artistic concepts of expressive singing and performance started to suffer. I don't think students noticed this—at least I hope not—but I began to feel that too much emphasis (and too much of my time) was spent in trying to objectively prove that the concepts and techniques were valid. The student didn't need that. They already trusted me. So, like any good actor, I decided to "trust the material, and not overplay it." I pulled way back in my use of technology to concentrate more on the artistic and expressive elements of voice technique. However, I do continue to video record any lesson that a student wants to review for their own self-study. And all of my sheet music (I mean *all* of it) is stored in "the cloud," where I can pull it down individually for use on my iPad Pro. Now, the only thing I have to carry is my iPad Pro and iPencil. I do highly recommend that.

What is in your future as a voice pedagogue?
I am often asked to write, and perhaps that is what's next for me: to be published. But my issue with that is similar to how I feel about the printed sheet music. Music happens in the air, in the room, long before it gets written down on paper. It is an experience, in both its creation and interpretation. That experience gets distilled down to a mathematical graph in order for others to begin to understand how to replicate it. But any great musician will know that you can't just do what's on the page. You must do more. You must bring yourself to it. You must understand the history and the common performance practice of the genre—and yes, CCM does have a common performance practice. So,

as clearly as I would (and do) try to write, I don't know if the experience of teaching voice can be distilled onto the page. Perhaps, like music itself, it has to be experienced in the room? I'm still deciding.

NOTE

1. Cultivated by castrati, the pharyngeal voice or *voce faringea* was a tool that was used in uniting the chest and head registers of the voice.

15

CATHRINE SADOLIN

Cathrine Sadolin is one of the leading voice researchers in the world. Her thirty years of research across all vocal styles, combined with her own experiences as a professional singer, have inspired innovative thinking within the field. She is regularly invited to voice conferences around the world and contributes to ongoing voice and vocal technique research. She has specialized in solving vocal problems, repairing worn-out voices, and teaching advanced singing techniques within all musical styles. She has worked with theater, opera, and record companies, both as a vocal coach and as a producer. She has also performed all over Europe as a classical, folk, and rock singer and has released several albums. In 2002, Ms. Sadolin launched a three-year singer/teacher diploma course for professionals who want to improve as singers as well as singing teachers. In 2005, she opened Complete Vocal Institute (CVI) in Copenhagen with branches in many other countries. CVI is today the largest singing institute for professional and semi-professional singers in Europe. ♪

Tell us a little about your background and what led you to become a teacher of contemporary commercial styles.
I never had a natural talent for singing.[1] In fact, I even had problems breathing. My first singing lessons were an attempt to overcome

breathing problems due to asthma. One way or another I had to develop techniques to get the sounds I wanted. The first step was to understand the anatomy and physiology of the voice, and this enabled me to distinguish between myths and truths about the voice. I then experimented with achieving the sounds in ways other than the traditional methods. The only natural talent I had was a love for music coupled with the belief that everything is possible and the energy to keep going. That is why I can truly say that if I was able to learn and achieve the sounds I wanted, then anybody can.

While I was working on my technical problems through the years, I always listened to all kinds of music. That was probably why many singers of popular music began asking for me to help them achieve certain sounds and overcome vocal problems, even though I was trained as and eventually performed as a classical singer. It seemed to me that they wanted the healthy aspect of the classical technique but without the classical sound. I thought that it must be possible to benefit from the technique without being constrained by the narrow ideals of the sound. To do this, however, I had to find out how sound was produced, and this encouraged me to study many styles of singing, speech and hearing science, acoustics, and spectral ear training.

Singing techniques were always presented with attached ideals regarding sound colors. If you wanted to use the technique, you had to accept these ideals. I did not want to accept that. I wanted to separate taste and technique in order to isolate the technique so that singers could combine the endless elements to create any sound they were looking for, without the interference of the specific taste of a particular technique or teacher.

What kinds of styles do you currently teach? How long have you been teaching these styles?

I teach all singers regardless of what style they prefer to sing, so I teach everything! In Europe, there is a big heavy metal culture, so I always get a lot of singers who are singing in various extreme styles. I have been teaching all kinds of singers for more than thirty years. I started out as a classical singer, but I have always listened to all styles of music, and this included a lot of rough metal styles. I was always interested in all sounds, from classical to sounds like screaming, growling, distortion, and grunting. I was also interested in ethnic styles and so on. I just thought that all extreme sounds were really interesting. I wanted to know how it could be done in a healthy way. Once I learned how to do this, singers began coming to me asking if I could teach them how to do it.

What, do you believe, are the criteria for teaching these styles well?

It is very important that the teacher thoroughly understands anatomy and physiology. It is also very important to study acoustics and voice science. I find that a lot of voice teachers do not study these things, and I think it is a pity. I feel that this kind of study has been severely neglected by both classical and contemporary voice teachers. Teachers in the past have been too subjective when they teach. They relied on charisma and modeling themselves instead of specifically identifying technical problems. A methodology was really needed, which is why I developed my approach. It is time for our profession to enter the new millennium. In all other disciplines, we look to science for answers, and singing teachers need to do that as well. We shouldn't be teaching the same way we were one hundred years ago, but that still happens too often. We wouldn't accept an intuitive approach from a physician—why should singing teachers be treated any differently? We need to have scientific expectations in the voice studio as well.

I think a lot of teachers are actually coaches as opposed to technique teachers. That is all fine as long as they inform the student about this. They develop good reputations because the singers they teach are very talented and sound good even without specific technical instruction. But what happens when a singer walks into your studio who isn't singing well and has real technical problems? Then the voice teacher needs to be able to know how to fix these issues and help a singer achieve the sounds they want with a healthy technique. Maybe they need to build their technique from the bottom up, stone by stone. With so much research and science available nowadays, there is no reason why every teacher shouldn't be benefiting from this information and be able to teach according to the knowledge we have from science, anatomy, and physiology.

How do you teach style to students who don't have a strong background in a given genre?
I never use the word "student" because that generally implies that the singer is on a lower level than the teacher, which I do not believe they are. A singer can and should be able to sing whatever he or she wants to sing. The human voice is capable of amazing flexibility, and too often that is not acknowledged. No one would suggest that just because a hand is used for writing that it can't also play piano! It is the same with the voice. I think all singers should be encouraged to cross-train. A singer who is trained classically can absolutely learn how to sing rock. So, when a singer comes to me wishing to explore a new style, I am always encouraging. I say, "Great! Let's get to work." However, they have to jump in with both feet and really understand the style. I never tell a singer how they should sound—that is their job. If I start changing their style, then it is not their style anymore. I don't impose my personal taste on them. A singer's uniqueness is what makes him or her special. My job is to listen and help the singer achieve the sounds, techniques, expressions, and improvisations that they want.

How did you come up with your method or approach? What does it consist of, and how is it unique?
I felt that I needed to come up with new terminology because the traditional terminology can be so confusing. For example, all voice teachers talk about "register," but they disagree on its definition. It means different things to different people. That's the way all voice terminology is. Our profession does not have standardized definitions. This is a problem because it interferes with our ability to communicate with one another.

My goal was to develop a terminology that is completely consistent. This is the concept behind Complete Vocal Technique™ (CVT). With CVT, every sound has only one term. Every term must mean only one thing and has only one definition. With this system, everyone is on the same page and we know exactly what we are talking about. The following chart from my book, also called *Complete Vocal Technique*, summarizes the entire method in one page (see figure 15.1).

CVT can be summarized by four main subjects: three *overall principles* to ensure healthy sound production; four *vocal modes* to choose the "gear" you want to sing in; *sound colors* to make the sound lighter

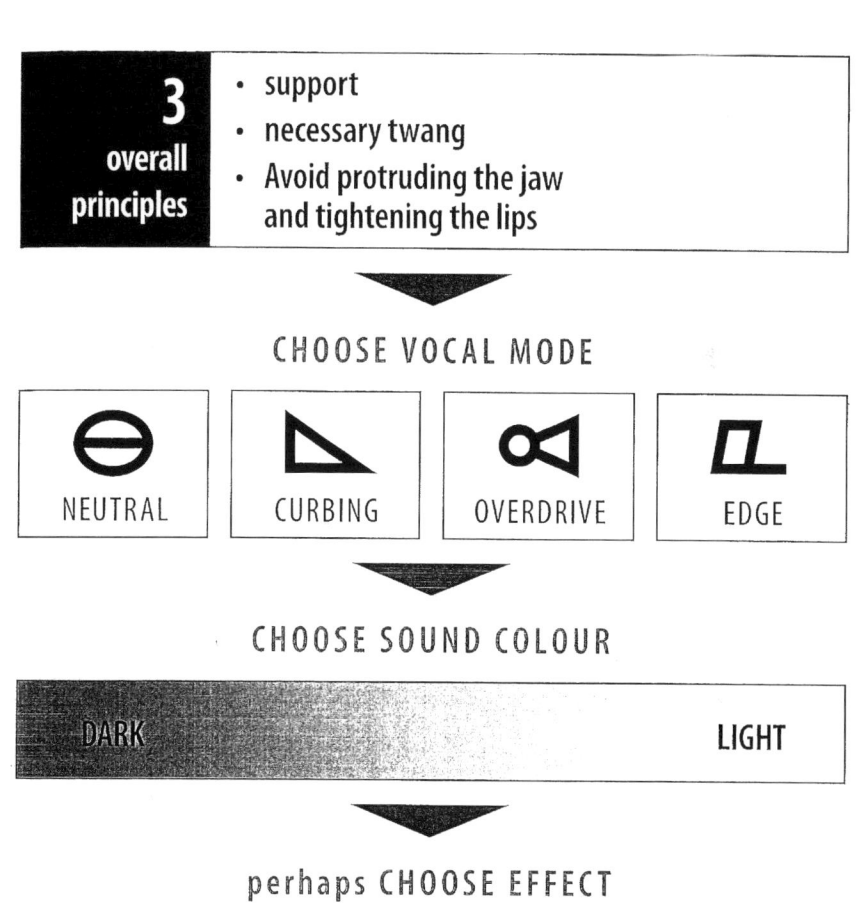

3 overall principles
- support
- necessary twang
- Avoid protruding the jaw and tightening the lips

CHOOSE VOCAL MODE

| NEUTRAL | CURBING | OVERDRIVE | EDGE |

CHOOSE SOUND COLOUR

DARK ──────────────── LIGHT

perhaps CHOOSE EFFECT

- distortion
- creak and creaking
- rattle
- growl
- grunt
- screams
- vocal breaks
- air added to the voice
- vibrato
- techniques for ornamentation

Figure 15.1. Chart for Complete Vocal Technique (CVT).

or darker; and *effects* to achieve specific sound effects. The three overall principles—*support, necessary twang,* and *avoid protruding the jaw and tightening the lips*—are the most fundamental and important to perfect. They make it possible to reach all the high and low notes within the range of the individual singer, to sing long phrases, to have a clear and powerful voice, and to avoid hoarseness. They must be obeyed regardless of *mode, sound color,* and *effect* (the other three subjects).

The use of the voice can be divided into four *vocal modes: neutral, curbing, overdrive,* and *edge.* The modes differ by having different amounts of metallic character. Most singing problems occur because of incorrect use of the modes. Each mode has a certain character, as well as advantages and limitations. To avoid mistakes and technical problems, it is important to know and control the modes, to use their advantages and to respect their limitations. It is also important to be able to change freely between the modes in order to make the most of their advantages. You can change smoothly or make abrupt changes to achieve vocal breaks. Each of the four *vocal modes* should be trained individually and in different ways. You need to remember to obey the three *overall principles* regardless of the mode.

All modes can be lightened or darkened, though some more than others. The *sound color* is created in the vocal tract, which is the space above the vocal folds extending to the lips and including the nasal passages. The form and size of the vocal tract is of great importance to the sound color. All singers have different vocal tracts so all singers have their own personal sound color. If the vocal tract is large, the *sound color* will be darker with more "body" to it. If it is small, the sound will be lighter and thinner. The shape of the vocal tract can be altered in many directions so there are many ways of changing the *sound color* of your voice. You need to remember to obey the three *overall principles* and retain control of the chosen *vocal mode* before changing sound color.

Effects are sounds that are not connected to melody or text but that underline the expression or style of a singer. Many *effects* are produced in the vocal tract. All singers are different. Consequently, every effect must be specifically designed to each singer, taking into account their anatomy, physiology, fitness, energy level, and temperament. Before you start working with *effects*, it is important that you can control the three *overall principles*, the chosen *vocal mode,* and the *sound color.*

This is obviously just a very basic introduction to Complete Vocal Technique (CVT). Readers who are interested in learning more can download the free introductory app for Complete Vocal Technique or get the full app/book, which goes into great detail about all of these topics and provides exercises for each. At the institute, we also offer various courses, including five-day courses, the Academy (which is a twelve-week course), the one-year course (offered over six weekends throughout a single year in various European cities), and the three-year CVT diploma course for singers and teachers (also offered in weekend format). All of these opportunities can be explored via the Complete Vocal Institute website.[2] ♪

What is your general philosophy of voice teaching? Summarize your core beliefs about vocal technique.

Singing is not difficult. Everyone can learn to sing, and you can sing whatever you want. You must trust yourself—singing should always feel comfortable. Also, the technique must have the intended effect right away; otherwise you are not working with it correctly. Finally, if an exercise hurts, feels uncomfortable, or feels wrong, it *is* wrong. Only you know how it feels, so trust your feelings. It is really that simple.

I also feel that teachers need to be clear and give concrete solutions for vocal problems. Also, do not fear sounds. You can't tell if a sound is vocally damaging based on how it sounds; how it is produced and feels to the singer is what is important. The sound in and of itself can never be damaging. A technique needs to be based in anatomy and physiology and supported by scientific evidence. I also believe that vocal technique should be *genre free*. A solid technique should allow a singer to sing in whatever style he or she desires. All sounds can and should be produced in a healthy way. Finally, personal taste needs to be completely separate from vocal technique.

What elements of vocal technique do you think are most important?

I think this depends on the individual singer. Every singer will have a different instrument, and different singers have different issues, wishes, and needs. For some people, support is very important; others may struggle with certain modes, and yet others may struggle with certain effects. It is important for the teacher to listen to the singers' wishes and help the singers achieve the sounds and expressions that they are looking for.

Have you sung in the past, and if so, which styles? Do you currently sing any of the styles you teach?
I was trained as a classical singer and that is how I got my start, but now I perform many other styles, including funk, hard rock, heavy metal, and folk music. As a teacher, I have to be able to demonstrate all sounds and styles in my teaching sessions to get certain points across. To be able to demonstrate all styles and sounds is also one of the requirements to become an authorized CVT teacher. I truly love all styles of music. I always have.

Who were your strongest influences, pedagogically, vocally, and musically?
Years ago, I read the book *Great Singers on Great Singing* by Jerome Hines. In this book, forty singers—all *wonderful* singers—were interviewed on how they did what they did. I thought it was an astonishing book because I couldn't find one thing that they all agreed upon or had in common. It was also interesting to see how all these wonderful singers had no clue physically of what they were doing and no mutual language to describe it. That experience had a profound impact on me and really influenced my pedagogical interests from that point on. I vowed to develop a methodology that was clear. Reading that book was the seminal event that in many ways marked the beginning of my quest for making singing technique more clear and efficient.

There are many singers across all styles who have influenced me and that I find very inspiring. Ronnie James Dio is someone who comes to mind right away. He sang with numerous heavy metal groups, most famously Black Sabbath. I have spent years studying his technique and recordings and am fascinated by how he used his voice. I also love Bob Dylan. Some people claim that he is not a good singer, but I don't know what they're talking about—he is a *wonderful* singer! Dick Gaughan is a Scottish folk singer whom I deeply admire. And then of course there are singers like Aretha Franklin and James Brown. There are so many people who are archetypes of their genre, and they have all taught me so much.

What is the primary goal when training your students?
To give them what they want to get. I always begin each lesson by asking them what they want to accomplish today. I don't have any ambition on their behalf. Often, they begin by singing a song. After they are finished, I say, "OK, what can I do for you?" Even if I hear six or seven things that I would do differently, they might choose to want to work on something completely different that never would have occurred to me. Whatever they want to work on, I will say, "Cool—we'll go there!" I really want to empower them to direct the lesson. I am just there to help. To achieve what *they* want. That is my primary goal.

What else is important to you in your work?
At Complete Vocal Institute, we are a large team of teachers. Working in a team is possible because we all have the same terminology, so we can precisely describe to each other what we hear. Therefore, many teachers can work effectively and efficiently with the same singer. I also believe it is very important that we are critical of ourselves. We are constantly giving input to one another and striving to make ourselves better. We are constantly scrutinizing our own method. I feel that it is extremely important to be open to new ideas. I am always interested in knowing more and being a better teacher every day. There should be no such thing as dogma or sacred cows in our industry. Everything is up for debate, and everything can be changed. ♪

I think it is important to have a healthy relationship with the singers. I like to have close relationships, but I also don't want to be "married" to a singer or feel like I "own" a singer. A teacher should not take credit for a singer's successes or be blamed for a singer's failures—the teacher should remain in the background. I don't like it when teachers are "name droppers" and take credit for famous singers. I don't want to do that, which is why we have client confidentiality at the Complete Vocal Institute. I never mention whom I work with. Physicians do not brag about their patients when they get healthy. I think that singing teachers should simply do their jobs to the best of their ability.

How has your approach been informed by life experience, and how has it evolved over the years?
I am a much better teacher now than I was thirty years ago because I know so much more than I used to. This is a result of years and years of research, and I am still evolving because I am continuing to do more research. Over the past ten years, I have done research with ENT doctor Julian McGlashan from Nottingham University Hospital in England. We meet for "research weeks" about twice a year and look into interesting aspects of the voice. Our meetings result in papers that we are publishing in the scientific community. To make the research more accessible for everyone, we have developed a "CVT Research Site" at our website and in the free app that is available online. Through these venues, we can share our discoveries with anyone who wants to read them.[3] We believe that this research should be shared, and I believe that singers should be actively engaged in research. This has become increasingly important to me as my career has progressed. ♪

What are your thoughts on professional organizations? Are you involved with any?
I frequently get invited to present my method and research at conferences. I usually attend three to ten conferences a year and have presented at many of the major singing conferences, including the Pan-European Voice Conference (PEVOC), European Voice Teachers Association (EVTA), British Voice Association (BVA), Pacific Voice Conference (PVC), and the Voice Foundation Symposium in Philadelphia. I also have presented at a variety of scientific conferences. I think it is very important to be a part of a larger community and share our research and ideas with one another.

Do you use technology in any of your teaching?
At Complete Vocal Institute, we teach a lot of Skype lessons and teach many singers who live and work outside of Copenhagen. Skype is a wonderful resource to connect with them. A lot of times in live lessons singers want to use a microphone because they always use one when they perform, and it is important to replicate the actual live situation as much as possible. Sometimes, they have very specific technological preferences, and I always honor their requests. I want them to feel as "at home" as possible when they work with me.

What is in your future as a voice pedagogue?
We have recently developed a free CVT app—Complete Vocal Technique: Introduction—as well as a full-version app that can be purchased on either the iTunes App Store or Google Play. We are very excited about it. It puts CVT in the palm of everyone's hand. I also plan on continuing to mentor a new generation of teachers through our CVT diploma course. We currently have 390 authorized teachers in twenty-four countries, and the number keeps growing. I also plan to continue conducting research and publishing scientific articles. We recently had a couple of articles published in the *Journal of Voice*, and we have several others that we are working on. It is so important to me to learn as much as I can and share my knowledge with as many people as I can. ♪

NOTES

1. These passages were originally published in my book, *Complete Vocal Technique* (Copenhagen: CVI Publications, 2012).
2. completevocal.institute/.
3. cvtresearch.com/.

16

MARY SAUNDERS BARTON

Mary Saunders Barton is professor emeritus in musical theatre voice and voice pedagogy at Penn State University. She currently resides in New York City, where she maintains a professional voice studio. Her students have been seen on Broadway in Book of Mormon, The King and I, Beautiful, Chicago, Pippin, Kinky Boots, Mamma Mia, Wicked, Newsies, Sunset Boulevard, *and* Miss Saigon *as well as in national tours and regional theaters. She is frequently invited to present her workshop "Bel Canto/Can Belto" in the United States and abroad. She has produced two well-received video tutorials for teachers of singing:* Teaching Women to Sing Musical Theatre *and its sequel* What about the Boys: Teaching Men to Sing Musical Theatre. *Mary is a member of the American Academy of Teachers of Singing (AATS).* ♪

Tell us a little about your background and what led you to become a teacher of contemporary commercial styles.
I grew up in the 1950s in Morristown, New Jersey, and sang and played piano by ear from as early as I can remember. It was a house filled with music and love. My mother encouraged me by introducing me at the age of nine to Mabel Doolittle, the choir director for the Presbyterian Church on the Green in Morristown, who listened to me sing and took

me into the children's choir. I remained in that choir through high school. My mother also arranged for me to take piano and singing lessons, which I continued through high school and college. I spent untold hours in our living room with the hi-fi blaring, singing along with Julie Andrews in *Camelot* and *My Fair Lady*. Although my parents loved music, they considered it strictly avocational at the time, and I dutifully followed an academic path through graduate school in Paris heading for a career as a French teacher.

While in Paris, I had the opportunity to audition for Pierre Bernac, the renowned baritone and teacher. I remember I sang Fauré's "Après un rêve." To my surprise and delight, he took me on, exclaiming with a twinkle to his accompanist, "Elle est enfant de choeur!" For the next year, I was the very fortunate recipient of his careful, always loving attention. To this day, every time I assign a French art song to one of my students, I cherish the memory of that time. Returning to the United States, my first job teaching French was at a professional children's school for actors and dancers on the upper west side of Manhattan next to Lincoln Center. I remember looking at those bored American Ballet Theatre students in the first row with their long legs stretched out in front of them and their eyes rolling heavenward as I tried to interest them in the magic of the imperfect tense. I began to envision other scenarios for myself.

Within two short years, I had registered at the Herbert Berghof Studios on Bank Street in the West Village, taking courses in music theater and Shakespeare. Soon after that, I began to study acting at the Michael Howard Studio and audition technique with Michael Shurtleff. In those days in New York City, training for music theater was strictly an à la carte affair. You took your dancing, singing, and acting all separately. I began auditioning for musicals, and the first thing I knew I was cast as Guenevere in *Camelot* and then Eliza in *My Fair Lady* opposite the man who would later become my husband. For the next ten years, I made my living as a performer in summer stock productions, regional tours, and Off-Broadway productions, ultimately making it to Broadway in the late 1970s. Everything about music theater felt right to me, and I couldn't believe I was being paid to do it. I began teaching voice in the most "natural" way, by helping friends prepare for their auditions. Word got around that I had a gift for solving vocal problems. Money started to exchange hands and I was off.

By the mid-1980s, I was married with two young children and teaching in our Brooklyn apartment. My studio grew and I relocated to a midtown Manhattan studio near Carnegie Hall where I still teach today. In 1999, I was hired to teach at Penn State University as their first music theatre voice "specialist" in a brand-new BFA music theatre program. My years at Penn State have provided me with a built-in laboratory. I have had the opportunity to formalize pedagogy for music theater singing through constant observation and interaction with talented colleagues and students in a rich and open learning environment. I have maintained my NYC studio all this time to keep in contact with current industry demands and because, well, it's where it happens.

What kinds of styles do you currently teach? How long have you been teaching these styles?
My orientation in the world of contemporary commercial music is almost exclusively theatrical. During the thirty-five years I have been teaching, music theater has continued to reinvent and renew itself by absorbing contemporary styles of singing to tell its stories. Rock, pop, hip-hop, country, operetta, golden age, and classical styles are all fair game for music theater composers today. The astounding success of Lin-Manuel Miranda's *Hamilton* on Broadway has given new life to the art form and new hope to our under-represented artists of color. This is an example of the power of theater to effect cultural change.

What do you believe are the criteria for teaching these styles well?
Any young performer dreaming of a music theater career needs to be a kind of vocal chameleon capable of reproducing the sounds of contemporary culture authentically and sustainably without injury. This is a tall order. Teaching such a flexible use of the voice depends in my view on conditioning the instrument top to bottom by a careful process of register balancing so that singers can rely on any amalgam of chest/head dominance on any given pitch.

How do you teach style to students who don't have a strong background in a given genre?
It can be disconcerting to be confronted with the need to support a kind of singing one has never even tried. A classical soprano who has

never or rarely carried a chest-dominant speaking quality beyond E4 or F4 can be understandably concerned about the wisdom of her students belting the F5 an octave above that! I certainly do recommend first and foremost giving it a try. Find a CCM teacher you trust and start experimenting. This does not mean you will have to model like Beyoncé, but it will certainly help alleviate some of the anxiety you may feel. There are workshops and summer intensives you can attend where you will find you are in the company of others who feel just the way you do.

Beyond the more obvious issues of dramatic shifts in registration/resonance, there are stylistic distinctions depending on the era a song represents that make the singing "authentic." There is no better way to train our ears and eyes than observing actual performers from the period living in the styles they sing. YouTube videos are an invaluable resource, along with Spotify, Pandora, and a host of digital music services.

Finally, we should all be comforted by the fact that there are experts in our community who can take some of the burden off our shoulders in terms of the nitty-gritty details of authenticity. As voice teachers, we should consider it our main obligation to train singers capable of optimal function regardless of style. Beyond that we can rely on the support of experts like Sheri Sanders (*Rock the Audition*), rock singing specialist Matt Edwards (*So You Want to Sing Rock 'n' Roll*), Melissa Cross (*The Zen of Screaming*), and Lisa Popeil, among other trailblazers like Jeannette LoVetri, who originally coined the term "contemporary commercial music" (CCM) and whose vision gave "nonclassical" pedagogy a legitimate foothold in the voice-teaching community. As the music theater art form continues to evolve, teachers need to recognize the importance of our "community" and share valuable information. We do not have to go it alone.

How did you come up with your method or approach? What does it consist of, and how is it unique?
My approach for teaching music theater singing has evolved quite naturally over the years out of my own singing and the observation of other singers I have admired. It has been an empirical study of what makes voices "speak" to us.

In music theater performance, the actor's allegiance is to dramatic context. That has always been my primary reference point. Soon after arriving at Penn State, my colleague Norman Spivey invited me to participate in a workshop called "Music Theatre and the Belt Voice" in New York City. This was a turning point in my professional life. I became aware of how many teachers in our NATS community had felt they were "flying blind" in terms of teaching music theater techniques, such as chest-dominant mixing and belting in particular. Their passionate interest spurred me to examine very seriously what I was doing and to try to codify certain principles. The approach is possibly unique because it is so easily accessible. It shares many of the same principles governing healthy dynamic speech even as voices ascend into the soprano stratosphere. The technique is vowel/resonance based and takes advantage of subtle laryngeal balancing between thyroarytenoid (TA or mode 1) and cricothyroid (CT or mode 2) functions. Speaking and singing become inextricably linked.

Describe your approach to training singers, including any specific exercises you would like to share with us.
It is a priority for me to train versatile singers capable of maintaining vocal health in spite of punishing rehearsal schedules and physical demands. The guiding principle of this pedagogy is register balancing. Optimal function depends on even wear of the laryngeal muscles. Every voice lesson is an opportunity to "work out" a young voice and to tire it in a good way. Endurance and conditioning are as vital to the health of these "vocal athletes"—as they are referred to in Wendy LeBorgne and Marci Rosenberg's book, *The Vocal Athlete*—as they are to dancers.[1]

I am always mindful that I am teaching actors to sing. The technique is speech-centered. The first thing I evaluate in a student is the speaking voice. Does it represent this person fully? How free is it? How much range is readily accessible? How authentic is the "emotional voice"? Speaking exercises, calling out, delivering a Shakespeare monologue are all ways to assess the flexibility of the speaking voice. My goal is to help students align their actor's voice with their singer's voice—in effect, to sing when you speak and speak when you sing.

In recent years, there has been a kind of global epiphany with regard to the notion of "gender neutrality" in training voices for CCM styles and, increasingly, for classical singing as well. In his presentation, "Training Mr. Soprano and Ms. Tenor" at the 2014 NATS summer conference in Boston, Robert Edwin laid out a compelling case for removing cultural bias from the training of singers. "Training the whole voice is simply good voice pedagogy. Limiting pedagogy to males making 'male sounds' and females making 'female sounds' is not."[2] As with any physical discipline, maximum conditioning and freedom of expression depend on all muscles being in play.

This realization takes a lot of the mystery and unnecessary complexity out of training singers. If we consider the size of the larynx—the only really significant difference between male and female voices—the similarity of their vocal terrain becomes easier to understand. The issue of terminology usually rears its head at this point. At the International Congress of Voice Teachers (ICVT) in Paris in 2009, a French team led by Bernard Roubeau redefined registers according to four vibratory "modes," or what we would commonly call *fry, chest, head,* and *whistle*. For those of us in the trenches trying to make sense of the information out there, this was a flash of genius. Adding to this, the American Academy of Teachers of Singing (AATS) delivered a paper, "In Support of Fact-Based Pedagogy," at the NATS Conference in Boston in 2014 reminding teachers that "regardless of what they are called, registration events for both women and men occur through the interaction of the larynx and the vocal tract and are not produced in the chest, head, or any other physical location."[3]

If we use these vibratory modes as a guide, we can train men and women according to primary register events between modes 1 (chest or thyroarytenoid) and 2 (head or cricothyroid) in a mixed continuum. For women, the primary register transition (at or around F4) is equivalent to the second register transition for men. Consequently the critical register balancing for men occurs higher in their range. They spend more time in chest voice (mode 2).

For any singer, it is of primary importance to build a strong "core" modal voice out of which the extended range blossoms. The metaphor of a tree with strong roots is my favorite. Leaves and branches can't survive without a trunk and roots.

The approach I use for developing a core to a male voice is virtually identical to that of my classical colleagues. I take the same approach with women. The difference in music theater training is that although I am interested in the individuality of every voice, I am not restricting singers to a voice "category." Actors are cast according to character rather than voice type. Sound technology makes vocal *Fach* unnecessary.

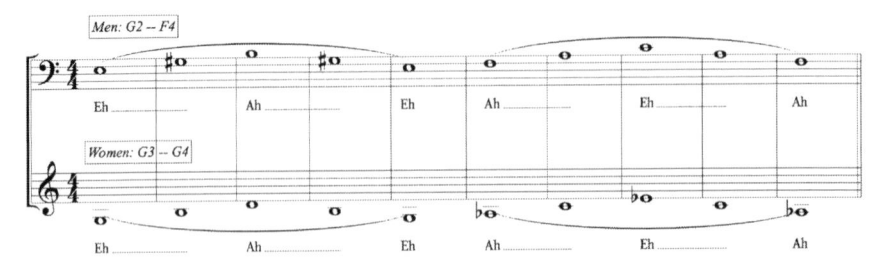

Figure 16.1. Exercise 1. Reinforcing the Core Voice.

In the following series of exercises, I have paired male and female versions of the same functional action for comparative reasons. The ranges indicated are suggestions, not expectations. Students will have varying degrees of facility or difficulty encountering some of them for the first time.

The issue of extending range begins right away for music theater singers. It is important to initiate the process of stretching and opening these young voices early on. Falsetto or mode 2 (cricothyroid-dominant function) for men is an essential quality in CCM styles. It simply can't be left out of the equation. It is the key to mixing and lightening the upper range and to developing dynamic control for both sexes. Again terminology fails us here because falsetto has been differentiated from a woman's soprano traditionally although it needs to be trained the same way.

If a young man's CT-dominant quality is weak or nonexistent, that treble part of the voice has to be developed right away. I will look for the "legit falsetto" (think classical soprano) first, starting with a "hoot" quality to encourage more vertical space (lower larynx) like a woman's lofty, energized "legit" soprano, bringing this sound down as low as it will go. It's usually pretty easy to elicit this quality by asking young men to cheer for a winning team as in "Woo-hoo!" The same thing will work for young women who are hesitant to open up and sing out in head voice. If the soprano is weaker than the chest voice, I will always start there and begin to build a bridge between treble and bass, just as I do for men. I will also begin to play with whistle register for young women. I have heard a few male singers who can access remarkable whistle tones and I am not counting this quality out for them either!

You will notice that the suggested exercises I am including here are intentionally very simple. Anyone could devise them. It is my belief that simple is always best in developing register balance. The student needs to identify and repeat these sounds with confidence. For men and

Figure 16.2.   Exercise 2. "Legit" Falsetto/Soprano.

women, it is important to be able to carry the classical soprano quality down as far as it will go. Women will need to integrate that quality into their middle voice.

Along with the classical or legit falsetto, men will need to find the more speechlike falsetto mix, sometimes called reinforced falsetto, which resonates in the mouth and nasopharynx with the larynx at speech level. Think *Jersey Boys*. The addition of more twang from the nasality reinforces this resonance substantially.

The male falsetto mix parallels a woman's all-important soprano mix, which gives her middle voice its speechlike power. The middle soprano or head-dominant mix (think Audra McDonald and Kelli O'Hara) between F4 and D5 can be a difficult quality for young women to achieve at first because the chest can easily overpower it.

Balance is key for women in the middle soprano (F4 to D5) because it gives them a smooth and effortless access to the upper extended soprano range above E♭5 and to the lower range below F4. It "prepares the way" both directions.

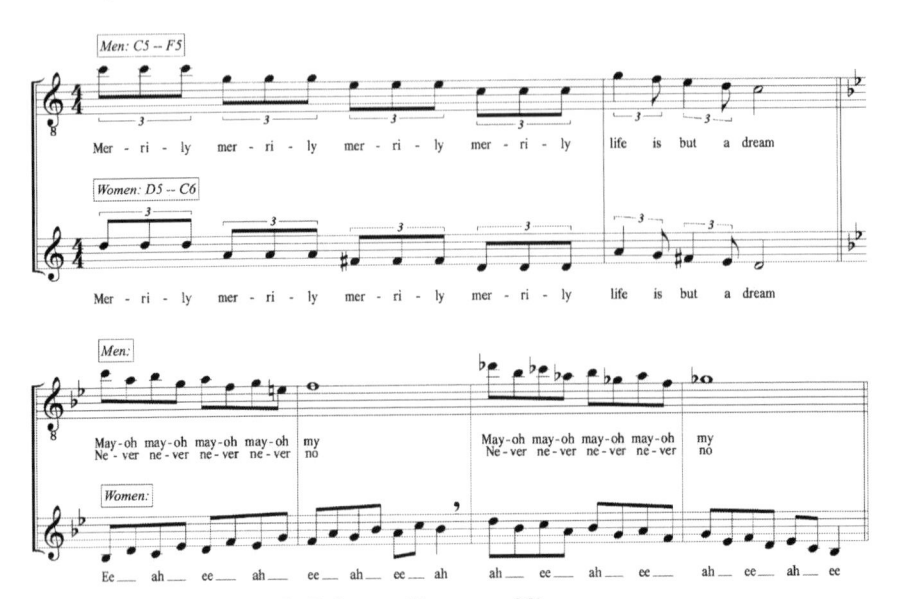

Figure 16.3. Exercise 3. Falsetto/Soprano Mix.

Once the cricothyroid function is actively engaged, men and women can start the process of opening up those speech-dominant sounds. Exercises I find invaluable for men and women include a combination of speaking and singing phrases one could compare to "barre work" for the vocal muscles. CCM teachers need to be gently insistent about encouraging healthy, versatile speech as a parallel vocal function.

The life, beauty, and buoyancy of a woman's voice in music theater and all CCM styles depends on the skillful coordination of her middle voice. Both women and men need to be able to move easily from chest- to head-dominant resonance and *know the difference* in speaking or singing.

Speech and speech-to-singing exercises can help teach the muscles of the vocal tract and larynx much more effectively than diagrams or anatomical models.

Here are two of my favorite exercises for coordinating chest-dominant speaking to singing in men and women:

Speak (in sung pitch range) then sing:

Figure 16.4. Exercise 4. Chest Dominant or Speech Mix.

What makes these phrases so useful is that the dramatic intention is so clear. The acoustic properties of the vowels used in these exercises are a great help in creating the desired resonance. With some encouragement, students will automatically energize the breath to say or sing them and extended range will be more accessible. Teachers need to be "cheerleaders" for their students. If you know what you want them to do, you can find creative ways to get the results without actually modeling the sounds.

Special Considerations for Women in the Middle Voice (It's All about Options)

As mentioned previously, the second *passaggio* for women in CCM styles occurs above D5, rather than at or around B♭4 where it occurs for classical sopranos. The distinction between a *soprano mix*—as in Laura Osnes or Julie Andrews singing "Ten Minutes Ago" from *Cinderella*—and a *speech mix*—as in Kristen Bell's version of "For the First Time in Forever" from the animated musical film *Frozen*—can sometimes seem very subtle. However, this distinction is essential for teachers to hear and understand because it defines the style of the music and honors the composer's intention. The ability to shift resonance/registration balance through the middle voice gives women a variety of options at the "exit" point above D5. Singing Julie Jordan's "If I Loved You" from *Carousel*, Kelli O'Hara chose to let her voice "bloom" into an opulent soprano on "how I loved you." But when she played the childlike Clara in *The Light in the Piazza*, the actress chose to retain a speechlike quality in that same range, minimizing the vowel space, to reflect the innocence and vulnerability of the character. Victoria Clark as her mother used a more mature speechlike soprano mix in the middle range and then opened up into a beautiful lofty soprano on the high notes. Then, of course, there is the option of a high belt above that D5, which has had young women longing to "defy gravity" since the late 1970s when *Evita* came on the Broadway scene and inspired composers to write increasingly higher belt tessituras for women.

The Belt

Ah, saving the best for last! Thanks to the continued efforts on the part of our colleagues in the realm of acoustics, we seem to be zeroing in on a description of belting as an acoustic phenomenon. Ken Bozeman calls it "skillful yelling" in his book *Practical Vocal Acoustics: Pedagogic Applications for Teachers and Singers*, and Ingo Titze speaks of "The Case of a Missing or Depressed Fundamental: Belting and Trumpeting."[4] We are also indebted to the ongoing work of Brian Gill in the area of vocal tract tuning for contemporary singers.

One thing is fairly certain, a belt can be a thrilling sound and should be part of the palette of colors for any singer of vernacular styles.

My own evolving definition is gender-neutral and range-specific. In a speech-dominant mix above the F4 *passaggio* for men and women, the floated "call" or belt can occur on open vowels as an optional resonance or color. It occurs in elevated speech, so we are making a direct transfer from the speaking voice. British singing teachers tell me they encourage their students to emulate the bright forward American "ah" natural to American music theater singers rather than the darker British vowel as in "father." It strikes me that they are seeking that "trumpet" formant. Americans are natural trumpeters.

In my experience, it is possible for women to carry an open belt quality as high as D5—think [ɑ] as in "hot" or [æ] as in "hat"—before it closes back into a speech mix and converges with the closed vowels—[i] and [u]—in a high chest-dominant mixed belt.

Coordinating open and closed vowels in speech-dominant singing is a critical element of technical control in CCM singing. The open vowel belt in music theater is a color or "spice" and can be used to great effect in that acoustic window between G4 and D5. But like any spice, the effect is lost if it is overused. With rock style as a notable exception, speaking a lyric intelligibly is of paramount importance in music theater. I think of the joke in the musical *Book of Mormon*: "You and Me But Mostly *May*."

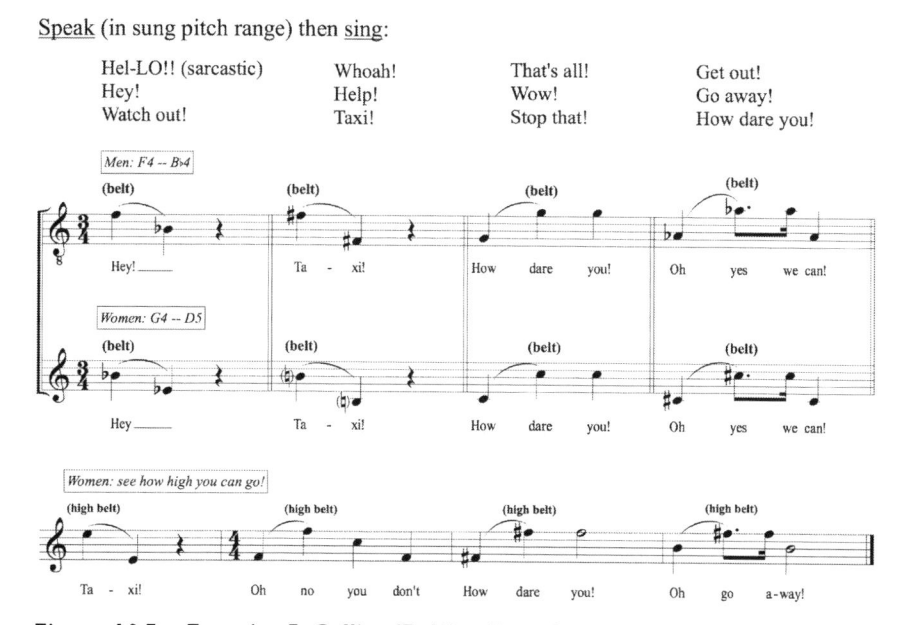

Speak (in sung pitch range) then sing:

Hel-LO!! (sarcastic)	Whoah!	That's all!	Get out!
Hey!	Help!	Wow!	Go away!
Watch out!	Taxi!	Stop that!	How dare you!

Figure 16.5. Exercise 5. Calling/Belting Exercises.

Obviously for men, the open belt quality is in a considerably higher range, but I am hearing some phenomenal male mixed singing these days and an open C5 or D5 is no longer freakishly rare.

These calls are just plain fun and great for energizing young singers. Make up your own! The vowels should be extended in duration to get as close to singing as possible and hovering in that F4–C5 range. To succeed in capturing an open belt resonance, singers will need to focus on maintaining the nuclear (primary) vowel and delay closing to the diphthong if one is present.

A belt is a mixed resonance and as such has dynamic flexibility like any other healthy vocal utterance. The word itself suggests triple forte but who hasn't marveled at the ability of elite female belters from Barbra Streisand to Cynthia Erivo to float a C5 belt that will melt your heart. The following exercise can be challenging, but if you stick with it, your students will eventually glide through these changes on every pitch from F4 to B♭4 and higher for women.

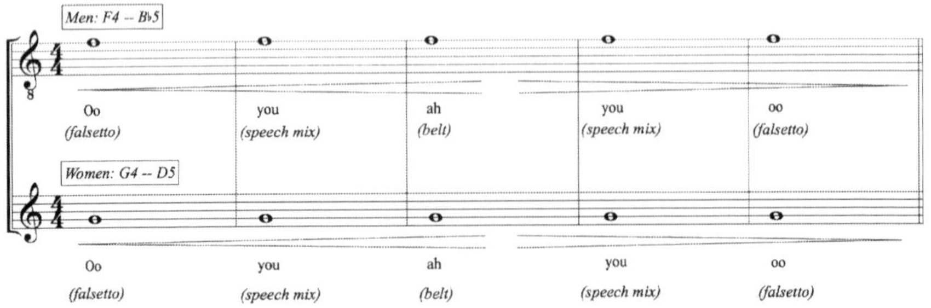

Figure 16.6. Exercise 6. *Messa di voce* for CCM Singers: "Circuit Training" for the Singing Voice.

Nasality can be a lifesaver when singers push to be heard in a very loud environment as when they are singing with an amplified rock band. Learning to manage the degree of nasality and twang by isolating the movement of the soft palate and narrowing the epilarynx respectively without straining is an important skill to develop. It acts as a guide for forward resonance and helps alleviate the impulse to overblow the voice. For actors, of course, it adds new character possibilities. (See figure 16.7.)

Figure 16.7. Exercise 7. Adding Twang or Nasal Resonance.

Vibrato

Many contemporary pop/rock styles need to be sung without or with only occasional vibrato. Because I am teaching music theater students who will be required to sing in so many styles, I advocate for training a consistent vibrato in developing singers. Once that skill is firmly established, they can begin to incorporate straight tone singing. It's important to keep reintroducing vibrato in order to ensure optimal function.

The Yodel or Cry

Many CCM styles, country music in particular, call for rapid laryngeal shifts. After working hard to smooth out registration, it can be challenging to create instability. But it's lots of fun and most young singers can access the quality fairly easily. Again it's important to keep rebalancing the voice so the singer controls the technique and not the other way around!

A lot of pop music requires facility in glottal and glottal fry onsets, similar to the prevalent *sanglot* or sob in operatic singing. They are part of the emotional communication but also facilitate an easier access to the chest connection. This is also true for belting.

What is your general philosophy of voice teaching?
Jennie Morton, an osteopath from London now teaching at Chapman University in California, said to me once, "What wears best wears evenly." This thought sticks with me and certainly sums up my philosophy of voice training. Training music theater performers involves the successful integration of many skills—acting, movement, dancing, and singing—all driven by creative energy. If we consider singing a kind of movement, and it certainly is, we can recognize the importance of conditioning the whole body, *including* the laryngeal muscles, to sing. The give and take between the action of diaphragm and the transverse abdominal muscle, or the interaction between external and internal intercostal muscles in breathing for example, mirror the give and take of the thyroarytenoid and cricothyroid muscles. Bringing these muscles into balance with each other seems to me to be the ideal way to condition a singing voice.

What elements of vocal technique do you think are most important?
Artfulness in singing certainly depends on a delicate and yet firm coordination of physical actions. When we work with very young beginning students, we can appreciate just how much they are being asked to do to achieve freedom of expression. I focus on the same guiding principles with any student, beginner or advanced. How are the elements of their "singing body" balanced? What might be holding them back? If the voice lacks treble, in other words has no dynamic control, I would go there first and begin to develop some buoyancy. If the voice has no power, I would begin to develop the core chest sound. Current vocal demands in music theater require both men and women to sing in chest-dominant qualities in higher and higher ranges. Balancing registration is the best way to keep these voices healthy.

Have you sung in the past, and if so, which styles? Do you currently sing any of the styles you teach?
I have sung classical and music theater styles, many golden age roles, Sondheim revues, and solo cabarets. I began creating one-woman shows during the 1990s because I longed to perform again and did not have the luxury of leaving home and family to do it. I love creating a solo

show—you never have to sing a bad song! The cabaret format can be anything you want and say anything you feel you need to say. You choose the lyrics that tell your story for you. My first show—*Stop, Time*—included songs by Lucinda Williams, Dar Williams, James Taylor, Maury Yeston, Steven Schwartz, Jacques Brel, Jason Robert Brown, Stephen Sondheim, Édith Piaf, Cy Coleman, and Harry Chapin.

Who were your strongest influences, pedagogically, vocally, and musically?
I am aware that I stand on the shoulders of so many teachers who have influenced me over the years. Sometimes I don't even remember where some of my ideas originated, and I imagine that is true for many of us. None of us "owns" any information exclusively. It is our obligation to share it. I do know that I owe a debt to Joan Lader and my beloved colleague Marianne Challis, who introduced me to some of the fundamental concepts of Jo Estill. I deeply appreciate Jo's flash of genius with regard to accessing vocal "qualities" in a conscious way. My first voice teacher in high school was the first woman president of NATS, Jean Ludman, a gracious and lovely teacher, who inspired me to consider the beauty of classical singing and took me to the first Met auditions I ever attended. My work with Pierre Bernac in Paris during my graduate study introduced me to the wonders of French art song. I remember his manner of modeling phrases with a sweet, floating high sound and the arm tracing the arc of the line. Looking back on this time, I sense that I was inspired as much by his personal grace, kindness, and empathy as a teacher as I was by his great musical artistry.

Joining the voice faculty at Penn State transformed my teaching because I became part of a community of dedicated classical voice teachers who welcomed me with open minds and hearts. A powerful synergy was created that has enriched us all.

As I began to teach myself how to belt back in those early days, my vocal role models were Barbra Streisand and my friend and colleague, Broadway actress Alix Korey. I was amazed by both of them. They had the ability to sing so effortlessly and powerfully in a high, buoyant soaring belt. They seemed to have complete dynamic control of the middle range of their voices. These two singers were in fact my introduction to the concept of mixed speech and the famous Broadway belt sound, and I have never looked back.

What is the primary goal when training your students?
My primary goal in training young music theater performers is to instill in them a respect for their budding artistry. We tell our students to "trust the process" as they train. This includes the care of the entire instrument—mind, voice, and body—as inseparable parts of a whole. Our young singers will need to represent a broad spectrum of sounds reflecting our shared human experience without actual harm to the instrument. I am grateful for the inspiration of Joan Melton, who reminds us that we make *all* sounds with "one voice" and that is the only one we have.

What else is important to you in your work?
I have had the good fortune to interact with voice teachers on several continents and will always value and cultivate a free and open exchange of ideas. We all move forward together.

How has your approach been informed by life experience, and how has it evolved over the years?
When I think back to my early teaching days, I am amazed how confident I was considering how little knew! I knew I had a gift for "hearing" voices and I adored the interaction with singers, but I had never taken a "voice pedagogy" class or been exposed to the work of other teachers in music theater. Back then, we were all flying by the seat of our pants, trying to figure things out as we went along. Because of the sense of community I have experienced at Penn State, where trusted colleagues interact, share information, and learn together, I have been able to find my own "voice" as a teacher and to create an MFA in musical theatre voice pedagogy. It has been a privilege to mentor these new teachers as they take their place in our universities and private studios.

What are your thoughts on professional organizations? Are you involved with any?
I have long been a member of SAG, AFTRA, and Actors' Equity. I joined NATS when I arrived at Penn State and owe any national or international standing I currently have to that organization. There was very little specific information about belting out there and what there

was created confusion and anxiety in the voice community. Norman Spivey had the foresight to see how important it would be to open up the conversation right in the heart of New York City. A workshop entitled "Music Theatre and the Belt Voice" was held at the New Yorker Hotel in New York City in 2001. Pioneers like Jo Estill and Jeannette LoVetri were in attendance, carrying the banner for alternative pedagogies. I had the opportunity to experiment with teaching classical singers to "belt" in a large public forum for the first time. I remember an article in the *Journal of Singing* by our then president Roy Delp entitled "Now That the Belt Voice Has Become Legitimate."[5] The event was certainly important for me, but I think it was the beginning of a huge change for NATS too, judging by the diversity of offerings at our regional and national conferences since that time. In addition to NATS, I am a member of the New York Singing Teachers Association (NYSTA), Musical Theatre Educators Alliance (MTEA), the Voice Foundation (TVF), and the American Academy of Teachers of Singing (AATS). ♪

Do you use technology in any of your teaching?
I teach acoustically in my studio. Students record their own lessons. I am working on conditioning voices primarily, and that is best achieved in an acoustic environment. The training does not include microphone technique, although I foresee it will be a required skill for music theater performers whose vocal health depends on the sensitivity of their sound technicians. A recent mainstage show at Penn State was Green Day's *American Idiot*. The voice teachers, director, music director, and sound design technicians devised strategies to prevent students from overblowing their voices in the loud rock environment. The lessons our young performers can learn from this experience will be a considerable benefit to them as they enter the profession.

  I do teach Skype lessons to international students and anticipate that we will see more online teaching as technology advances to support it. There is no substitute for being in the room with singers, but I am aware of the power and potential of online teaching resources. I do not use programs like VoceVista in my own studio teaching but have seen the value of auditory feedback for voice training.

What is in your future as a voice pedagogue?
I have recently retired from Penn State, and it is my intention to return to my teaching in New York City. I look forward to having more time to reflect on what I have learned, read more, write more, and, of course, learn more. ♪

NOTES

1. Wendy D. LeBorgne and Marci Rosenberg, *The Vocal Athlete* (San Diego: Plural, 2014).
2. Robert Edwin, "Training 'Mr. Soprano' and 'Ms. Tenor'—Gender Neutral Voice Pedagogy," Breakout Session at the 2014 NATS National Conference in Boston, Massachusetts.
3. www.americanacademyofteachersofsinging.org/academy-publications.php.
4. Ingo Titze, "The Case of a Missing or Depressed Fundamental: Belting and Trumpeting," *Journal of Singing* 73, no. 1 (2016): 53–54.
5. Roy Delp, "Now That the Belt Voice Has Become Legitimate," *Journal of Singing* 57, no. 5 (2001): 1–2.

⓱

DANIEL ZANGGER BORCH

Daniel Zangger Borch is one of Sweden's most recognized voice professionals. He has regularly appeared as a high-profile vocal coach for popular television shows such as Idol, True Talent, X-Factor, and Eurovision. He is considered a top vocal coach in both Sweden and internationally. He holds a PhD in music performance and is an established professional singer and songwriter. Dr. Zangger Borch has been the lead singer for many bands and projects and has recorded six albums. As a songwriter, he has reached number one on the Swedish album chart. His vocal versatility is evidenced by his ability to present a wide range of styles within popular music. His doctoral thesis is titled "Singing in Popular Music Genres: Artistic, Physiological, and Pedagogical Aspects." Dr. Zangger Borch's book, Ultimate Vocal Voyage, is one of the world's best-selling vocal instruction books, with approximately fifteen thousand copies sold worldwide. As a vocal coach, he has coached many of Sweden's most prominent vocal artists, has achieved numerous gold and platinum records, and is the CEO of Voice Centre and Zangger Vocal Art, an organization through which he also certifies vocal coaches and instructors. ♪

Tell us a little about your background and what led you to become a teacher of contemporary commercial styles.

My lifelong interest in music began when I started playing drums at the age of nine or ten and picked up guitar shortly thereafter. When I was fourteen, I began writing songs, and I realized that I was more skilled as a singer than I was as a guitarist or drummer. I ended up getting a record deal as a singer in a band when I was eighteen. However, I began struggling vocally. I had trouble finishing recording sessions because my voice had issues and was fatiguing. So I began looking for a vocal coach, but every singing teacher I could find was a classical teacher. I began taking classical voice lessons and did that for several years while I continued to work as a professional singer. I did all of the classical vocal exercises I was assigned, my voice was feeling better, and I thought things were going well.

Then, about two years later, I read a review of my singing that said, "Daniel is a good singer, but he sounds like a music theater singer in a rock band." I was crushed! That review was a personal catastrophe for me. I knew it was a result of my classical lessons since my background was entirely rock—I had no background in music theater. The classical lessons were not giving me the result that I wanted vocally. I stopped taking lessons, modified my approach, and began having some commercial success.

When I was twenty-four, I was approached by some colleagues who asked if I would be willing to make an instructional video on rock singing. This was a new venture, but they were convinced of its market potential. It was this opportunity that made me begin thinking about pedagogical issues: *What* should I teach and *how* should I teach these styles? *What* should a student know and *how* should I present this information? I recorded a video called *Vocalist*, but through the process of putting it together, I realized that we as a profession did not have a lot of knowledge or research on the pedagogy of popular and commercial styles.

In 1995, I began working with Johan Sundberg to try to unlock some answers to my questions. My research under his guidance eventually resulted in my book *Ultimate Vocal Voyage*, which I published in 2005. I continue to do research today and just published my second book, *Vocal*

Workout of the Day. My daily routine of all three of these activities—singing, research, and coaching—is something I plan on continuing to do. Each one benefits the other two.

How do you define contemporary commercial music?
For me, contemporary commercial music is popular music singing—rock, pop, soul, and all of its subgenres. I personally do not include music theater and jazz singing under the CCM umbrella. It's perhaps clearer to simply label the styles I teach as popular music singing so there's no confusion. "Contemporary" is also a problematic word—what do you mean by contemporary? But we have made some good progress with the CCM label. In the science world, these styles are still being called "nonclassical." I read this vocabulary all the time in scientific papers.

What kinds of styles do you currently teach? How long have you been teaching these styles?
All popular music styles: rock, pop, soul, and all of their subgenres. Lately, more and more students are also wanting to rap. I don't teach rap per se, but I give them some techniques that they can use. I have now been teaching for more than twenty years.

What, do you believe, are the criteria for teaching these styles well?
First and most important, you need to *love* the music and the singing style. You also have to be able to sing and model the styles, but I don't think you necessarily need to be a great singer yourself. But you have to love and embrace the styles you are teaching. And, to teach the styles well, I also think you need to gain experience doing it, but experience alone doesn't necessarily mean that you're good at it. You need to thoroughly understand the music itself and the realities of the commercial industry. There is also a difference between a coach and a singing teacher, however. Coaches can help singers a great deal, but to work with someone technically, teachers have to go a step further and study the physiology of the voice so that they understand the principles of voice production. ♪

How do you go about teaching authentic style to students?
To sing popular styles well, you have to be genuine. Your singing needs to be an extension of who you are. It has to match your personality. A student will never be able to sing authentically unless he or she loves the music and thoroughly understands the style inside and out. They also have to sing material that shows their voice to best advantage and doesn't exceed their abilities or technical facility. Students should never try to guess what someone wants to hear—they should sing authentically with a unique and personal style that they have developed themselves. Try not to copy someone else's style. Be great—don't imitate!

How did you come up with your method or approach? What does it consist of, and how is it unique?
My personal experiences—singing in a rock band, encountering vocal issues, studying classically, and learning that I couldn't find the answers there—have informed everything that has occurred since then. I had to come up with my own approach because there was nothing out there at the time that could help me do what I wanted to do. An important element in my teaching is grounding my exercises in the style that the singer is trying to sing. Using classical exercises to try to sing rock is worthless because the transition from one style to another is too vast and too difficult. You can't practice ping pong exclusively if you want to become a future tennis player. They both use a racket, but they're not the same game. The foundation of my whole teaching approach is the development of specific exercises that are directly connected to the styles I sing and teach. The melodies and harmonies that I use are as close as they can be to real songs. This is not always possible or necessary—warm-ups and cooldowns come to mind—but it is usually possible and beneficial. Second, I make every effort to ensure that my exercises make sense physiologically and are grounded in current scientific research. This is the result of my extensive study of voice production and voice science. Finally, I like to integrate musicianship building into my exercises: singing progressively more difficult intervals, increasingly complex rhythms, and so forth. This threefold approach summarizes my personal approach to voice teaching; I refer to this as the "Zangger-essence." ♪

 Another thing that I think is unique and that distinguishes me from other CCM voice teachers is my extensive background as a successful rock singer. I have recorded six albums and have reached number one on the Swedish album chart as a songwriter. I am a product of the industry, and that brings a certain authentic quality to my teaching and informs my philosophy and approach. My interest in voice science and PhD with Dr. Sundberg is another aspect of my background that I feel is unique and beneficial to my work.

What is your general philosophy of voice teaching? Summarize your core beliefs about vocal technique.

I think my overarching philosophy is to treat everyone who comes to me as a unique individual with different vocal instruments, personalities, and dreams. You really have to love people and everything about them to be a great voice teacher. I think this is the most important thing. I also believe that the more knowledge you have about everything related to singing, the more effective you can be as a teacher. The more knowledgeable you are, the better you can usually pinpoint what a person needs. Sometimes it is a technical issue, but there are so many other things that go into singing as well. A great teacher needs to be able to see the whole picture.

What elements of vocal technique do you think are most important?

That's a hard question because technique doesn't really exist in the abstract. It is always used in combination with repertoire and aspects of musicianship (pitch and rhythm, etc.). In terms of the different physiological elements—breath, articulation, resonance, and so forth—probably registration is the most important for commercial singers. The registration strategy is so different than classical. I also think that it is very important for CCM singers to routinely do warm-up and cooldown exercises. This is not practiced universally, but it is important and should be.

Have you sung in the past, and if so, which styles? Do you currently sing any of the styles you teach?

As I mentioned earlier, I have been a rock singer since I was a teenager and have never stopped performing. I continue to actively perform rock and model popular styles for my students. I occasionally teach a student who wants to sing a style that I don't actively perform. I can teach those less familiar styles up to a certain level, and I am always happy to work with a student on a technical level, but eventually an advanced singer will need to move on to a vocal coach who specializes in that particular style.

Who were your strongest influences, pedagogically, vocally, and musically?
Johan Sundberg is my greatest pedagogical influence. I would not be who I am today without him. Ingo Titze has also taught us so much. Vocally, I am a great admirer of Stevie Wonder. He is wonderful! And musically? That would be Stevie too. But there are many other singers that I admire as well, such as Donny Hathaway, Chris Stapleton, Beyoncé, and of course Michael Jackson. Both vocally and musically I love Sting as well.

What is the primary goal when training your students?
To meet the career goals and needs of the student I am teaching. It is not about my goal; it's about their goal. They are seeing me so that they can get results. I have done my job when—as you say in America—"the lightbulb goes on" and they understand how to do something. Sometimes we can do that by spending thirty minutes talking and ten minutes singing, or sometimes it's the opposite: thirty minutes of singing and ten minutes talking. It doesn't matter how you get there, but the student needs to learn something at each and every lesson.

What else is important to you in your work?
It's important to me to stay abreast of the latest revelations in voice science and technical innovation. These are very exciting times in the world of voice research, and we are learning so much more each and every year. I am always curious to learn all I can about new and exciting developments.

How has your approach been informed by life experience, and how has it evolved over the years?
I have lived an intense life and done a lot of different things. These varied experiences have been invaluable in helping to address the needs

of students when they walk in the door. The longer I have lived and the more I have experienced, the more I have to offer my students. Over the years, I have found that it becomes easier to connect with my students personally, which leads to also connecting with them on a technical level. The more you know about everything life has to offer, the easier every task becomes.

What are your thoughts on professional organizations? Are you involved with any?
I have presented at many conferences and do this as often as I can. I was the keynote speaker for CCM styles at the International Congress of Voice Teachers (ICVT) in Brisbane, Queensland, Australia, in 2013 and am currently on the planning committee for ICVT 2017, which will be hosted here in Stockholm. I would love to attend more, but the biggest barrier to me is the cost. Since I run a private practice and am not affiliated with a university, I do not have travel funds for conferences. They are very expensive, so unless someone brings me in, I have to pay my own way.

Do you use technology in any of your teaching?
I used to use all kinds of technology, but I have actually pared back a bit. Ultimately, the most important factor is the teacher as the guide. But I still use technology with some degree of regularity. Recording technology and microphones are very important to the CCM singer. I've done Skype sometimes, but it doesn't replicate the live experience and I find it to be lacking. I think that apps are the way of the future—many interesting ones are emerging. In my scientific work with Dr. Sundberg, I did a lot of acoustic analysis and used software for that research, but I honestly don't use that in my current practice. It's too complicated for most voice students, and if they don't understand it, then it is not helpful.

What is in your future as a voice pedagogue?
I have recently published a new book, *Vocal Workout of the Day*, and have launched a companion website to go along with it. My first book, *Ultimate Vocal Voyage*, was about obtaining skill, but this one is about a daily workout regimen. I am excited about launching these resources, and my plan for the near future is to promote them so that people are

aware that they are available. My long-range plan is to become more involved in app development. I have some ideas for app software that will be of great benefit to voice students. I am keeping some of my ideas secret at this point, but they will be revealed when the time is right. ♪

CONTEMPORARY COMMERCIAL MUSIC

Past, Present, and Future

18

EFFORTLESS SINGING

SLS™ and Its Influence
Darren Wicks

Speech Level Singing™ (SLS) is an approach to singing developed by Los Angeles teacher Seth Riggs. Few teachers can claim to have Riggs's track record, and few pedagogies have been applied like SLS—Riggs's students have achieved success at the highest levels of the industry and across multiple musical genres. In his sixty-plus years of teaching, Riggs has taught four winners of the Metropolitan Opera National Council Auditions (New York), some 120 Grammy Award winners, and countless Broadway performers.[1] His television and movie credits include roles as voice consultant for Madonna (*Dick Tracy*, 1990), Val Kilmer (*The Doors*, 1991), Whoopi Goldberg (*Sister Act*, 1992), and Michael Jackson (*This Is It*, 2009) and voice coaching for the *American Idol* television series. At the time of writing this chapter, Riggs is eighty-six years old and continues to operate a busy home studio in Hollywood, working with performers, actors, serious amateurs, producers, and teachers. In addition, he maintains an international profile as a voice consultant, teacher educator, and workshop presenter. ♪

Riggs's contribution to CCM singing and pedagogy has been immense, and any publication on current CCM practice would be incomplete without considering his legacy. This chapter seeks to explain something of the background, formulation, core principles, and impact of the SLS technique. Another purpose of this chapter is to account for how this approach continues to inform current CCM practice. From the outset, I must stress that I am not a spokesperson for Seth Riggs or for the Speech Level Singing organization. I was fortunate, however, to study singing with Riggs and with several of his master teachers and to have been a certified SLS teacher for several years. Along with many colleagues, I left the SLS organization in 2013 to become a founding member of the Institute for Vocal Advancement (IVA). I will discuss this transition in more detail later in this chapter. ♪

My experience with SLS was profoundly formative and set me on the path to developing an approach to voice pedagogy that is based on functional principles and vocal balance. Although I am aware of controversies surrounding the SLS technique, I found Seth Riggs to be an exceedingly passionate and inspiring teacher who dedicated his career to helping individuals find vocal freedom. He was also a strong supporter of other teachers who wanted to achieve great results with their students. As a graduate student researching the practice of exemplary teachers, I was privileged to interview Mr. Riggs for my doctoral thesis. This chapter has been constructed from personal conversations and my experiences with the SLS organization. I also gratefully acknowledge the assistance of former SLS master teachers Greg Enriquez, Spencer Welch, and Guy Babusek, who provided information and advice for this chapter.

This chapter fills a void since very little about SLS has been published or subjected to scholarly research. Typically, singers learn the technique by taking classes with a certified SLS teacher. Teachers certify in the pedagogy via mentoring, attending seminars, working on their voice with a master teacher, and supervised on-the-job training. This process reflects the way Riggs likes to teach—he does not see himself as an academic or a voice scientist. In fact, Riggs was often critical of scientists, whom he felt had a lot of knowledge but could not demonstrate good singing technique. Moreover, Riggs does not believe someone can learn to sing or to teach singing from a book. Conversations with him about singing might start out conceptually but would inevitably result in him singing to demonstrate concepts—or asking you to sing!

BACKGROUND

Seth Riggs was born on September 19, 1930. As an only child, he grew up outside Baltimore, Maryland. Showing an inclination toward singing from a young age, he joined the choir of the Washington National Cathedral at the age of nine. Upon graduating high school, he received an opera scholarship to the Peabody Conservatory of Music at Johns Hopkins University and later completed a master's degree in opera theater at the Manhattan School of Music in New York. Among his vocal teachers and musical influences, Riggs cites the American baritones John Charles Thomas (1891–1960) and Robert Weede (1903–1972), the Italian tenor Tito Schipa (1888–1965), and the Danish tenor Helge Rosvaenge (1897–1972). An interesting training ground for one of the quintessential icons of CCM pedagogy!

Riggs began working professionally as a singer after graduating. He sang with the New York City Opera (NYCO) company on 55th Street for five years and was a member of the first NYCO at Lincoln Center in 1966. He spent three years in Broadway shows playing leading roles, including Lun Tha in *The King and I*, Starbuck in *110 in the Shade*, and the juvenile lead in *Do Re Mi*. Beginning in 1949—and while performing in New York City—Riggs started teaching singing and quickly built up a studio of clients, many of whom were Broadway performers. However, in 1967, he moved to Los Angeles to take up a college teaching post and commence his doctoral studies in voice. He never completed these studies or stayed in a college teaching post and—in a personal interview—cited the poor quality of teaching in these schools and the inability of any of his teachers to "get through their bridges" as his reasons for dropping out.[2]

In the early part of his teaching career, Riggs began formulating his approach to vocal technique. SLS was born out of frustrations with his own vocal journey and his assessments of the deficit in technique among professional singers he encountered. He described his frustration to me in these words:

> Why is it that the greatest singers could go from the bottom of their voice to the top with pure vowels, even legato, and consistent vibrato? What

could they be doing that I'm not? I had all these bits of paper that said I should be able to do it, but I couldn't.[3]

Riggs was disgruntled with his vocal education, which he felt had not prepared him for life as a professional singer. Despite obtaining a graduate degree and taking lessons with many teachers, he was unable to find a teacher who could show him how to "put his voice together." He explained further,

> That's really what good singing is about. How do you get from your chest voice where you talk and not drag it up to the top into your head voice, which is for the higher pitches? The masters of [the] *bel canto* [period] could do this and, somewhere along the line, we lost that wisdom.[4]

Another frustration for Riggs involved problems with word intelligibility, vowel quality, and the poor diction he observed among professional singers. Riggs felt that by forcing the voice, singers were destroying the beauty of the legato line, improperly handling their registers, and consequently distorting their words.

> The great *bel canto* singers could maintain pure vowels as they sung through the *passaggi* and could do so without yelling or disconnecting into falsetto. So many pop singers don't seem to understand that yelling distorts all the vowels. I would prefer to take a sound that is not so heavy on a G4 and then have access to the A, B♭, and high C above it, but most important—be able to understand the words.[5]

For answers to his frustrations, Riggs looked back to the practices of the great singers of the past, particularly those used during the Middle Ages in the training of the *schola cantorum*, the professional Roman papal choir. He followed that lineage of teachers through to the Italian *bel canto* school. Among his pedagogical influences, Riggs cites the Italian baritone and celebrated voice teacher Antonio Cotogni (1831–1918) as well as the Italian baritones Mattia Battastini (1856–1928), Riccardo Stracciari (1875–1955), and Giuseppe De Luca (1876–1950), whom he felt demonstrated flawless technique and the ability to perfectly sing through their *passaggi*.

Riggs's greatest influence, however, was the Italian tenor Edgar Herbert-Caesari (1884–1969), who studied at the Santa Cecilia Academy in Rome alongside Riccardo Daviesi (1839–1921)—the great Sistine Chapel singer of the nineteenth century—and the celebrated Italian tenor Benjamino Gigli (1890–1957). Settling in London in 1925 as professor of singing at the Trinity College of Music, Caesari became an eminent teacher of opera known for his research and efforts to restore the teachings of the *bel canto* school. Riggs cites Caesari's writings as the genesis for Speech Level Singing, particularly *The Science and Sensations of Vocal Tone* (1936), *The Voice of the Mind* (1951), and *The Alchemy of Voice* (1965).

While building his studio and clientele in Los Angeles, Riggs was engaged as a vocal consultant for laryngologists Henry Rubin, Hans von Leden, and Edward Kantor, who referred postoperative patients to Riggs to assist with voice rehabilitation. Out of the many referrals Riggs worked with, one patient was to change the course of his career—Stevie Wonder. Stevie came for postoperative care after undergoing voice surgery. His producer, Quincy Jones, was so impressed with Stevie's progress that he began sending artists such as Michael Jackson, Luther Vandross, and Natalie Cole to Riggs to improve their voice technique. From there, Riggs's reputation expanded to the world of film and theater, and he received engagements from actors, directors, and producers, including Steven Spielberg, Bob Fosse, Oliver Stone, and Martin Scorsese. Through his continued success with high-profile clients, Riggs established his reputation as the "teacher of the stars."

CORE VALUES

Riggs defines Speech Level Singing as "a way of using your voice that allows you to sing freely and clearly with maximum power and clarity."[6] The central idea behind SLS is that singing should be produced as easily and freely as natural speech. "You should be able to sing through your entire range—from the lowest notes of your chest voice, up through the highest notes of your head voice—in a smooth, even, or what we call connected manner, and still maintain a relaxed speech level posture [of the larynx]."[7]

In a personal conversation, Riggs noted "the simplest definition of Speech Level Singing is the absolute refusal to help pitch in any way."[8] The absence of "helping" that he refers to is in fact the stabilization of the larynx in its natural "resting" posture during singing. Riggs believes that the larynx should remain "stable but not locked" during vocalization, regardless of pitch and vowel changes. He further clarifies this idea:

> So many people think that to sing they have to reach up for high notes or go down for low notes when actually the pitches are made on a horizontal—they are not made on a vertical. Now, the resonance may be on an up and down . . . when it's speech level, you don't "reach." The cords will make the pitches. So, the technique I teach enables the cords to make the pitches without the performer having to kill themselves to sing high or to sing low.[9]

Speech Level Singing differentiates between the function of the extrinsic laryngeal muscles and the intrinsic muscles during singing and asserts that efficient vocalization can only occur in the absence of interference from the extrinsic (the laryngeal elevator and depressor) muscles. As he describes in a 2010 interview with Babusek, "Most of us who are teaching SLS have to get rid of extraneous muscles that other teachers have induced [in an attempt] to make a bigger sound. You've got to do the work with resonance—with co-ordinating and compounding the resonance in the bridges [*passaggi*]."[10]

Another hallmark of the Riggs approach is his rejection of subjectivity and imagery in the teaching of singing. In the preface to his book *Singing for the Stars*, he protests, "The language of voice teachers and choir directors abounds in such confusing and dangerous clichés."[11] When asked to clarify his thoughts on this topic, he explained, "When teachers say, 'Put it in the mask,' that makes me so mad because they imply that a student knows where and how to 'put' it. You don't 'put' anything. You allow it to go into that condition."[12]

In the absence of imagery, how are voice concepts taught using the SLS technique? Riggs is famous for his adage "Expect it; don't direct it," meaning that voice technique is best taught through principles of cause and effect. To achieve this, teachers should avoid describing singing in terms of a tonal ideal or an end result. Instead, they ask a singer to perform an exercise that enables the experience of the desired result. As Riggs explains, "I prefer to use exercises that have a definite cause and effect relationship, producing a desired result, rather than relying on the nebulous descriptions of someone else's personal experience."[13] When a student discovers a sound or coordination for himself, the teacher can ask him or her to describe and compare this result in a way that makes sense to the individual singer.

At some point, Riggs became increasingly critical of approaches to singing that put a heavy emphasis on breathing or that prescribed breathing exercises as a panacea for technical problems. Consequently, SLS deemphasized breathing in favor of registration and vocal fold function. Riggs taught that singers should attend to their posture, maintaining an elevated sternum/rib cage and abdominal flexibility, but apart from this, there was no need to practice specific breathing exercises in isolation. He felt that attempts by singers to "support the breath" usually resulted in unhelpful constrictions in the vocal tract, rather than the desired result of better singing. In a 2004 interview with Buescher, Riggs clarified, "If the larynx is not in the right condition regarding position and vocal fold structure as it relates to registration, it will not receive the air in a proper manner."[14] Thus, correct breathing and breath management occurs spontaneously and naturally as a result of Speech Level Singing.

EDUCATION

Riggs's repeated success in studio teaching led to requests for him to teach others his methods. In 1985, he published *Singing for the Stars*, a workbook and audio-based instructional course outlining his approach and the only officially endorsed publication on SLS. In 2007, in association with the *American Idol* television series, Riggs produced a further audio instruction course, *The Singer's Advantage*. Attempts by teachers to employ these methods often produced mixed results. However, Riggs was steadily amassing a community of teachers around him that wanted to emulate his approach. There was a need for more comprehensive training. In the late 1990s, Riggs developed Speech Level Singing International with a group of associates. This company was designed to promote the benefits of the SLS technique and to oversee the training of voice teachers who wanted to align themselves with this approach. In 2009, SLS International published the *Instructor Manual*, the most detailed work ever published on the technique, but it was used internally for teacher education and never released to the public.

Over the next twenty years—from the inception of SLS International—some seven hundred teachers from all over the world studied the techniques at teacher education events or entered the Speech Level Singing certification program. Certified teachers agreed to a code of conduct and invested considerable time and finances in professional development, private coaching, attending seminars and conferences, and licensing fees. Depending how far a teacher chose to progress with this program, the education could involve up to ten years of supervised on-the-job training to advance from student teacher status through to Level 5, the highest level of certification before "master teacher" status. Certified teachers were permitted to use the SLS branding. However, there were restrictions on what SLS practitioners could say, write, or teach about the approach until they reached senior levels of certification, giving the perception that the pedagogy was an exclusive or closely guarded secret.

Several teachers who reached Level 5 certification were promoted to the master teacher level by Riggs and given responsibility for the education of other teachers. Among this team were Jeffrey Skouson, Greg Enriquez, Spencer Welch, Dave Stroud, Linda Tomkinson, Kathy Kennedy, Stephanie Borm-Krueger, and Guy Babusek. Master teachers were not employees of SLS International but maintained their Level 5 certification and their own studios. However, many achieved significant success working in the industry with recording artists and performers. At different points, both Stroud and Skouson held positions as CEO of SLS International.

CRITICISM AND CONTROVERSY

Riggs once remarked to me that there are as many different methods for teaching singing as there are teachers. So it wasn't surprising that he received criticism from teachers who employed other methods or had different tonal preferences. Riggs has strong views on what constitutes good singing and best practice in the teaching of singing. What some know to be his passion and desire to find better or more efficient methods has at times been mistaken for egotism. However, he is not afraid to speak his mind or tell someone he thinks they are wrong. Riggs is critical of teachers and university voice programs that do not teach registration to their singers. In his 2014 interview with Schneider, he describes being fired from several tertiary teaching positions and—in his 2004 conversation with Buescher—Riggs admitted to being outspoken at teacher events. This candor eventually resulted in him being ejected from NATS.[15] It is unfortunate that, to this day, this relationship has never been repaired.

Misunderstanding has often surrounded the terminology used by SLS teachers, which was viewed by some as in-house jargon. For example, the term "speech level" has regularly been misunderstood with critics confusing it with the Schoenbergian term *Sprechstimme*. Some also argue that singing is not like speech and therefore the foundations of SLS are wrong. Riggs's intention, however, was not to liken singing to speech, only to remind us that good singing should feel effortless and easy—like talking. To cite another example, Riggs's use of the term "bridges" to describe the *passaggi* is confusing to some, but this word choice reflects his intention that vocal concepts should be taught from the perspective of the singer. Riggs also teaches that when the voice ascends in pitch, the vocal folds "zip up" or "dampen" along their length. This idea was challenged by some as being inaccurate on scientific grounds.[16] However, Riggs maintained that the concept came from the *bel canto* tradition and was taught by Caesari. This alludes to a further source of criticism in that Riggs appears to resist voice science if he feels that scientific truth does not directly benefit the singer. It is true that he believes that scientific information might be interesting but is of little use to singers unless they can use it to sing better or—as he puts it—"get through their bridges."

Riggs has been criticized by those who feel the technique does not allow singers to sing with a loud or full voice. In particular, he discourages belting in favor of the mix voice, claiming that the chest voice taken too high is an unattractive sound and injurious to the long-term vocal health of a singer. Riggs asserts that a strong mix can achieve the same or better quality than a belt. In conversation, he has mentioned being fired by record producers because he discouraged artists from producing strong or harsh sounds.[17] Riggs does not allow his students to abuse their voices (even if that is a sound that is currently popular) and will not endorse other teachers or approaches that he believes compromise a singer's vocal health or the longevity of their singing career.

Another source of controversy surrounds internal politics and rifts within the SLS organization. During its history, several prominent voice teachers, once closely associated with the organization, broke away to start their own singing schools. Among these were Brett Manning, Randy Buescher, John Henny, Roger Love, Dave Stroud, Wendy Parr, and Leigh McRae. Legally, they are prevented from using the term "Speech Level Singing" or the name of Seth Riggs in their marketing, but in many cases, there is a clear connection. Others have built upon the foundation of Riggs's technique, adapting it and reframing it in light of current voice science or to meet the needs of their clientele. The most dramatic of these rifts occurred in 2013 when Skouson, then CEO of the organization, resigned publicly. This was followed by mass walkouts by nearly all the master teachers, senior staff, and finally the bulk of certified teachers. Over time, they formed a new professional association for teachers of singing, the Institute for Vocal Advancement (IVA), which has focused on establishing comprehensive teacher education programs, adapting and building upon the foundation of Riggs's technique and incorporating voice science and a greater breadth of topics. Although SLS International still offers teacher certification, Riggs has downsized his operations, focusing mostly on private studio teaching and running retreats for singers and teachers. ♪

SIGNIFICANCE

Speech Level Singing is often discussed in relation to its core beliefs or the controversies surrounding its implementation. However, little attention has been given to the significance and impact of the SLS technique for CCM singing and the music industry, which I believe to be immense. Riggs's achievements include pioneering one of the first teacher education programs in CCM pedagogy, inspiring a generation of CCM teachers who approach working with voices from a common mind-set, and changing the sound of CCM singing by teaching his technique to so many artists in the industry.

Riggs contributed much to demystifying the teaching of CCM styles by showing that the sounds that are evident in good CCM singing can be broken down and taught. They are not based on subjective opinions or dependent on the singer having a talent for contemporary singing but on the function of the vocal mechanism. Riggs focuses on certain vowel and register configurations, and he uses the terms "chest voice," "head voice," "mix," and "falsetto" to describe these qualities. Although voice pedagogues have continued to debate the terminology and existence of certain vocal registers, Riggs is adamant that singing should be taught from the singer's perspective and that science (as much as possible) should be kept out of instruction. To do this, he uses terminology borrowed from historical pedagogy and relates things directly to the singers' experiences and personal perception of their tone quality.

The simplicity of the technique is also its sophistication. SLS teachers are taught to listen analytically to voices and respond to individual needs. They prescribe tools, which are specific combinations of vowels, consonants, and musical patterns, to elicit and train vocal qualities in singers. This means that the technique is experiential rather than informational. Teachers consciously resist talking or explaining too much during lessons but rather focus on singing. Singers are taught to build their awareness of what their voices are doing and to adjust their voice on the fly—during the act of singing.

Riggs approaches voice technique from the perspective of vocal balance, teaching singers to sound natural and unforced. The mix voice and even registration are hallmarks of the SLS sound. Using Riggs's techniques, CCM singers learn to sing lightly and easily across a wide vocal range. By teaching this sound to hundreds of Grammy Award–winning artists as well as new artists who emulate these sounds, it is undoubtable that Riggs has affected a significant change in the current sound of CCM singing and in the tonal preferences of at least one segment of the music industry.

Although Riggs advocates that his techniques are applicable to the performance of any style or genre of music, he was most troubled by some of the opera teachers of his day who asserted that a person who has a grounding in "classical technique" could sing anything. Riggs felt they were teaching a pedagogy that was not conducive toward CCM singers meeting their goals.[18] He saw a gap in the market for competent CCM teaching and began attracting many clients who were contemporary singers and popular recording artists, adapting his pedagogy to suit the demand. Riggs never felt he was inventing something new but rather reapplying successful techniques used by the great singers of the past to meet the needs of the present. Accordingly, Riggs's most significant contribution is probably the reframing of *bel canto* techniques to suit the needs of CCM singers. He was among the front-runners in the profession to present a structured pedagogy for the teaching of contemporary voice technique.

FINAL THOUGHTS

My strongest impression of Seth Riggs—after attending seminars and voice lessons with him—is his unmistakable passion for singing and for helping people achieve their vocal goals. He was never content to learn techniques merely to improve his own singing. Rather, he is an educator at heart with a sincere desire to improve the profession of teaching and quality of singing in the music industry. There are thousands of singers and teachers around the world who have been helped by Riggs and regard his techniques as revolutionary. At the same time, there are also critics. In his 2010 interview with Babusek, Riggs responded to his critics by saying, "What we do has a better track record usually than those people who try to put us down."[19] Regardless of individual opinions of his teaching, Riggs was one of the first to develop a systematic pedagogy for teaching CCM singing. Additionally, he was a front-runner in a new wave of teachers who approach CCM voice pedagogy from the standpoint of registration and vocal fold function. Any discussion of the history of CCM pedagogy would be incomplete without mentioning Seth Riggs as one of the discipline's principal founders and most iconic figures.

NOTES

1. Randy Buescher, "An Interview with Seth Riggs," *Journal of Singing* 60, no. 5 (2004): 457–90.

2. "Getting through their bridges" is Riggs's way of saying that a singer can't handle his or her registers properly or—in other words—that the voice is not connected and even. He often judged a teacher's capacity by what he or she could do with his or her own voice.

3. Seth Riggs, personal communication with the author (May 18, 2012).

4. Ibid. Brackets inserted by the author.

5. Ibid.

6. Seth Riggs, "The Method" (2007), last accessed July 9, 2017, www.sethriggsvocalstudio.com/sethriggs/themethod.html.

7. Seth Riggs, *Singing for the Stars*, 5th ed. (Van Nuys, CA: Alfred Publishing Company, 1992), 32. Brackets inserted by the author.

8. Riggs, personal communication with the author.

9. Danny Schneider, "Seth Riggs" (2014), last accessed July 9, 2017, www.youtube.com/watch?v=WGREQ670LrU.

10. Guy Babusek, "Voice Lesson: Seth Riggs on Breath Support" (2011), last accessed July 9, 2017, www.youtube.com/watch?v=b5W3_Otvm4U.

11. Riggs, *Singing for the Stars*, ix.

12. Seth Riggs, personal communication with the author (May 18, 2012).

13. Guy Babusek, "Voice Lesson: What Is Speech Level Singing?" (2010), last accessed July 9, 2017, www.youtube.com/watch?v=_vHUCwibNfM.

14. Buescher, "An Interview with Seth Riggs," 488.

15. Schneider, "Seth Riggs"; Buescher, "An Interview with Seth Riggs," 457–90.

16. Buescher, "An Interview with Seth Riggs," 457–90.

17. Riggs, personal communication with the author.

18. Buescher, "An Interview with Seth Riggs," 457–90.

19. Babusek, "Voice Lesson: What Is Speech Level Singing?"

19

WHY IT'S TIME TO ADD CCM TO YOUR STUDIO

Matthew Edwards

In 1985, Robert Edwin wrote an article for the *Journal of Singing* titled "Are We the National Association of Teachers of Classical Singing?"[1] At that time, if you read through the articles in the journal, the answer would be yes. Thankfully, the climate of NATS has changed drastically over the past thirty years. Music theater and CCM adjudication opportunities now exist alongside classical auditions at NATS events. NATS workshops and conferences regularly offer opportunities to explore CCM styles and pedagogy, and—of course—there is now a NATS-sponsored book series dedicated primarily to CCM styles. Even though NATS has made great strides toward the inclusion of all types of voice usage, there are still some circles in which resistance remains. This chapter will present a theory about why this may be the case, offer data to support the need for increased attention to CCM styles, and offer suggestions for continuing education to help you enter this world of teaching if you are so inclined.[2]

A RAPIDLY CHANGING MARKETPLACE

Before we get into the more detailed discussions outlined above, let us first take a moment to examine the ever-changing music market.

Music Theater

Broadway itself has been doing very well over the past few years. The 2016–2017 Broadway season brought in $1.37 billion in ticket sales with attendance reaching 13.3 million, a 35 percent increase from 2010. National tours were also notably successful, grossing $1 billion, a 7 percent increase from 2010, and bringing 13.9 million people to the theater.[3] Those figures do not include Off-Broadway and Off-Off-Broadway shows, regional theater, cruise ships, or international tours. The closest estimate of sales for productions outside of New York City can be found in an article published by *American Theatre* magazine, which states that in 2005 approximately 1,200 nonprofit theaters presented more than 13,000 productions (plays and musicals) with an economic impact of $1.4 billion.[4] Clearly, music theater is a multi-billion-dollar industry, and with the increases displayed in Broadway box office sales, it appears that we will continue to see growth.

Commercial

Even though physical record sales have declined in the past decade, a report by the Recording Industry Association of America found that U.S. recorded music revenues totaled $7.7 billion in 2016.[5] Of these sales, 1 percent account for classical music.[6] Live concert sales reached $7.3 billion in 2016, bringing total commercial sales to at least $14.9 billion in 2016.[7] The statistics indicate that despite rumored declines, the commercial music market is still robust.

Church Music

Church music is worth mentioning as it has served as a great source of employment for musicians all the way back to the earliest days of our art form. Due in part to the rise of contemporary worship music, choral singing appears to be declining in the church. In 1998, approximately 72 percent of churches had a choir; by 2012, that number had fallen to 57 percent according to the National Congregations Study. There has also been an uptick in the use of drums and guitar, which indicate a move toward contemporary praise and worship music.[8] *Christianity Today* reports that 22 percent of churches now have contemporary worship services and 43 percent offer a blended worship service that contains both traditional and contemporary music. The number of traditional-only services is reported to be 35 percent.[9]

Classical

Opera America's report on the 2015 season estimates that the total operating budget of its member companies and the Metropolitan Opera totaled approximately $1.11 billion. A survey of ninety member companies (62 percent of membership) showed that box office sales covered 27 percent of their budget. Therefore, we can estimate that box office sales totaled around $300 million, which is in line with previous research estimating 2011 box office sales at $246.3 million.[10]

What People Are Singing

The industry data clearly shows that consumer dollars are overwhelmingly being spent on music theater and commercial genres. But what type of music are people singing? According to the National Endowment for the Arts Survey of Public Participation in the Arts, approximately 20.4 million adults in the United States practiced singing in 2012. A cross-tabulation of the data shows of those who said they "perform or practice singing," 14.6 percent "perform or practice classical music," and 2.6 percent "perform or practice opera." After accounting for those who sing both classical and opera, the data shows that 89 percent of Americans are singing styles outside of the classical domain.[11]

An examination of listening habits sheds light on the music preferences of Americans. Nielsen reports the percentages of recorded music consumption in 2016 with rock at the top (29 percent), followed by R&B/hip-hop (22 percent), pop (13 percent), country (10 percent), dance/electronic (4 percent), Christian/gospel (3 percent), Latin (3 percent), holiday/seasonal (2 percent), and jazz, classical, and children's music accounting for 1 percent each.[12] It is reasonable to assume these are the genres that likely account for the other 89 percent Americans are singing outside of classical music. However, as you will read in the following pages, we are not educating young musicians for the genres that 89 percent of them are going to sing.

A BRIEF HISTORY OF MUSIC AND POST-SECONDARY EDUCATION

When trying to understand why academic music programs continue to be predominantly classical, it is helpful to examine how they were created. Post-secondary education in the United States was modeled after the European system and funded primarily by religious institutions. As the American upper class grew, many of the nation's wealthiest citizens gave generously to expand religiously affiliated institutions. Those who preferred to develop an education system outside of the church joined together to form secular universities.[13] In religiously affiliated schools, the purpose of musical training was to prepare students to glorify God. In secular institutions, the purpose of musical training was to elevate the cultural standing of American youth so that they were not seen as inferior to the Europeans.[14] The secular model gained a boost after WWII with the return of veterans who were able to take advantage of the GI Bill, while performers and composers were eager to accept university positions as a way to supplement their careers.[15]

In the time before student loans and the GI Bill, students relied heavily on their parents for tuition support, which relegated a college education to the upper and upper-middle class. From 1900 to 1910, college enrollment was only 4 to 5 percent of the student-age population. Parents who were willing and able to send their children to college believed that a formal education would lead to upward mobility.[16] Voice pedagogy, which emerged during the nineteenth century, was seen by some as a way to elevate those of the lower class to middle-class status through the development of the "cultivated voice."[17] Parents who were willing to fund the education of musically inclined children wanted them to be trained in the European tradition as a means of elevating or maintaining cultural status. Thus, our American music education system developed, and it has stayed nearly the same through the present day.

Current Enrollment Figures

According to the Higher Education Arts Data Services Project, there has been a decline in the number of vocal performance majors. In the fall of 2010, there were 7,078 voice majors at the undergraduate level and a total enrollment of 9,093 when accounting for graduate and doctoral students. By 2016, however, the number of undergraduate voice performance majors had fallen to 5,428 with a total enrollment of 7,038 when accounting for graduate and doctoral students. Those statistics indicate a 30 percent decline in the number of undergraduate vocal performance majors and a 23 percent decline overall.

Music theater programs, however, saw robust growth during this same period. In 2010, there were seventy-one NASM/NAST institutions offering a bachelor's degree in music theater with 2,302 students enrolled. By the fall of 2016, there were eighty-seven NASM/NAST institutions with 3,057 students enrolled. These statistics indicate a 33 percent increase in music theater majors since 2010.[18]

There are no National Association of Schools of Music (NASM) enrollment statistics for commercial voice degrees. The best estimate we have comes from researcher and pedagogue Jessica Baldwin, who has identified twenty-three music degrees with a CCM component. When one compares the number of classical voice programs (386) to the number of music theater (87) and commercial degrees (23), it is clear there is a large imbalance in the degrees we are offering compared to the music Americans are listening to and performing.[19]

Disproportionate training opportunities are not only problematic for aspiring performers but also budding pedagogues. While undergraduate enrollment in vocal performance programs fell by 30 percent, enrollment in DMA programs fell only 17 percent. Students enrolled in DMA programs are traditionally interested in pursuing full-time university positions. However, if the undergraduate marketplace for classical teachers is decreasing at a greater rate than the number of DMA students, it is highly likely that an already competitive job market for those with a doctorate degree will only become more competitive. This is further complicated by the fact that there is not a single doctoral degree in the United States solely dedicated to music theater or commercial music. Those who want to teach in those fields must be able to sing classically well enough to be admitted into a traditional DMA program. That requirement creates a barrier that prevents qualified CCM performers from earning the required credential to share their experience and skills in academia and create industry-focused degree programs for future performers.

THE RISE OF POPULAR MUSIC

Early popular music in the United States arose primarily from rural musicians who lacked formal training. America has always been a cultural melting pot, and soon those cultures began to evolve into distinct styles including hillbilly, folk, gospel, and blues. These styles are the bedrock upon which today's popular music genres are built. One of the more controversial elements of some early styles was "shout singing." Shout singing relied on chest-dominant vocal production and was primarily associated with black Americans.[20] In the early twentieth century—when racism was even more widespread than today—there were obvious biases against vocal usage that was strongly associated with people of color. It is no wonder that universities were hesitant to offer formal training in this type of vocal production.

The invention of the phonograph and the radio made it easier for different cultures and races to experience each other's music. In 1951, a disc jockey named Alan Freed learned that white teenagers were increasingly buying "rhythm and blues" records at a local record store. At this time in history, R&B records were also known as "race records," and they were exclusively associated with black artists and audiences.[21] Freed saw an opportunity, and he created a new late-night program called "The Moondog Show" where he could play the records teens were buying, regardless of the race of the performers.[22] However, he knew that due to the social climate of the time, he needed a racially neutral term to use on air. Thus, he began using the term "rock 'n' roll."[23]

During the mid-twentieth century, rock 'n' roll and R&B were considered lower-class forms of music than their classical counterparts. However, they had great appeal to the youth market. Parents of that era were troubled by numerous aspects of rock 'n' roll, including the term itself, which was a black euphemism for sex. In the 1950s, the thought of pre-marital relations was one of a parent's worst nightmares.[24] Parents had witnessed a rise in the unwed mother birthrate that peaked in the 1920s due in part to a move toward social dancing in major cities during the big band era.[25] Popular music was therefore associated with immoral behavior and was not regarded as "art." It is not surprising that styles carrying such connotations were not accepted within a higher education system that prided itself on creating opportunities for upward mobility through religious and European models.

TECHNIQUE

While social attitudes more than likely had a significant impact on the resistance to popular music in higher education during the twentieth century, there is also a reluctance to teach this music due to misconceptions about the technique. Two adages continue to be disseminated by some voice teachers: "good singing is good singing" and "it is all the same technique; the only difference is style." Let us begin with the "good singing is good singing" statement.

Explanations of what this statement means can vary widely. Is Pavarotti a "good" singer? Is Randy Blythe's approach to screaming when performing with Lamb of God symbolic of good singing? It depends on who you ask, and that is part of the problem. When teachers use the phrase "good singing is good singing," it automatically indicates subjectivity. If we instead ask, "Is this voice functioning correctly for the style the artist is singing?" then the conversation shifts from the subjective to the objective. Many of those who specialize in commercial and music theater styles use a functional approach for this very reason. A teacher's personal bias can have a detrimental impact on a client. This is more likely to occur when the teacher is working outside of their preferred music style(s) and they approach the student's training with the philosophy that "good singing is good singing." If the teacher's and student's tonal goals are not in line with each other, problems are likely to occur, and the student could easily end up singing in a manner that is not congruent with their personal aspirations.[26]

That brings us to the second saying—"it is all the same technique; the only difference is style." Scientific research shows that this statement is not accurate. Differences in technique begin at the vocal fold level. Christopher Barlow, Jeannette LoVetri, and David Howard investigated CQ (closed quotient) ratios in adolescent females singing in both classical and CCM styles. The investigators found that in 76 percent of the singers, CQ was greater in mix than in head voice.[27] The findings also suggest that the closed quotients are indeed different between the two styles. An analysis of distorted singing in a single subject found that there were vibrations in both the glottis and the supraglottal mucosa, which was vibrating at one-third of the fundamental frequency. Subharmonic frequencies were present in the spectrographic readings, and subglottic pressure was measured at 20–45 cm compared to 4–36 cm found in classical singers.[28] Vibration of the supraglottal mucosa is rarely if ever advocated in classical pedagogies, yet the quality is essential in many commercial styles.

Vowel qualities are different between commercial, music theater, and classical styles. Spectral analysis of country and rock singers has shown that the resonance strategy in this repertoire closely resembles speech and lacks activity within the singer's formant range.[29] Also, an analysis of music theater and classical singers found that words produced without a singer's formant had increased intelligibility, suggesting that a singer's formant may, in fact, be counterproductive to effectively communicating the text in speech-based singing styles.[30] Therefore, a forward "ringing" quality associated with the *chiaroscuro* of many classical techniques could be counterproductive to the needs of these singers.

There are specific physiological requirements for producing these different resonance strategies. Ingo Titze has written about the physiological benefits for a widened pharynx in classical singing, including lowering the first formant, boosting the singer's formant, and isolating the glottis from the effects of vowel changes.[31] However, these "benefits" are counterproductive to the characteristics found by Cleveland, Sundberg, and Stone in country singers.[32] In a later article, Titze states that a slightly raised larynx allows the first formant frequency of vowels such as [a] and [æ] to rise with pitch, thus surpassing the second harmonic and providing an acoustic advantage for the CCM singer. He goes on to say that the belt voice has been shown to benefit from a slightly higher laryngeal position.[33] New insights continue to be presented at conferences every year. While the results vary, the studies consistently indicate that there are differences in the techniques used by classical and CCM singers.

Finally, breathing strategies are another important aspect of vocal production that need to be studied in depth. A study of respiration patterns of country singers found that the subjects used a breathing strategy similar to that employed while speaking with only a 5 to 10 percent increase in lung capacity from speech to song.[34] Investigators studying classical singers saw significant differences in lateral rib cage movement when the singers were projecting their voices, indicating a more robust inhalation and use of their lung capacity.[35]

There is still much research to be done in all of these areas; however, the papers published so far clearly demonstrate significant differences between CCM and classical singers. These differences indicate unique technical approaches, refuting the statement that "it is all the same technique." In 2008, the American Academy of Teachers of Singing published a position paper in which they state the following:

> Since there are significant and measurable acoustic differences between classical singing styles and popular singing styles, the Academy proposes that the techniques used to train singers in those styles should be tailored to the particular performing needs of the singer. . . . Though many singers perform successfully in both classical and CCM styles, the vocal techniques required to produce those styles are not likely to be interchangeable.[36]

AUDIO TECHNOLOGY

In the past, voice teachers have expressed concerns about singers performing commercial music for fear they will ruin their instruments. Barbara Doscher suggested that the reason rock singers run into vocal difficulties lies in the fact that they phonate at volume levels that are beyond the threshold of pain, which is approximately 120 dB.[37] However, researchers interested in commercial styles have produced data that suggest our perceptions may be skewed. A study on intentional vocal distortion conducted by Daniel Zangger Borch and Johan Sundberg found that an experienced pop/rock singer is able to produce distorted sounds at amplitude levels between 90 and 96 dB.[38] Researchers working with country singers have reported amplitude levels at 30 cm that rarely exceed 90 dB.[39] Both sets of measurements are well below the maximum amplitude of 112 dB found in opera singers. The same authors also reported that their operatic subjects sang ≥ 90 dB anywhere from 37 to 53 percent of the time.[40] With pop/rock and country singers peaking around 90 dB, it would seem operatic singers are actually more likely to be singing near the threshold of pain.

Technology is a major contributing factor in creating the perception that commercial singers are singing loudly all the time. Live rock concerts regularly reach amplitude above 100 dB, with one of the highest readings coming in at 132.5 dB.[41] College students have been found to listen to music through headphones at 94.8 dBA + 8.2 (SD), indicating that some students are surpassing 100 dB. It is quite possible that biases against the loud singing of CCM performers may in part be due to a misunderstanding of how audio enhancement can alter our perception of vocal effort (see chapter 5).

In the past, it was common for performers to capture a vocal track in the studio that was difficult to reproduce on stage. However, companies such as TC-Helicon manufacture digital vocal effects processors that allow singers to replicate recording studio tricks in live performance. For instance, the TC-Helicon VoiceLive can simultaneously double or triple the lead vocal while also compressing and equalizing it. The unit can then add Auto-Tune and create harmonies at a fifth, an octave, and a tenth above the lead. The VoiceLive can be programmed so that each song has its own preset with preprogrammed changes in vocal effects for the verse, bridge, and chorus. The results produced by this type of technology can really skew our impression of a singer's natural vocal ability.

Another way performers can make their music appear "larger than life" is through the layering of multiple tracks. When artists record a song in the studio, it is not uncommon for them to record more than one pass of their voice. For example, according to recording engineer James Porte, Boyz II Men recorded "I'll Show You" with six vocal parts each recorded six times, for a total of thirty-six vocal tracks on the final recording.[42] Those prerecorded tracks can be synced with the live performance, allowing a group of four to sound like thirty-six. According to Matt Rifino, principal mixer for NBC's *The Today Show*, 80 percent of the bands that perform on the show utilize backing tracks to enhance their performance.[43] A high school men's quartet cannot sound like the Boyz II Men recordings unless they clone themselves. It is important for young singers to understand that if they try to reproduce acoustically what was created electronically, they may be increasing their risk of vocal injury. However, if they learn to utilize audio technology correctly, they can easily enhance their natural voice without compromising it during performance.

PERFORMANCE DEMANDS AND VOCAL DAMAGE

There remains a perception that it is primarily CCM singers who get injured, and the belief continues to be perpetuated by some in the classical community. In 2016, the Royal Opera House created a program to use opera with primary school children in an attempt to "combat unhealthy singing styles." Jillian Barker, director of learning and participation, states:

> I have a particular beef about kids in schools singing like they're trying to be on *The X Factor*—hardly using any notes and really sliding onto the note the whole time. . . . I think young people can tend to sing a very narrow range of notes, and to imitate the pop style. Which is great, it's fine, but it's not really extending the vocal range and it's not teaching good technique or diaphragm support, or all the things a professional singer would do. . . . There is a risk that you would damage your voice. If you're trying to belt out and you're not supporting your voice properly, you can strain your vocal cords.[44]

While it is true that improper technique can lead to vocal pathologies, stylistic choices such as sliding into notes, singing in a narrow range, and imitating pop styles are not to blame. Furthermore, as the classical and CCM voice teachers of the American Academy of Teachers of Singing (AATS) have stated, the techniques necessary to sing pop and classical are not interchangeable.[45] Programs like the one created by the Royal Opera House are helping perpetuate myths that have been proven false by researchers. In order to move our profession forward, we must let go of our personal biases and acknowledge the facts.

It appears that some in the classical community forget that opera singers are not immune to injury themselves: Sherill Milnes, Simon Keenlyside, Christine Goerke, Natalie Dessay, and Luciano Pavarotti have all struggled with highly publicized vocal injuries. However, for some reason, this is not talked about to the same extent as when a CCM performer gets injured. Football players are not shamed for having improper tackle technique when they get hurt. Instead, it is just an accepted fact that they are extreme athletes who are at a higher risk of injury. The same forgiving nature should apply to CCM singers. As professional educators, we need to ask ourselves why anyone is shamed for their vocal injuries. We could have a much stronger impact on our profession if we examined how we can we help this population instead of "armchair quarterbacking" on social media every time someone gets hurt.

While a busy opera career may consist of seven to nine performances in a month, performers on Broadway regularly perform eight shows a week, which is at least thirty-two per month. There is a significant difference in performance demands on these two sets of stage performers. While most operatic and Broadway performers get to stay in one city for a month or more, commercial singers are constantly on the road when performing. Adele scheduled 121 performances between February 29, 2016, and June 29, 2017.[46] She also performed in fifty-one cities in nineteen countries on four continents. In comparison, world famous operatic soprano Anna Netrebko sang seventy-five performances in seventeen cities in nine countries on two continents during that same period.[47]

Between tour buses, airplanes, hotels, and performance venues, performers like Adele are exposed to a wide range of humidity levels and many different allergens that can have a detrimental impact on the vocal folds. While opera and music theater performers will often get to spend time off stage between scenes, commercial artists regularly perform sets that are between an hour and a half and two hours long. It is not unusual for some performers in the early stages of their careers to gig for three hours or more in a noisy bar or at a summer festival. These circumstances have a significant impact on the entire body, and it is no surprise that many commercial artists develop health issues while trying to meet the impossible demands that are placed upon them.

It should also be noted that there is research supporting the notion that CCM styles are not inherently more dangerous than classical styles. Wendy LeBorgne has found that approximately 33 percent of incoming vocal performance and music theater students at an elite institution have a vocal pathology.[48] A survey in Australia examining opera, music theater, and commercial singers (rock 'n' roll excluded) found that there was no statistically significant difference in the prevalence of voice problems among the three groups. While we need more research to generalize the overall population, this preliminary data does not support the argument that CCM performing is inherently more dangerous than classical singing.

MUSICAL PREFERENCE

Debates regarding the value of musical literature being studied and performed have surely existed since the beginning of our art form. One quote in particular comes to mind when I consider this subject. The text comes from an 1892 speech to the New York State School Music Association (NYSSMA) by famed musician Louis Lombard:

> The well-known fact that Europe has educated all our good musicians, native or alien, proves beyond question the superiority of its system of education. A reason frequently given for the lack of musical culture in America is that Americans possess less musical genius than Europeans. Were it not more logical to censure the methods used here? With the same thorough training, Americans may equal Europeans in music as they have done in other fields. Girls and boys that have a good ear, heart, and mind abound around us, and they also have artistic temperaments. The main reason for their seeming inferiority is that they have been denied the advantages which others have enjoyed for centuries. Why should a country so fruitful in almost all other desirable ways be so deficient musically? No one caring for the moral and intellectual improvement of mankind can overlook the civilizing influence of musical culture; yet, while we ought to do much for musical education, we have done little.[49]

While this article dates from the nineteenth century, there are still authors today who express similar sentiments with statements that laud the past. For instance, "all good vocal technique comes from a classical foundation." To many, this includes using foreign-language repertoire with all students, a practice that is even found in some popular music degree programs in the United States. But is this really beneficial to students?

Jennifer Hamady touches on the problems that occur when students who are primarily interested in commercial genres are forced to sing classically in her book *The Art of Singing*. She discusses the limited number of opportunities for commercial performers to pursue a college degree and notes that many end up going into a classical program. Lacking the necessary vocal characteristics required for classical singing, many of these singers develop tensions to create sounds their bodies do not desire and are not developed enough to make.

> This is to say nothing of the lack of interest of many teenagers in classical repertoire, the lack of understanding of the languages in which they are sung, and the lack of opportunity to study, practice, and develop the voice and repertoire that inspired them to apply to and attend a music school in the first place. Learning new and unfamiliar material is a wonderful way to broaden a young singer's mind, but certainly not when it comes at the expense of all other styles of music.[50]

Author Neil Postman says there are two types of musical curricula that our students encounter, the first and most influential being what they receive through the media. The second and less influential is what they receive through school or—in the case of the voice teacher—through their private lesson. Since students spend most of their time being educated through the media, the voice teacher will always encounter the two-curriculum model of music education. Whether we embrace it or resist it can have lasting effects on students. A 2002 study of adults' reflections on their singing experience in secondary school found that 50 percent of females did not enjoy singing in choir. Of those participants, 100 percent said the reason they did not enjoy school singing was because the ensemble "didn't sing my style of music." Fifty percent of those participants who did not enjoy school singing no longer sing.[51] These statistics raise an important question—had these students had an opportunity to sing music they enjoyed, would they have kept singing? The data does not answer that question, but it is worthy of consideration.

It is helpful for teachers to understand that the student's choice of music in this secondary curriculum often reflects their developing personality. For instance, heavy metal fans tend to be more resistant to authority, while students who prefer light pop music tend to be conscientious and emotionally reserved.[52] Researchers suggest that the motivation for listening to music can be divided into two categories: (a) satisfaction of individual needs, and (b) satisfaction of social needs. When an adolescent chooses music for their individual needs, it usually serves as an emotional outlet. When choosing music for social needs, it is a vehicle for fitting in with other students. Song selection can, therefore, have implications beyond technique.[53] If a student is struggling emotionally, we may get better results by allowing them to choose songs that help them work through their emotions. If a student is just beginning to find their place in the social strata of high school through their love of country music, we could significantly improve their chances of being accepted into that social circle by helping them become one of the best country performers at their school. When we embrace the student's preferred musical style(s), we do more than just improve their satisfaction in lessons; we create an atmosphere where students have an opportunity to express their authentic selves and share their human experience. Some students will find that classical music does just that for them and will fall madly in love with Italian art songs. However, when the student shows no connection to that music and merely goes through the motions until they can eventually sing the music they want to sing, are we actually serving them as best as we can?

IMPLICATIONS FOR HIGHER EDUCATION

For those in academia, it is increasingly evident that a classical-only approach is insufficient for our students. Music therapists are primarily singing nonclassical music, music educators in K–12 settings are integrating world and popular music as they adapt to keep music programs relevant, and music theater performers are now being asked to sing pop/rock or pop-based music theater selections at auditions more than 50 percent of the time.[54] Even classical singers are finding themselves being required to cross over as more opera companies produce musicals and more churches embrace contemporary and blended worship. If we are not exposing our undergraduates to healthy approaches for CCM styles, we are not preparing them for the world they will enter upon graduation.

There is a mistaken belief by some that the National Association of Schools of Music (NASM) requires classical repertoire in degree programs. Several sections of the NASM Handbook make it very clear that this is not the case.

WHY IT'S TIME TO ADD CCM TO YOUR STUDIO 279

Section III. L. 1.
NASM standards address bodies of knowledge, skills, and professional capacities. At times, the standards require breadth, at other times, depth or specialization. However, the standards do not mandate specific choices of content, repertory, or methods.

Section III. L. 2.
With regard to specifics, music has a long history, many repertories, multiple connections with cultures, and numerous successful methodologies. Content in and study of these areas is vast and growing. Each music unit is responsible for choosing among these materials and approaches when establishing basic requirements consistent with NASM standards and the expectations of the institution.[55]

For music therapists, Section III. N. 3. c. recommends developing the following:

Skills in voice, especially as related to group singing. Ability to communicate using a basic repertory of traditional, folk, and popular songs.[56]

The NASM guidelines are broad and there are no explicit barriers to including commercial and music theater repertoire for students taking private voice lessons at the university level. The only barriers are those that we have created for ourselves. Perhaps one of the largest roadblocks to improving the situation lies in the requirement of a terminal degree to teach at most universities. The pathways for a CCM performer to attain a doctorate are extremely limited, to the point that many explore degrees outside of the voice department to obtain their credential. We desperately need more universities to offer graduate degrees in CCM pedagogy while creating pathways for students without an undergraduate degree in voice to enter these programs.

HOW TO IMPROVE YOUR SKILLS

Most of us who have taken the vocal performance path were not exposed to the type of information necessary to teach commercial and music theater students during our degree programs. Regarding technique, a lot depends on how you were trained as a classical singer. While the terms "classical" and *bel canto* are often used to identify technique, there is no universally accepted, codified approach that falls under either category. There have been hundreds of writings by famed teachers, but within those writings, you will find many contradictions. Many of these differences have to do with national tonal goals, as described in Richard Miller's book *National Schools of Singing*.[57] Therefore, one of the first steps in transitioning to teaching commercial and music theater singers is to begin thinking functionally instead of dogmatically.

There are many pedagogical texts that will guide you in this direction. To begin, I suggest *The Vocal Athlete* by Wendy LeBorgne and Marci Rosenberg. However, reading alone is often insufficient to completely understand the concepts if you have never been trained functionally yourself. For teachers looking to get firsthand experience in a functional approach, there are now many helpful conferences and workshops that are worth attending, including the following:

- NATS National Conferences and Summer Workshops
- The Voice Foundation Annual Symposium
- The Southeastern Theatre Conference (SETC)
- The Musical Theatre Educator's Alliance (MTEA)
- The International Voice Teachers of Mix (IVToM)
- Ingo Titze's Summer Vocology Institute (SVI)
- The CCM Voice Pedagogy Institute at Shenandoah University
- Estill Voice Training (EVT)
- The LoVetri Institute for Somatic Voicework™ (SVW)
- Lisa Popeil's Voiceworks™

To gain a better handle on styles, the So You Want to Sing series is a great starting place. It is also beneficial to learn the history of CCM styles as you venture into this territory. Books including *Rock of Ages: The Rolling Stone History of Rock and Roll* by Ed Ward and Geoffrey Stokes, *What's That Sound?: An Introduction to Rock and Its History* by John Covach and Andrew Flory, *The Theatre Will Rock: A History of the Rock Musical, from Hair to Hedwig* by Elizabeth Lara Wollman, and *The Rise and Fall of the Broadway Musical* by Mark N. Grant are all full of interesting and useful information. ♪

If you are interested in teaching music theater or improving your current skill set, there are several additional books that you should check out. It is important to understand the types of acting techniques students will encounter to be highly effective with music theater performers in the voice studio. A great book to begin with is *The Great Acting Teachers and Their Methods* by Richard Brestoff. The author takes you through the history of acting techniques as a time traveler, allowing you to observe sample classes with the great teachers to understand why they did what they did. The reader learns how gesture-based acting evolved into realism while covering most of the significant evolutions along the way. Once you understand the foundations of acting, you will want to explore how those techniques are applied to song. *Acting in Musical Theatre: A Comprehensive Course* by Joe Deer and Rocco Dal Vera is a comprehensive guide that belongs on every teacher's bookshelf. The exercises are clear, and the authors make sure every possible detail is covered. Finally, to help prepare students for auditions, pick up Jonathan Flom's *Get the Callback: The Art of Auditioning for Musical Theatre* and *The Enraged Accompanist's Guide to the Perfect Audition* by Andrew Gerle. These texts illuminate the small details casting directors look for and help students learn to walk into the room as young professionals. ♪

FINAL THOUGHTS

I will conclude with a few thoughts from Bennett Reimer, professor emeritus of music education at Northwestern University:

> Music is thriving in America, in its rich array of types and styles and ways to be involved that our multi-musical culture makes so readily available to all. Music education is not thriving comparably. We have tended to hunker down with our narrow preferences and limited opportunities and then, because we are dangerously irrelevant, we advocate, advocate, advocate—not for fundamental change in music education but for unquestioning support for what we have traditionally chosen to offer. . . . Our most urgent task, our way out of our unreality, is to more fully satisfy the actual musical needs and enthusiasms so plentiful all around us while adding to people's musical satisfactions the breadth and depth we are professionally qualified to help them achieve.[58]

Indeed, many educators have embraced change and are making waves in our profession. However, there is still room for more educators to join in this effort. The entire music industry is changing whether we like it or not. With numerous studies showing that American audiences overwhelmingly prefer CCM styles, sales data suggesting the greatest opportunities for employment are in CCM styles, studies showing music can have a significant impact on emotional development, and numerous respected pedagogues supporting the need and validity of CCM pedagogy, there is no reason not to embrace these styles.

There was a point in time, at the end of my undergraduate training and the beginning of graduate school, that I was of the belief "it is all the same technique" and a serious singer should not want to sing CCM styles anyway because they are inferior. I was training at a classical-only conservatory where all CCM styles were looked down upon and never performed on campus. After my first year of graduate school, I found myself at a summer stock theater where I was required to sing in *Fiddler on the Roof*. I resisted very strongly at the beginning of the rehearsal process—I was a classical singer, not a music theater performer! I remember very well the night I was backstage and realized I was taught to think that way and those were not my true feelings. I actually loved musicals and commercial music. That was when I started my journey with CCM pedagogy. I began reading, the research changed my mind-set, and I fully embraced CCM and music theater styles.

If you are still not sure whether it is time to add CCM to your studio, I have one final thought: we all sing because we desire to communicate the human experience through song. The diverse styles of CCM enable performers from all cultures to be part of this beautiful art form and share their unique experiences. If we embrace them all and teach students the music they want to sing, we just might make the world a better place.

NOTES

1. Robert Edwin, "Are We the National Association of Teachers of Classical Singing?" *Journal of Singing* 41, no. 5 (1985): 40.

2. An earlier version of this article, "Why It's Time to Add Pop-Rock to Your Voice Studio," was originally published in *VOICEPrints: The Journal of NYSTA* in 2013 (vol. 11, no. 2). This chapter, however, has been greatly revised and expanded, incorporating a significant amount of new data.

3. "Statistics: Broadway in NYC," The Broadway League, accessed August 10, 2017, www.broadwayleague.com/research/statistics-broadway-nyc/; "Statistics—Touring Broadway," The Broadway League, accessed August 10, 2017, www.broadwayleague.com/research/statistics-touring-broadway/.

4. "Going National: How America's Regional Theatre Movement Changed the Game," American Theatre League, accessed August 10, 2017, www.americantheatre.org/2015/06/16/going-national-how-americas-regional-theatre-movement-changed-the-game/.

5. "News and Notes on 2016 RIAA Shipment and Revenue Statistics," Recording Industry Association of America, accessed August 10, 2017, www.riaa.com/wp-content/uploads/2017/03/RIAA-2016-Year-End-News-Notes.pdf.

6. "Nielsen Music Year-End Report U.S. 2016," Nielsen, accessed August 19, 2017, www.nielsen.com/content/dam/corporate/us/en/reports-downloads/2017-reports/2016-year-end-music-report-us.pdf.

7. "Live Nation Leads the Charge in Concert Business' Booming Revenue," *Variety*, accessed August 10, 2017, variety.com/2017/music/features/live-nation-concert-business-1201979571/.

8. "Religions Congregations in 21st Century America," National Congregations Study, accessed August 5, 2017, www.soc.duke.edu/natcong/Docs/NCSIII_report_final.pdf.

9. "Worship Music: The Latest Research," *Christianity Today*, accessed August 17, 2017, www.christianitytoday.com/pastors/2001/september-online-only/cln10926.html.

10. David Meyer and Matthew Edwards, "The Future of Collegiate Voice Pedagogy: SWOT Analysis of Current Practice and Implications for the Next Generation." *Journal of Singing* 70, no. 4 (2014): 437–44.

11. "A Decade of Arts Engagement: Findings from the Survey of Public Participation in the Arts, 2002–2012," National Endowment for the Arts, accessed July 30, 2017, www.arts.gov/sites/default/files/2012-sppa-feb2015.pdf.

12. "Nielsen Music Year-End Report," Nielsen, accessed August 19, 2017, www.nielsen.com/content/dam/corporate/us/en/reports-downloads/2017-reports/2016-year-end-music-report-us.pdf.

13. Gretchen D. Starr-LeBeau et al., *American Eras: Westward Expansion, 1800–1860*, vol. 6 (Farmington Hills, MI: Gale, 1998), 361.

14. Irving Lowens and Louis Lombard, "Louis Lombard's 'Our Conservatories (1892),'" *American Music* 3, no. 3 (1985): 347–51.

15. Richard Crawford, *An Introduction to America's Music* (New York: W. W. Norton, 2001), 555.

16. Randall M. Miller, *The Greenwood Encyclopedia of Daily Life in America*, vol. 2 (Westport, CT: Greenwood Press, 2008), 760.

17. Grant Olwage, "The Class and Colour of Tone: An Essay on the Social History of Vocal Timbre," *Ethnomusicology Forum* 13, no. 2 (2004): 203–26.

18. HEADS Data Summary 2016–2017, accessed August 15, 2017, secure3.verisconsulting.com/HEADS/ReportOverview.aspx.

19. Jessica Baldwin et al., "A Survey of Curriculum in Commercial Music Degree Programs," Voice Foundation 47th Annual Symposium: Care of the Professional Voice, June 4, 2017; HEADS Data Summary 2016–2017.

20. While most slaves came from Africa, some came from the Caribbean Islands. Therefore, some argue that "black" is the more appropriate term. To keep in line with other historical writings and the wishes of many of my students and colleagues, I have chosen to use the word "black."

21. Crawford, *An Introduction to America's Music*, 555.

22. John Covach, *What's That Sound?: An Introduction to Rock and Its History* (New York: W. W. Norton, 2009), 566.

23. Crawford, *An Introduction to America's Music*, 555.

24. David P. Szatmary, *A Time to Rock: A Social History of Rock and Roll* (New York: Schirmer Books, 1996), 367.

25. Miller, *The Greenwood Encyclopedia of Daily Life in America*, 760.

26. James R. Wigginton, "When Proper Is Dead Wrong: How Traditional Methods Fail Aspiring Artists," *Journal of Singing* 66, no. 4 (2010): 447–49.

27. Chris Barlow et al., "Voice Source and Acoustic Measures of Girls Singing 'Classical' and 'Contemporary Commercial' Styles," Proceedings of the International Symposium of Performance Science (2007), 195–200.

28. Daniel Zangger Borch et al., "Vocal Fold Vibration and Voice Source Aperiodicity in 'Dist' Tones: A Study of a Timbral Ornament in Rock Singing," *Logopedics Phoniatrics Vocology* 29, no. 4 (2004): 147–53.

29. Thomas F. Cleveland et al., "Long-Term Average Spectrum Characteristics of Country Singers during Speaking and Singing," *Journal of Voice* 15, no. 1 (2001): 54–60.

30. Johan Sundberg and Camilla Romedahl, "Text Intelligibility and the Singer's Formant—a Relationship?" *Journal of Voice* 23, no. 5 (2009): 539–45.

31. Ingo R. Titze, "The Wide Pharynx," *Journal of Singing* 55, no. 1 (1998): 27–28.

32. Thomas Cleveland et al., "Estimated Subglottal Pressure in Six Professional Country Singers," *Journal of Voice* 11, no. 4 (1997): 403–9.

33. Ingo R. Titze, "Belting and a High Larynx Position," *Journal of Singing* 63, no. 5 (2007): 557.

34. Jeannette D. Hoit et al., "Respiratory Function during Speaking and Singing in Professional Country Singers," *Journal of Voice* 10, no. 1 (1996): 39–49.

35. C. William Thorpe et al., "Patterns of Breath Support in Projection of the Singing Voice," *Journal of Voice* 15, no. 1 (2001): 86–104.

36. "In Support of Contemporary Commercial Music (Non-Classical) Voice Pedagogy," American Academy of Teachers of Singing (2008), 9–10.

37. Barbara Doscher, *The Functional Unity of the Singing Voice* (Lanham, MD: Scarecrow Press, 1993), 352; Vern J. Ostdiek and Donald J. Bord, *Inquiry into Physics*, 7th ed. (Boston: Cengage Learning, 2012), 576.

38. Zangger Borch et al., "Vocal Fold Vibration and Voice Source Aperiodicity," 147–53.

39. Cleveland, et al., "Estimated Subglottal Pressure in Six Professional Country Singers," 403–9.

40. Anick Lamarche et al. "The Singer's Voice Range Profile: Female Professional Opera Soloists," *Journal of Voice* 24, no. 4 (2010): 410–26.

41. "Gallows Become the World's Loudest Band!" Kerrang.com, accessed August 11, 2017, web.archive.org/web/20070626212835/http://www2.kerrang.com/2007/06/gallows_become_the_worlds_loud.html.

42. Blair Jackson, "Recording Vocals," MixOnline.com, accessed August 17, 2017, mixonline.com/recording/applications/audio_recording_vocals/.

43. Blair Jackson, "Live Music Challenges 'Today Show' Mixer," MixOnline.com, accessed August 17, 2017, mixonline.com/post/features/live_music_challenges_today_show_mixer.

44. "Royal Opera House to Teach Children to Sing 'Healthily' over X Factor Voice Strain Fears," *Telegraph*, accessed August 15, 2017,
www.telegraph.co.uk/news/2016/10/18/royal-opera-house-to-teach-children-to-sing-healthily-over-x-fac/.

45. "In Support of Contemporary Commercial Music (Non-Classical) Voice Pedagogy," American Academy of Teachers of Singing (2008), 9–10.

46. en.wikipedia.org/wiki/Adele_Live_2016, accessed August 15, 2017.

47. annanetrebko.com/en/schedule/, accessed July 1, 2017.

48. Wendy LeBorgne, CCM Vocal Pedagogy Institute Session I at Shenandoah University, delivered July 15, 2017.

49. Louis Lombard, *The Art Melodious: Observations of a Musician* (Philadelphia: Theodore Preser, 1894), 104.

50. Jennifer Hamady, *The Art of Singing: Discovering and Developing Your True Voice* (New York: Hal Leonard, 2009), 5.

51. Angela Turton and Colin Durrant, "A Study of Adults' Attitudes, Perceptions, and Reflections on Their Singing Experience in Secondary School: Some Implications for Music Education," *British Journal of Music Education* 19, no. 1 (2002): 31–48.

52. Kelly D. Schwartz and Gregory T. Fouts, "Music Preferences, Personality Style, and Developmental Issues of Adolescents," *Journal of Youth and Adolescence* 32, no. 3 (2003): 205–13.

53. Dave Miranda and Patrick Gaudreau, "Music Listening and Emotional Well-Being in Adolescence: A Person- and Variable-Oriented Study," *European Review of Applied Psychology* 61, no. 1 (2011): 1–11.

54. Kathryn Green et al., "Trends in Musical Theatre Voice: An Analysis of Audition Requirements for Singers," *Journal of Voice* 28, no. 3 (2014): 324–27.

55. NASM Handbook (2016–2017), 83.

56. Ibid., 114.

57. Richard Miller, *National Schools of Singing: English, French, German, and Italian Techniques of Singing Revisited* (Lanham, MD: Scarecrow Press, 1997).

58. Bennett Reimer, "Reconceiving the Standards and the School Music Program," *Music Educators Journal* 91, no. 1 (2004): 34.

20

THE FUTURE OF CCM PEDAGOGY

Matthew Hoch

Much has changed since many of the pioneers profiled in this book began their quest for contemporary commercial styles to obtain recognition and legitimacy in the voice teaching profession. Over the past twenty years, CCM pedagogy has flourished. While the student of commercial singing a generation ago had few places to turn to find quality instruction, there are now hundreds—if not thousands—of well-qualified singing teachers who are successfully teaching contemporary styles. Summer workshops in CCM pedagogy, conferences, degree programs, and online resources have exploded. With more academic programs embracing commercial styles and industry statistics sending a loud and clear message to singing teachers, one wonders if CCM pedagogy will eclipse classical pedagogy in the coming decades, a prospect that would have been unthinkable only a short time ago.

In his famous 1982 book, *Great Singers on Great Singing*, Jerome Hines interviewed some of the world's greatest opera singers in an attempt to shed light on how these artists did what they did. One of the most fascinating aspects of this book is that—even though every singer interviewed was inarguably great—there was little consensus at the time on what constituted greatness. The singers, especially when discussing their technique with Mr. Hines, often seemed to contradict one another. Now, thirty-five years later, there seems to be much greater consensus among classical pedagogues on the fundamentals of healthy classical technique. This is in large part due to our understanding of vocal function and the major strides that have been made in the field of voice pedagogy and science in recent decades. ♪

This book, with its twelve profiles of CCM pioneers, is in some ways a direct descendant of Mr. Hines's book: a "Great Singers on Great Singing" for the CCM world, if you will. While some confusion and contradictions still abound within the CCM community—particularly on disagreements over pedagogical philosophy, preferences in regard to breath management strategy, and opinions over the nuances of technique—there is no question that our greater understanding of voice function, as well as vocal health, acoustics, resonance, anatomy, and physiology, has contributed greatly to increasing consensus among CCM pedagogues over technical matters and the legitimization of CCM singing among the classical voice teaching community. It is likely that this trend will continue in the coming decades.

One particular challenge that the CCM community faces has to do with the lack of a unified terminology. Unlike the medical community, singing teachers do not have "industry standard" terms when teaching their students, and various teachers often use different terminology to describe the same phenomena. Historically, this has been a problem in the classical community as well, although it seems as if more and more consensus is coalescing among classical singing teachers, who are increasingly choosing "fact-based" terminology that corresponds with our current knowledge of voice function. This is perennially a moving target, as our knowledge is always limited by our current scientific understanding. Few teachers in 2017 would select Vennard's book, *Singing: The Mechanism and the Technic*, as their textbook for a college-level voice pedagogy course, but this book was a landmark achievement in its day—"truth" as we understood it fifty years ago. By extension, it would be naïve to think that many of our pedagogical ideas will not become dated fifty years from now, in 2067. While no one can predict what new terminologies will emerge between now and then, it seems likely that we are headed in a direction of greater consensus as opposed to less.

Where the CCM community currently seems to differ most from the classical community is in the abundance of trademarked methodologies, each with its own lexicon of (often trademarked) terms. While some of these terminologies are shared by the classical community, others are unique to a specific CCM methodology or teacher. Some are also more fact-based and rooted in voice science than others. Even if some of these diverse terms are foundational in their agreement about vocal function, the fact that we sometimes have four or five different terms to describe the same phenomena is not helpful to the profession, and this plethora of jargon can lead to confusion among singers and voice teachers. It will be interesting to see whether consensus will eventually be achieved due to the proprietary nature of large segments of the CCM pedagogy community. My prediction is that—eventually—this will indeed occur. It has already begun to happen, thanks in large part to organizations like NATS and the Voice Foundation, who have championed the fact-based movement in voice pedagogy. ♪

No one can predict the future, but it is probably safe to say that CCM has found legitimacy and a permanent place in the field of voice pedagogy. This would not have been possible without the toil and perseverance of the pioneering teachers profiled in this book. They are the ones who laid the cornerstone for future generations of singing teachers. It is now up to us to build upon their work. Twenty, forty, and sixty years from now, people will still be singing, and it is fascinating to think about what the world of CCM pedagogy will look like.

GLOSSARY

Acoustic Efficiency: The specific acoustic envelope formed by the vocal tract that brings out the greatest boost of energy (intensity) in any given combination of vowel, pitch, and volume level. Related to but not the same as formant/harmonic ratios. In singing, teachers often refer to this phenomenon as resonance.

Belt: (1) A belt quality is the modal or chest register quality, carried above approximately E/F/G4, at a loud volume or with increased intensity, and without vowel modification. Belting is using that sound quality. A belter is someone who can easily make this sound and is comfortable in material written to be sung in this quality. This is the only term that can be used multiple ways to describe vocal output: "I am a belter, belting out a belt song." (2) One of the six voice qualities of the Estill Voice Model (EVM). According to the EVM, belt quality is "a loud voice quality heard in American music theater, ethnic music, pop music, and in children's voices on the playground."

CCM: Abbreviation for contemporary commercial music.

Chest Register: In pedagogy, chest voice, chest tone, chest resonance, heavy mechanism, speaking voice, TA dominant, or lower mechanism. Also called modal in voice science. Chest register is the lower speaking voice in most adults. The quality is considered to be stronger, louder, more authoritative, and declarative.

Complete Vocal Technique (CVT): A vocal technique developed by Danish pedagogue Cathrine Sadolin (b. 1958). The primary philosophy behind Complete Vocal Technique is that singing is not as difficult as many people think it is and that the most important aspect of the technique is expression, which allows singers to convey their individual artistic choices through the music they choose to sing. The method idiosyncratically uses four basic technical "modes" of singing: neutral, curbing, overdrive, and edge.

Contemporary Commercial Music (CCM): An umbrella term for all styles and genres that fall outside of classical singing. The term "CCM" was coined by Jeannette LoVetri (b. 1949) as a more positive alternative to its pejorative predecessor, "nonclassical."

Curbing: One of the four vocal modes of Cathrine Sadolin's Complete Vocal Technique (CVT). Curbing is the only half-metallic mode. There is a slight "metal" on the notes. Curbing is the mildest of the metallic modes. It sounds slightly plaintive or restrained, like when one moans because of a stomachache. Curbing can be found by establishing a "hold."

CVT: Abbreviation for Complete Vocal Technique.

Edge: One of the four vocal modes of Cathrine Sadolin's Complete Vocal Technique (CVT). Edge—formerly called "belting"—is one of the two full-metallic modes, along with overdrive. The character of edge is light, aggressive, sharp, and screaming, like when one imitates a diving airplane. Edge can be found by twanging the epiglottic funnel (i.e., sounding like a duck).

Estill Voice Model (EVM): A pedagogical method developed by Josephine "Jo" Estill (1921–2010). The EVM includes thirteen figures that are combined into six voice qualities.

Estill Voice Training (EVT): Training program built around the Estill Voice Model (EVM). Estill voice training is based on four operating principles: (a) knowledge is power—understanding how the voice works is a good thing; (b) voice production begins before the voice is heard—muscle effort makes it happen; (c) the breath must be allowed to respond to what it meets on the way out; and (d) voice training is optimized when separated into three disciplines: craft, artistry, and performance magic. A certification program exists for teachers wishing to be trained in the Estill method.

EVM: Abbreviation for Estill Voice Model.

EVT: Abbreviation for Estill Voice Training.

Falsetto: (1) The upper extension of the male voice that is produced in a head register quality. It means "a little false" because it does not sound like the mature adult male voice; however, it is a perfectly normal vocal production and not false in that respect. In most men, it is not used in average speech; hence it seems to be a bit "false" and the name derives from that. In the vocal folds, the behavior is the same as in head register in women. (2) One of the six voice qualities of the Estill Voice Model (EVM). According to the EVM, falsetto quality is "a breathy voice heard in the voices of children, boy choirs, and certain early music singers."

Figures: In the Estill Voice Model (EVM), specific exercises designed to isolate voice quality variations according to anatomy and physiology. The thirteen figures are as follows: true vocal fold (onset/offset), false vocal fold, true vocal fold (body-cover), thyroid cartilage, cricoid cartilage, larynx, velum, tongue, aryepiglottic sphincter, jaw, lips, head and neck, and torso. Although named for specific anatomical structures, each figure takes on an idiomatic definition within the Estill Voice Model (EVM).

First *Passaggio*: See *Primo Passaggio*.

Four Vocal Modes: In Cathrine Sadolin's Complete Vocal Technique (CVT), the four basic uses of the voice. The modes differ by having different amounts of metallic character. In CVT, most singing problems occur because of the incorrect use of the modes. Each mode has a certain distinct character, as well as advantages and limitations.

Head Register: In pedagogy, head voice, head tone, head resonance, light mechanism, CT dominant, or upper mechanism. Also called loft in voice science. Head register is a softer, lighter quality associated with most children, some women, and falsetto in men. Often called "pure" or "angelic" in children.

Legit: The theater community's term for classical vocal production. Word comes from the early days of music theater, at an indeterminate date, and refers to "legitimate" singing as would be found in a trained voice. The alternative to this was the belt sound. Belters were considered to be "shouters" who were not refined, elegant, and trained. The word continues to be in use in the contemporary theater industry.

Loft: The term for head register in voice science.

Mix: A descriptor of a sound quality that is neither an obvious chest or head quality, or that quality found most often in average voices. It has characteristics of both chest and head simultaneously. Mix can be further described as head/mix or chest/mix by pedagogues, which implies that the sound is predominantly but not completely colored by one register more than the other.

Modal: The term for chest register in voice science.

Neutral: One of the four vocal modes of Cathrine Sadolin's Complete Vocal Technique (CVT). Neutral is the only non-metallic mode. There is no "metal" in the sound. The character is often soft, like singing a lullaby. Neutral is the only mode where one can sing using a breathy quality without causing damage. Neutral is found by establishing a loose jaw.

Opera: One of the six voice qualities of the Estill Voice Model (EVM). According to the EVM, opera quality is "heard in the heightened stage speech of classically trained actors (e.g., Shakespearean) or in the ringing quality of singers on the operatic stage."

Overdrive: One of the four vocal modes of Cathrine Sadolin's Complete Vocal Technique (CVT). Overdrive is one of the two full-metallic modes, along with edge. The character of overdrive is often direct and loud, like when one shouts, "Hey!" at somebody in the street. Overdrive can be found in the beginning by establishing a "bite." It is usually used when speaking or singing loudly in the low part and middle part of the voice.

Pharyngeal Voice: See *Voce Faringea*.

Primo Passaggio: Italian term for the lower of the two primary points of transition in singing. Also called first *passaggio*.

Register: A group of pitches or notes that have the same quality or texture, differing from another group of a recognizable quality or texture.

Resonance: See Acoustic Efficiency.

Second *Passaggio*: See *Secondo Passaggio*.

Secondo Passaggio: Italian term for the higher of the two primary points of transition in singing. Also called second *passaggio*.

Six Voice Qualities: In the Estill Voice Model (EVM), six categories of vocal production, each of which was original chosen for its association with a specific genre of music. Speech, sob, twang, and opera were the initial four qualities established in 1981. Falsetto and belt were added in 1986. Each quality combines some of the thirteen Estill figures in a specific combination to produce the desired sound.

SLS: Abbreviation for Speech Level Singing.

Sob: One of the six voice qualities of the Estill Voice Model (EVM). According to the EVM, sob quality is "heard in mournful conversation, in the singing of lullabies, or in the classical singing style of art songs."

Somatic Voicework (SVW): Method created by American pedagogue Jeannette LoVetri (b. 1949). The three levels of Somatic Voicework certification are offered through period workshops, including an annual summer institute at Baldwin Wallace Conservatory.

Speech: One of the six voice qualities of the Estill Voice Model (EVM). According to the EVM, speech quality is "heard in the everyday speaking of most newscasters and in the singing of popular and folk songs."

Speech Level Singing (SLS): Vocal technique created by Seth Riggs (b. 1930) that dovetails traditional *bel canto* concepts with contemporary industry terms and CCM styles. Speech Level Singing (SLS) is a trademarked term, and only certified teachers are licensed to use it or claim that they are SLS teachers.

SVW: Abbreviation for Somatic Voicework.

Twang: One of the six voice qualities of the Estill Voice Model (EVM). According to the EVM, twang quality is "heard in the speech of many cultures, modern music theater, bluegrass, and some country music."

Vocal Function: The way the vocal folds and surrounding muscle and tissue respond to the brain's command to produce vocal sound. Breath movement, both exhalation speed and pressure, and the resistance to same through the sound itself, can be thought of as a correlate of vocal production having an effect upon vocal function.

Vocal Power Method: A system of vocal technique developed by American pedagogue Elisabeth Howard (b. 1932). Howard disseminates her method through a series of "Vocal Power Academy" workshops and several books, including *Sing!* (1980) and *The ABCs of Vocal Harmony* (2006).

Voce Faringea: Cultivated by castrati, the pharyngeal voice or *voce faringea* was a tool that was used in uniting the chest and head registers of the voice.

Vocology: The science and practice of voice habilitation. Vocology parallels audiology as the study of vocalization as opposed to hearing. The term was coined by Dr. Ingo Titze, who founded the Summer Vocology Institute (SVI) at the National Center for Voice and Speech (NCVS), currently located in Salt Lake City. At this summer program, enrolled students earn 9.0 graduate credits in four courses: Principles of Voice Production, Singing Voice Habilitation, Instrumentation for Voice Analysis, and Voice for Performers. Students who successfully complete all coursework receive the Certificate in Vocology.

Voiceworks: A system of vocal technique developed by American pedagogue Lisa Popeil (b. 1956). Popeil disseminates her method through a series of "Total Singer" workshops and several books, including *The Total Singer* (1996) and *Sing Anything* (2012).

Zipper Effect: The zipper effect is a concept developed by American pedagogue Seth Riggs (b. 1930), the creator of Speech Level Singing (SLS). The term is used to describe the zipper-like process in which the vocal folds dampen along the posterior two-thirds of the folds, thus only using the front third of the folds for vibration at the *primo passaggio*. The zipper effect theory was challenged in 2011, when a study published in the *Journal of Singing* by Randy Buescher (b. 1961) reported that no such action exists in the vocal folds.

INDEX

AATS. *See* American Academy of Teachers of Singing
The ABCs of Vocal Harmony (Howard, E.), 148
abdominal muscles, 36–38, 37–38
a cappella, 29
Accademia Vocal Power Italia, 148
Accent Method, 118, 177–78, 179, 184
acne, 57
acoustic analysis programs, 122, 247
acoustic efficiency, 291
acoustics, 121–22, 213, 288
acting, 24–25, 27, 175, 206, 225–26, 281
Acting in Musical Theatre: A Comprehensive Course (Deer & Dal Vera), 281
activism, 108–9
Adam's apple. *See* larynx
adduction, 40, 118, 188
Adele, 275

affect, 61
Africa, 284n20
Agresta, Katie, 4, 97–109
airflow, 38–39
air flow, 155, 176, 177, 178
air pressure, 34–36, 38–39, 118, 141, 143, 176–78
alcohol, 59, 66
Alexander Technique, 150, 180
alignment, 63, 64, 117, 119, 155, 161
allergies, 55–56
American Academy of Teachers of Singing (AATS), 132, 171, 222, 227, 272
American Idiot, 23, 239
American Idol, 257
American Theatre, 265
amplification, 69, 92, 122, 170; in Broadway shows, 22; formant/harmonic ratios and, 46–47; performance and, 72; pop music and, 148; resonance and, 45–46;

self, 203–4; unamplified singing and, 21–23. *See also* microphones
amplitude, 73
amplitude response, 79–81, *81*
anatomy, 153, 183, 217, 288
ANATS. *See* Australian National Association of Teachers of Singing
Andrews, Julie, 223
Annie, 151
ANS. *See* autonomic nervous system
anti-anxiety medication, 60
anticipation, 138
antidepressant medication, 60
anxiety, 60–62, 116, 225
AOTOS. *See* Association of Teachers of Singing
aphonia, 41
apple cider vinegar, 56–57
appoggio technique, 126, 179
art funding, 17
articulation, 33, 48–49, 130, 199, 202, 204
artistic freedom, 88
artistic temperaments, 276
artistry, 6, 118
The Art of Singing (Hamady), 277
arytenoids, 41, *42*
Association of Teachers of Singing (AOTOS), 173, 183
asthma, 212
audiation, 129–30
audience, 20–22, 122, 282
audio enhancement, 273
audio signal, 73. *See also* signal chain
audio technology, 20, 22, 272–74
auditions, 142, 145, 146, 164, 207, 281
Austin, Howard, 137, 144
Australian National Association of Teachers of Singing (ANATS), 110

Australian Voice Association (AVA), 121
authenticity, 139, 163, 187, 205, 206, 225; emotions and, 226; of styles, 115, 244; of teaching, 245; technique and, 12
autonomic nervous system (ANS), 61
Auto-Tune, 90–91, 113, 273
AVA. *See* Australian Voice Association
avant-garde, 187

background tracks, 273
"Back to Rock," 5
Baldwin, Jessica, 268
Baldwin Wallace Conservatory, 7, 295
Balk, Wesley, 104
Barker, Jillian, 274
Barlow, Christopher, 10
baroque principles, 200
Bartlett, Irene, 110–23
Barton, Mary Saunders, 4, 11, 222–40
behavior, 61
Behlau, Mara, 159
bel canto, 200, 222, 254, 262
bellies (muscles), 36
belting, 3, 20, 189, 204, 291, 292, 295; calling/belting exercises, *233*; exercises, 191, 232–34, *233*; legit, 239; methods, 203; open, 234; range and, 203, 234; resonance and, 234; technique, 119; tessituras, 232; workshop, 5, 195
Bernac, Pierre, 223, 237
Beyoncé, 225
bias, of teachers, 270
biographical musicals, 24
The Black Crook, 22

INDEX

Black Sabbath, 218
Blood, 137
blues, 101, 104, 127, 269
bluetooth, 65
Blue Tree Publishing, 157
Blythe, Randy, 270
body mapping, 118
body type, 39
Bon Jovi, Jon, 106
Book of Mormon, 233
Boone, Daniel R., 168
Borch, Daniel Zannger, 9, 241–48, 272
Born to Sing, 144
box office sales, 17
Boyle's Law, 34
Boyz II Men, 273
Bozeman, Ken, 205, 232
brain/voice research, 122
breath, 117; control, 199; flow, 119; management, 39, 63, 118, 129, 177–78, 257; pressure, 38–39; support, 190; vocal folds and, 118
breathing, 63, 141, 143, 165, 166, 292, 295; artistry and, 118; Boyle's Law, 34; demands, 39; diaphragm, 35–36; different ways of, 39; exercises, 64; misconceptions about, 34; oxygen and, 34; posture and, 39; problems, 211–12; registration and, 257; strategies, 39, 177–78, 271; technical problems and, 257; technique, 39, 62
breathlessness, 60
Brestoff, Richard, 281
bridge, 45
British Voice Association (BVA), 173, 183, 184, 220
Broadway, 100, 104, 198

Broadway shows, 18, 22, 205, 222, 253, 265
Brodnitz, Friedrich, 152–53
Brooklyn, 198
The Brotherhood of Angels and of Men (Hodson), 107
Brown, Oren, 4, 153
Buckley, Betty, 200
Buescher, Randy, 296
BVA. *See* British Voice Association

cabaret, 112, 205, 236
caffeine, 56, 58–59
California Institute of the Arts, 186
Callas, Maria, 104, 207
calling/belting exercises, *233*
Camelot, 223
Caplan, Liz, 5
Caplan, Norman, 5
carbonation, 59
carcinogens, 66
cardioid microphones, 81, *82*
cardiovascular fitness, 59–60, 69
Caribbean, 284n20
Carnegie Hall, 205, 224
cartilages, of larynx, 41, *42*
casting, 148
casting directors, 281
castrati, 210n1
Cats, 22
cause and effect, technique and, 256–57
CCM (contemporary commercial music), 291, 292; acceptance of acronym, 16–17, 30–31; acting in, 27; classical and, 272; community, 288; controversy about word commercial in, 17–18; dance in, 27; definition of, 16, 243; employment and, 282; genres,

16, 30; language/text in, *27*; marketplace, 265; music theater *vs.*, 10–11, 15–32, 175; origin of term, 5–6, 15–17, 225; other skills required for, *28*; pedagogy, 125; persona for, *28*; pioneers, 288; storytelling for, *28*; teachers, 11; training, *26*; universities and training programs for, *28*; venues, *26*; vocal demands of, *27*
cell phones, 65
Challis, Marianne, 237
Chapman, Janice, 179, 180–81
character development, 67, 197–98, 206
charisma, 213
Charles, Ray, 101
Charnin, Martin, 151
chest register, 189, 210n1, 227, 259, 261, 291; exercises, 231, *231*; glottis in, *43*; head voice and, 201, 254; music theater and, 179; speech and, 162; vibrations in, *43*; vocal damage and, 164–65; vocal extremes and, 88
chiaroscuro, 271
Chicago, 198
Chicago Lyric Opera, 192
choirs, 29
chord patterns, 130
chord structure, 163
choreography, 60
Christianity Today, 265
church music, 104, 265–67
cigarettes, 62, 66
circle of fifths, 130
classical, 104, 139–40; acting in, *27*; CCM and, 272; community, 288; dance in, *27*; exercises, 242, 244; language/text in, *27*; marketplace,

265, 266; other skills requires in, *28*; persona in, *28*; storytelling in, *28*; styles, 199; technique, 19, 125, 126, 212, 261–62, 288; training, 8–9, *26*, 112, 162; universities and training programs for, *28*; venues, *26*; vocal demands, *27*, 277; vocal production, 3, 293
closed quotient. *See* CQ
closed vowels, 233
coaches, 243
cognition, 61
color, 139, 143, 176, 212; emotions and, 138; sound, 214, *215*, 216. *See also* timbre
coloratura exercises, 67
comfort zone, 127
commerce, 17
commercial, 17–18
communication, 162, 199
community, 288
Complete Vocal Institute (CVI), 211, 217, 219, 220–21
Complete Vocal Technique (CVT), 8, 214, *215*, 216–17, 292, 293, 294
composer, intentions of, 232
compression, 73, 73, 86–88, 87
condenser microphones, 76–78, *78*
conferences, 280, 287
confidence, 190
conflict, 206
consonants, 93, 202, 204
consumers, 17, 18, 266
contemporary commercial music. *See* CCM
contemporary pop, 20–21
continuing education, 18, 29
contour, 206
cooldowns, 64, 99, 108, 245
coordination, 166

INDEX

coping strategies, 29
copying, 139
copyright, 131–32
counseling, 66
countertenors, 198, 199, 202
CQ (closed quotient), 10, 201, 270–71
craft, 6
creative energy, 236
creative process, 20, 25, 238
creativity, 175, 193
cricoid cartilage, 41, *42*
cricothyroid dominant, 43, 118, 226
crooning, 21–22
crossover singing, 119
cross-training, 67, 119, 127, 153–54, 214
crying exercises, 235
CT muscles, 42
culture, music, 115, 281
curbing, *215*, 216, 292
CVI. *See* Complete Vocal Institute
CVT. *See* Complete Vocal Technique

Dal Vera, Rocco, 281
dance, *27*, 29, 60, 125, 269
Daviesi, Riccardo, 255
Davis, Richard, 113
decibels, 73, 80, 272–73
deep lamina propria, *40*
Deer, Joe, 281
degree programs, 287
dehydration, 54, 55
delay, 89–90, *90*
Delp, Roy, 239
DeMain, John, 144
dialogue, 19
diaphragm, *35*, 35–36, 129, 236, 274
diaphragm, of microphones, 76, 80
diction, microphones and, 93

diet, 52–53, 58, 59
digestive system, 38, 58
digital effects, 113
digital reverb, 88–89
digital voice processors, 91, 273
Dio, Ronnie James, 218
diphthongs, 49, 234
disappointment, 157
disease, 53
doctoral dissertations, 18
donations, 17–18
Doscher, Barbara, 272
dramatic context, acting and, 225–26
drones, 44
drugs, 66
dryness, 53, 57–58
Dwyer, Edward J., 97, 98, 99, 101, 102, 104
Dylan, Bob, 218
dynamic control, 228, 236
dynamic microphones, 76, 77, 93
dynamics, 48, 69, 88, 118, 143

eating disorders, 52
edge, *215*, 216, 292
education, 169, 174; church and, 267; continuing, 18, 29; higher, 30, 267–68, 269–70, 278–79; music, 267, 276, 277; post-secondary, 267–68; of Riggs, 254, 257–58; of teachers, 258
Edwards, Matthew, 10
Edwin, Robert, 4, 5, 8–9, 124–33, 226–27, 264
effects, 113, 139, *215*, 216
elastic recoil, 36
electronic manipulation, 170
electronic music, 108
emotional baggage, 189–90

emotions, 130, 143; authenticity and, 226; color and, 138; extremes of, 69; fear and, 60–61; language/text and, 69; microphones and, 69, 72; neurology and, 61–62; repertoire and, 277–78; singing and, 105
empathy, 102
employment, 282
engineers, 69
The Enraged Accompanist's Guide to the Perfect Audition (Gerle), 281
Entertainer's Secret, 54
enunciation, 188
environment, 121–22
epiglottis, 41, *42*
epithelium, *40*
equalization (EQ): graphic, 84, 86, 87; interface, *85*, 87; parametric, 84–85, *85*; shelf, 83–84, *84*, *85*, 86; utilizing, 86
esophagus, 58
Estill, Jo, 4–6, 151–53, 156, 180, 237
Estill Voice Model (EVM), 291, 292, 293, 294–95
Estill Voice Training (EVT), 6, 150, 154, 292, 293
ethics, 131–32
Europe, 276
European Voice Teachers Association (EVTA), 220
Evita, 232
EVM. *See* Estill Voice Model
EVT. *See* Estill Voice Training
EVTA. *See* European Voice Teachers Association
excitation, 206
exercise. *See* physical exercise
exercises, 120, 155, 184, 226–27; articulation, 202; belting, 191, 232–34, *233*; breathing, 64; calling/belting, *233*; chest voice, 231, *231*; classical, 242, 244; coloratura, 67; cry, 235; disconnected, 129; *Messa di voce*, *234*; musicianship, 244; music theory and, 130; pitch, 103; pressure lips, 191, *192*; reinforcing core voice, *228*; SOVT, 155; speech, 226, *231*; styles and, 9, 139, 244; teaching and, 9; tongue, 103; vibrato, 234–35; yodel, 235
exhalation, 36, 39
exhaustion, 157
experience, of singers, 261
experimentation, 94, 156, 165, 186, 225
expiratory muscles, 38
expression, freedom of, 227, 236
external intercostal muscles, 36, 37, 143, 236
external obliques, 37, 38

failure, 182
falsetto, 88, 198, 228, 229, 293, 295; gender and, 230; glottis in, *43*; reinforced, 230; soprano and, *230*; speech and, 230
falsetto/soprano mix, *230*
Faria, Carlo, 98
fatigue, 29, 53, 68–69, 99, 117, 122, 242
fear, 60–61, 161
feedback, 76, 92
feeling, 152
Feldenkrais, 180
Fiddler on the Roof, 282
figures, 293
first formants, 46–47, *47*
first *passaggio*. *See primo passaggio*
Fischer-Dieskau, Dietrich, 180

INDEX

fitness, 59–60, 180
Fitzmaurice Voicework, 150
flattery, teaching and, 189
flexibility, 103, 166, 214
Flom, Jonathan, 281
flow, 117, 119, 155
food, 52–53
forced resonance, 44–45
foreign-language repertoire, 276
formant/harmonic ratios, 45–48, 47, 161, 271, 291
four vocal modes, 8, 214, 216, 293
Freed, Alan, 135, 269
freedom, 166, 175, 227, 236, 252
free resonance, 44, 45–46
frequency, 43, 65, 73, 75, 75, 78–79, 79, 81

gargling, 56–57
Gastroesophageal reflux (GERD), 58
Gaughan, Dick, 218
gender, 129; audience and, 21–22; bending, 11–12; falsetto and, 230; formant/harmonic ratios and, 46–47; neutrality, 226–27, 232; registration and, 11–12, 228, 230; speech and, 65
genres. *See* styles
GERD. *See* Gastroesophageal reflux
Gerle, Andrew, 281
Get the Callback: The Art of Auditioning for Musical Theatre (Flom), 281
GI Bill, 267
gigging singers, 29
Gigli, Benjamino, 255
Gilbert and Sullivan, 151
Gill, Brian, 232
glottis, 10, 40, 43, *43*, 271
Goettling, Gisela, 186

good singing, 270
Gotti, Anna, 148
Gould, Wilbur James, 153
Grabscheid, Eugene, 152
Grammy Awards, 251, 261
grants, 17
graphic equalizer, 84, 86, 87
The Great Acting Teacher and Their Methods (Brestoff), 281
greatness, 287–88
Great Singers on Great Singing (Hines), 143, 218, 287–88
Green Day, 23, 239
Griffith University, 113

Hagen, Uta, 146
Hair, 10, 22, 138
Hamady, Jennifer, 276–77
Hamilton, 23, 199, 224
harmonics, 74, 75
harmonic series, 45
harmony, 91
Harris, Sara, 181
Harris, Tom, 181
headphones, 273
head register, 201, 210n1, 254, 293
healing, 99, 102, 105–6, 162
health, 156, 161, 165, 178, 200, 259–60, 288; issues, 275; problems, 107, 164; sound technicians and, 239; technique and, 207; of throat, 56–57; training and, 114; warm-ups and, 64
hearing, 129, 152
heartburn, 58
heavy metal, 212
Herbert Berghof Studios, 223
Herbert-Caesari, Edgar, 255
herbs, 57, 59
hertz (hz), 43, 73

higher education, 30, 267–68, 269–70, 278–79
Hines, Jerome, 143, 218, 287–88
history, 101, 132–33, 261, 267–68
hoarseness, 66, 186, 216
Hodson, Geoffrey, 107
Hofstra University, 98, 99, 104
holds, 292
Holiday, Billie, 162
home neutral, 179
honey, 56–57
hop-hop, 23
hotels, 55
Howard, Elisabeth, 4, 8, 134–49, 295
human experience, 238
Humidflyer, 55
humidification, 54–55
Hunter, Kim, 147
Hunter College, 136
Hutchinson, Linda, 178
hydration, 53–56, 64, 70
hyoid bone, 42, 49, 189
hypercardioid pattern, 82
hz. *See* hertz

Iannotta, Antonio, 98
ICVT. *See* International Congress of Voice Teachers
ideals, technique and, 212
identity, 116, 199, 207
If in Doubt, Breathe Out! (Morris & Hutchinson), 178
imagery, teaching and, 256
imitation, 128, 187, 199–200, 206
improvisation, 115, 127, 135, 214
income, 136
industry, 12, 16–18, 113, 224, 282
in-ear monitors, 92
inflammation, 41, 56, 57
inhalation, 39, 118, 272

inharmonic overtones, 44
injuries, 51–52, 62, 65, 68–69, 117, 224, 274–75
inner life, 205
insecurity, 190
Inside the Light, 97
inspiration, 118
instant gratification, 206
Institute for Vocal Advancement (IVA), 252, 260
Instructor Manual (SLS), 258
instruments: elements of, 33; pitch and, 74; resonance and, 33, 74–75, 75; voice as, 120, 142
intermediate lamina propria, *40*
internal intercostal muscles, 36, 37, 143, 236
International Congress of Voice Teachers (ICVT), 194, 227, 247
Internet, 131, 171, 239
intervals, 130, 244
interviews. *See* specific people
intimacy, 20–22, 69, 203–4
intuition, 120
irritants, 62, 66
Italian language, 109
IVA. *See* Institute for Vocal Advancement

jaw, 49, 117, *215*, 216
jazz, 98, 113, 138, 162, 176, 200
Jersey Boys, 100, 175, 179, 230
Jesus Christ Superstar, 20
Joe Papp's Public Theater, 137
Jones, Quincy, 255
Journal of Singing, 5, 124, 126, 131, 133, 185, 239, 264, 296
Journal of Voice, 16, 185, 221
joy, 181
judgment, teaching and, 105

INDEX

Juilliard, 98, 134, 135, 136, 144, 147, 151, 165
jukebox musicals, 20–21, 24

Kane and Glory, 137
kidneys, 54
Kingston Polytechnic, 174
knowledge, 6, 292
Korey, Alix, 237

Lader, Joan, 4, 6, 11, 150–58, 237
La Gran Scena Opera Company, 197–98
lamina propria, 41
language/text, 27, 69, 109, 206
Lanza, Mario, 140
laryngeal pathologies, 52, 66
laryngitis, 41
laryngopharyngeal reflux (LPR), 58
larynx, 38, 155; breathlessness and, 60; cartilages of, 41, *42*; dryness of, 53; fatigue and, 117; height of, 177; movement of, 161; muscles of, 178–79, 226, 236, 256; position of, 154; range and, 255; rigidity of, 49; stabilization of, 256; structures of, 41; style and, 114–15; as vibrator, 39–44
latissimi dorsi muscles, 39
Lauper, Cyndi, 100, 106
Lawrence, Van, 53
learning, singing, 252
learning models, 121
LeBorgne, Wendy, 226, 275, 280
legato, 19, 24, 140, 163, 204, 254
legit, 3–4, 10, 19, 138–39, 228, *229*, 289, 293; belting, 239
Lessac, Arthur, 150
lessons, 142, 156, 166, 184, 277
licensure, 169

licks, 139
life experience, 116, 132, 146–47, 156–57, 170, 182–83, 193, 208, 220, 238, 246–47
lifestyle, 59, 107
Lincoln Center, 205, 223, 253
lips, 48–49, *215*, 216
listening: habits, 266; motivation for, 277–78; to music, 104–5, 111; styles and, 163; technology and, 108
Little Steven, 106
live cell treatment, 107
live concerts, 17
live performance. *See* performance
live sound systems, 91–93
loft, 43, 204, 207, 294
Lombard, Louis, 276
longevity, 63–64, 143, 156, 182, 260
loudness, 72, 73
LoVetri, Jeannette, 4–7, 13n3, 15–16, 125, 159–72, 181, 292, 295
LoVetri Method. *See* Somatic Voicework
LPR. *See* laryngopharyngeal reflux
Luciano Pavarotti International Voice Competition, 198
Ludman, Jean, 237
lungs, 39, 272
Lupone, Patti, 200
lyrics, 127, 163, 206

MacRae, Gordon, 131
mainstream culture, 23
Manhattan School of Music, 160, 164, 253
Man of La Mancha, 186
Manuel, Lin, 23
marijuana, 66
marketplace, 264–66

Massapequa Music Center, 97, 98
Mathieson, Lesley, 181
Mathis, Johnny, 104
maturity, patience and, 208
McArthur, Edwin, 98
McCoy, Scott, 205
McGlashan, Julian, 220
Means-Weekly, Edrie, 6, 15–16
media, 277
medical management, 56, 58
medication, 53, 57–58, 60
meditation, 68
melismas, 127
melody, 138
Melton, Joan, 238
memorization, 206
mental focus, 60, 68
mental health, 68
mental library, 132
mental wellness, 60–62, 68
Merrill, Robert, 131
Messa di voce exercises, *234*
methodologies, 6–8, 288–89. *See also* teaching
Met Opera Competition, 198
Metropolitan Opera, 135, 147, 266
Meylan, Mark, 11, 173–84
Michael Howard Studio, 223
microphones, 69, 75, 148, 158, 247; amplitude response of, 79–81, *81*; cardioid, 81, 82; condenser, 76–78, *78*; diaphragm of, 76, 80; diction and, 93; dynamic, 76, 77, 93; electric, 21; emotions and, 69, 72; frequency response of, 78–79, *79*, 81; head-mounted, 88; hypercardioid pattern of, 82; intimacy and, 20, 21–22, 69; invention of, 21; manufacturers, 79; omnidirectional pattern of, *83*; phantom power, 77; placement of, 86; polar patterns of, 79–80, *80*, 81, 82, *83*; proximity effect, 81; sensitivity of, 81–83; shotgun pattern of, *83*; supercardioid pattern of, 82; technique, 72, 86, 93, 194; types of, 22; vocal qualities and, 72; wireless, 22
Middle Ages, 254
middle soprano, 230, 231
middle voice, women in, 231–32
Miller, Donald, 201, 205
Miller, Richard, 5, 125, 128, 131, 179, 280
mistakes, 105, 142
misuse, 51–52
mix, 20, 141, 161, 226, 259, 294; falsetto/soprano, *230*; soprano, 230, 232; speech, 232, 233
mixer, 92
modal, 291, 294
modal voice, 43
Monbo, Helena, 4, 124–25, 128
monitors, 92
Monteith, Cory, 66
"The Moondog Show," 269
Moore, Melba, 141
morality, pop music and, 269–70
Morris, Ron, 178, 181
Morton, Jennie, 235–36
motor control, 39
Motown, 192
mouth, 48–49, 75, 187–88
mouth shapes, 187–88
MPA. *See* musical performance anxiety
mucus, 53–54, 55, 56, 64, 66
multiband compressors, 88

INDEX

muscles: entanglement, 99; function, 100; of larynx, 178–79, 226, 236, 256; memory, 63, 67, 139. *See also* specific muscles
muscular antagonism, 39
muscular tension, 117
music: appreciation, 112; culture, 115, 281; education, 267, 276, 277; inner response to, 163; listening to, 104–5, 111; motivation for listening to, 277–78; race and, 269; respect for, 102, 203
musical directors, 177
musical inventions, 116
musical performance anxiety (MPA), 60–62, 116
musical preference, 276–77
musical supervisors, 177
music history, 101, 200, 267–68
musicianship, 48, 112, 244, 245
The Music Man, 160, 186
music theater, 104, 114, 138–39, 145, 173, 197, 207; acting in, 27; CCM *vs.*, 10–11, 15–32, 175; chest register and, 179; contemporary, 19–20; dance in, 27; goal of, 207; intricacies of, 19–21; language/text in, 27; marketplace, 265; National tours, 265; other skills required for, 28; persona and, 28; programs, 268; radio *vs.*, 23; storytelling in, 25, 28; subgenres of, 19; technique, 226; tonal goals for, 24–25; traditional, 19, 20; training, 26, 236; universities and training programs for, 28; venues, 26; vocal demands of, 27
"Music Theater and Popular Music Symposium," 4

music theory, 130, 187
music therapy, 29, 278–79
My Fair Lady, 223
mystery, 140, 193

naps, 66
nasal irrigation, 55–56
nasality, 188, 230, 234
nasal passages, 55–56
nasal resonance, 235
NASM. *See* National Association of Schools of Music
nasopharynx, 230
National Association of Schools of Music (NASM), 278–79
National Association of Teachers of Singing (NATS), 5, 50, 108, 121, 125, 126, 147–48, 157, 171, 193, 196, 208; climate of, 264; conference, 227; Riggs and, 259
National Center for Voice and Speech (NCVS), 50, 296
National Endowment for the Arts, 266
National Schools of Singing (Miller, R.), 280
National Student Auditions, 6
NATS. *See* National Association of Teachers of Singing
natural harmonic series, 45
natural reverb, 88
naturopathy, 59
NCVS. *See* National Center for Voice and Speech
Neti pots, 55–56
Netrebko, Anna, 275
neurology, 49, 61–62
neutral, 215, 216, 294
New Orleans, 168

New York City, 4, 5, 240
New York City Opera (NYCO), 253
New York Singing Teachers Association (NYSTA), 4–5, 109, 157, 171, 173, 196, 208
New York State School Music Association (NYSSMA), 276
nicotine, 66
nosebleeds, 57
notation, 115, 205
nutrition, 52–53, 70
NYCO. *See* New York City Opera
NYSSMA. *See* New York State School Music Association
NYSTA. *See* New York Singing Teachers Association

objective, 206
objectivity, in teaching, 270
Off-Broadway, 204–5
Oliver, 178, 192
omnidirectional pattern, 83
online teaching resources, 239
opera, 18, 104, 114, 200, 294
Op'ra to Pop'ra, 144
oral hydration, 54–55
oral hygiene, 56–57
orchestras, tuning of, 43
overdrive, *215*, 216, 292, 294
overhydration, 54
oversinging, 92, 163
overtones, 43–44, 74
overuse, 51–52
oxygen, breathing and, 34

Pacific Voice Conference (PVC), 220
pain, 272–73
palate, 49
Pan-American Vocology Association (PAVA), 171

Pandora, 225
Pan-European Voice Conference (PEVOC), 173, 183, 194, 220
parallel vocal function, 231
parametric equalization, 84–85, *85*
parents, 269
patience, maturity and, 208
PAVA. *See* Pan-American Vocology Association
Peabody Conservatory of Music, 253
pedagogy, 3–4, 5
Penn State University, 24, 150, 238, 240
pentatonic scale, 138
Pepperdine University, 137
perfection, 142, 146
performance, 6, 84, 111, 273; amplification and, 72; demands, 25–29, 62, 69, 274–76; identity, 116; longevity, 117
performance anxiety. *See* musical performance anxiety
"Performance Day," 108
personal style, 149, 244
personas, 28
PEVOC. *See* Pan-European Voice Conference
phantom power, 77
pharyngeal voice. *See voce faringea*
pharyngitis, 54
pharynx, 9–10, 53, 57, 114–15, 125
philosophy, of teaching, 102, 116–17, 129, 131–32, 154–55, 178, 189–90, 202–4, 217, 235–36, 245
phonation, 115, 117, 119, 126, 129, 176; diaphragm and, 36; PTP, 54; straw, 202; vocal folds and, 40–41
phonation threshold pressure (PTP), 54
phonograph, 269

INDEX

phonotrauma, 51, 62, 65, 69
phrasing, 115, 136, 138, 163, 188, 207
Phyland, Deb, 181
physical exercise, 59–60, 67, 70
physiology, 61, 217, 243, 288
pitch, 73; Auto-Tune, 90–91, 113, 273; exercises, 103; formant/harmonic ratios and, 46–47; frequency and, 75; hearing and reproducing, 129; instruments and, 74; names of, 44; tuning, 43–44; vocal folds and, 41
point of view, 206
polar patterns, 79–80, *80*, 81, *82*, *83*
polypoid degeneration, 66
pop culture, 142
Popeil, Lisa, 7, 185–95, 296
pop music, 186; amplification and, 148; contemporary, 20–21; genres, 269; higher education and, 269–70; morality and, 269–70; rise of, 269–70
pop/rock musicals, 20–21, 23
post-secondary education, 267–68
posture, 39, 64, 129, 161, 166, 180, 188, 257
power, 6
power source, 33, 34–39
Practical Vocal Acoustics (Bozeman), 205
Practical Vocal Acoustics: Pedagogic Applications for Teachers and Singers (Bozeman), 232
practice sessions, 67
pre-marital relations, 269
pressure lips exercise, 191, *192*
prevention, of injuries, 62
Price, Henry, 137
Prime of Miss Jean Brodie, 147

primo passaggio, 115, 294, 296
professional organizations, 121, 132, 147–48, 157, 171, 183–84, 193–94, 208, 220, 238–39, 247
pronunciation, 136, 138, 139
proximity effect, 81
psychology, 190
PTP. *See* phonation threshold pressure
pulmonary system, 34–39, 271–72
PVC. *See* Pacific Voice Conference

race, music and, 269
racism, 269
radio, 21–22, 23, 104, 269
range, 103, 129, 189, 203, 234, 255, 274
rarefaction, 73, *73*
R&B, 269
recitation, 206
Reckford, Leo, 152
Recording Industry Association of America, 265
recordings: lessons, 184; sessions, 68–69; technology, 20, 113, 247
record labels, 17
record sales, 17
recovery, 67
rectus abdominis muscles, 36, *37*, *38*
reflux, 58–59, 62
registration, 204, 262, 294; appropriate, 24; balance, 161, 224, 226, 229, 236; breathing and, 257; configurations, 261; cross-training with, 70; definition of, 129–30, 202, 214; gender and, 11–12, 228, 230; low, 115; modeling, 199; permutations, 191; problems, 189; resonance and, 201; Riggs and, 263n2; shifts in, 225; strategy, 245;

teaching, 137–38, 179, 263n2; transitions, 19, 191, 227; vocal folds and, 257. *See also* specific registers
rehabilitation, 110, 117, 152, 181, 255
Reid, Cornelius, 167
Reimer, Bennett, 281
reinforcing core voice exercises, *228*
religion, 267
repertoire, 112, 115, 125, 128, 276, 277–78
repetition, 67, 69, 128, 166
research, 18, 100–101, 246
resonance, 70, 118, 119, 130, 161, 176, 288; amplification and, 45–46; appropriateness of, 117, 188; belting and, 234; communication and, 199; definition of, 44, 202; forced, 44–45; formant/harmonic ratios and, 48; free, 44, 45–46; impact of, 48; instruments and, 33, 74–75, *75*; mouth and, 75, 187–88; nasal, 235; patterns, 115; qualities, 199; registration and, 201; sound source and, 44; speech and, 271; spoken, 199; strategies, 199–200, 201, 203, 204, 207, 271; throat and, 75; vocal tract and, 42–48, 201; 208; vowels and, 226, 232–33
resonator, 33, 44–45, 187–88
respect, 13, 102, 156, 169–70, 203
respiration. *See* breathing; pulmonary system
rest, 66, 67
reverb, 89, 89–90, 148
rhinosinusitis, 56
rhythms, 67, 129, 206, 244
ribs, 36

Riggs, Seth, 7, 251–52, 296; background of, 253–55; *bel canto* and, 262; core values of, 255–57; criticism and controversy, 258–60; education of, 254, 257–58; Herbert-Caesari and, 255; NATS and, 259; passion of, 262; registration and, 263n2; reputation and clients of, 255; as vocal consultant, 255; voice science and, 259
rock 'n' roll, 269
Rock of Ages, 23
rock singers, 99, 100, 245
roots music, 4
Rosenberg, Marci, 226, 280
Roubeau, Bernard, 227
Royal Opera House, 274
runs, 139

Sabella, David, 196–210
Sadolin, Cathrine, 8, 211–21, 292, 293, 294
safe space, 166, 182
sales data, 282
saliva, 58
sanglot, 235
Sataloff, Robert T., 167
scales, 130, 138
schola cantorum, 254
science, 213, 244
second formants, 47–48
Secondo Passaggio, 231, 294
seeing, 152
self-amplification, 203–4
self-talk, 190
Semer, Neil, 5
semi-occluded vocal tract (SOVT), 155
sense of self, 206

sensitivity, of microphones, 81–83
sex, 269
shelf equalization, 83–84, *84*, *85*, 86
Shenandoah Conservatory, 7
Shewell, Christina, 181
shotgun pattern, *83*
shout singing, 269
Show Boat, 160
Shurtleff, Michael, 223
sight singing, 130
signal chain, 75–91
SING! (Howard, E.), 134, 141, 144, 148
singers, 29, 99, 100, 261
The Singer's Advantage, 257
singer-songwriters, 199
singing. *See specific entries*
The Singing Actor (Balk), 104
Singing and Teaching Singing (Chapman), 179, 181
singing exercises. *See* exercises
Singing for the Stars (Riggs), 256, 257
singing lessons, 112
six voice qualities, 294–95
skill development, 67–68, 279–80
Skype, 157, 171, 194, 220, 239, 247
slaves, 284n20
sleep, 68
SLS. *See* Speech Level Singing
Smith, Svend, 177
smoking, 66
Snider, Dee, 99
sob, 295
social dancing, 269
social media, 275
social needs, 277–78
soft palate, 234
software, 157, 194, 201, 205, 247, 248

Solfège, 130
Somatic Voicework (SVW), 7, 159, 167, 295
songs, 174–75, 277–78
songwriting, 25
soprano, 228, *229–30*, 230–32
sore throat, 54
sound, 73, 227
soundboards, 29, 44–45, 77, 84
sound colors, 214, *215*, 216
sound engineers, 69
sound equipment, 29
sound pressure level (SPL), 80
sound source, 33, 44
sound technicians, 239
SOVT. *See* semi-occluded vocal tract
speakers, 92
specialists, 30
spectrum analysis, 48, 271
speech, 19, 120, 295; chest register and, 162; exercises, 226, *231*; falsetto and, 230; frequency of, 65; gender and, 65; mix, 232, 233; range and, 255; resonance and, 271; singing and, 207, 226, 231, 271; vocal folds and, 65
speech-language pathology, 113, 152–53, 160, 169
Speech Level Singing (SLS), 7, 251–52, 295; breath management in, 257; certification program, 258, 260; core beliefs, 260; definition of, 255–56; *Instructor Manual*, 258; internal politics at, 260; significance, 260–61; terminology of, 259
spirituality, 107
Spivey, Norman, 5, 225–26, 239
SPL. *See* sound pressure level
spontaneity, 50, 167

Spotify, 225
Sprechstimme, 259
spring reverb, 88
stamina, 64, 67, 69, 103, 166
steam inhalers, 54–55
Steinfort, Edwin Robert, 125
sternum, 35
stomach, 58
Stop, Time, 237
storytelling, 25, 28, 199
straight tone singing, 235
straw phonation, 202
Streisand, Barbra, 136, 237
strength, 103, 166
strength training, 59–60
stress management, 68, 169
stretching, 64, 228
The Structure of Singing (Miller, R.), 179
students, 6; auditions, 281; backgrounds and teaching, 101, 119–20, 128, 138–39, 153–54, 162–63, 176–77, 187–88, 200, 214, 224–25; parents of, 267
student-teacher relationships, 105, 107, 116
styles, 3, 7, 18, 111–12; authenticity of, 115, 244; classical, 199; cultivation of own, 12; definition of, 9, 162; elements of, 189; exercises and, 9, 139, 244; immersion in, 100–101, 163; larynx and, 114–15; legitimacy of, 4–5; listening and, 163; mastering, 187; personal, 149, 244; pharynx and, 114–15; researching, 100–101; teaching, 113–14, 116–17, 119, 127, 128, 137–38, 138–40, 153–54, 160–61, 162–63, 167, 174–75, 180, 187, 189, 199, 212–13, 218, 224, 236–37, 243, 245–46; technique and, 126; technique vs., 8–10, 160, 270; tonal goals of, 24–25; tradition and, 205
subglottal pressure, 201
sub-harmonic frequencies, 10, 271
subjectivity, 213, 256, 270
Summer Vocology Institute (SVI), 296
Sundberg, Johan, 242, 245, 246, 247, 272
supercardioid pattern, 82
superficial lamina propria, 40
supplements, 59
support, 117, 119, 141, 143, 161, 190, 199, 204
supraglottal mucosa, 10, 271
SVI. *See* Summer Vocology Institute
SVW. *See* Somatic Voicework
Sweden, 241
syncopation, 138

Take Them Along, Our Songs, 131
taste, technique and, 212
TC-Helion, 91, 273
tea, 56–57
teachers, 25, 30, 112, 277; background of, 127–28; bias of, 270; CCM, 11; commitment of, 155; education of, 258; fear and, 161; interacting with other, 238; knowledge of, 245; licensure of, 169; as models, 180, 213; role and place of, 219; strictness of, 155; student-teacher relationships, 105, 107, 116; subjectivity of, 213; successful, 142–43
teaching: authenticity of, 245; criteria for, 100–101, 114, 127–28, 153, 161, 175–76, 187, 199–200, 213,

INDEX

224, 243; environment, 182; exercises and, 9; explaining, 261; flattery and, 189; goals, 117–18, 129, 131, 145–46, 156, 168–69, 181–82, 193, 206, 219, 238, 246, 270; imagery and, 256; judgment and, 105; methods, 115–16, 128–29, 154, 163–64, 177–78, 188–89, 200–201, 214–15, 225–26, 244; objectivity in, 270; philosophy of, 102, 116–17, 129, 131–32, 154–55, 178, 189–90, 202–4, 217, 235–36, 245; register, 137–38, 179; registration, 263n2; standards of, 141–42; student backgrounds and, 101, 119–20, 128, 138–39, 153–54, 162–63, 176–77, 187–88, 200, 214, 224–25; styles, 113–14, 116–17, 119, 127, 128, 137–38, 138–40, 153–54, 160–61, 162–63, 167, 174–75, 180, 187, 189, 199, 212–13, 218, 224, 236–37, 243, 245–46; subjectivity in, 256, 270; technique, 100; technology and, 108, 121–22, 132–33, 148–49, 157–58, 171, 184, 194, 209, 220–21, 239, 247; traditional models of, 113; at universities, 114, 120; videos, 188–89

technical problems, 102, 212, 213, 257

technique: absence of, 200; acting, 281; application of, 204; *appoggio*, 126; authenticity and, 12; belting, 119; breathing, 39, 62; cause and effect and, 256–57; classical, 19, 125, 126, 212, 261–62, 288; comfort and, 202; dance and, 29; definition of, 9, 178; drills, 64; elements of, 103, 129–30, 155, 166, 178–79, 190–91, 217–18, 236, 245; as foundation, 102–3, 116, 119, 145; four legs of, 202; fundamentals of, 143; genres and, 217; health and, 207; ideals and, 212; identification of, 279–80; improper, 274; as journey, 182; lack of, 158; longevity and, 143; methods for, 101–2; microphones, 72, 86, 93, 194; music theater, 226; poor, 117; repertoire and, 125; shortcuts, 183; styles and, 126; style *vs.*, 8–10, 160, 270; taste and, 212; teaching, 100. *See also* teaching

technology, 48; audio, 20, 22, 272–74; history of, 132–33; Internet and, 239; listening and, 108; recording, 20, 113, 247; sound, 227; teaching and, 108, 121–22, 132–33, 148–49, 157–58, 171, 184, 194, 209, 220–21, 239, 247

television, 74, 111, 112, 187
tempo, 127
tension, 49, 190
terminology, 214, 219, 259, 261, 288
tessituras, 232
text work, 67
therapeutic "chewing" technique, 153
thinking outside the box, 193
thorax, 35, 36, 37
Thorendahl, Eric, 140–41, 144
threshold, 86–87, 87
threshold of pain, 272–73
throat, 41, 49, 54, 56–57, 75, 164
Throat Coat, 54
throat singing, 44
thyroarytenoid muscle, 42, 43, 118, 226
thyroid cartilage, 41, *42*

timbre, 22, 25, 42–43, 44, 75, 75
Titze, Ingo, 23, 168, 201, 232, 246, 296
tobacco, 66
tonal goals, 24–25, 270
tonal quality, 89
tongue, 48–49, 103, 117, 141, 154
Toscanini, Arturo, 98
Total Singer, 185
Total Singer Workshop, 7, 185
toxins, 66
trachea, 41, *42*
tradition, styles and, 205
Traficante, Marie, 197–98, 205
training, 226–27; CCM, *26*; classical, 8–9, *26*, 112, 162; for classical, 28; goals, 105; health and, 114; music theater, 236; for music theater, 28; vocal longevity and, 63–64. *See also* exercises; teaching
transverse abdominis muscles, 37, 37–38
trauma, 62
travel, 55
truth, 105
tuning, 43–44; Auto-Tune, 90–91, 113, 273; of orchestras, 43
Tuvan throat singing, 44
twang, *215*, 216, 230, *235*, 295
tweeters, 92
Twisted Sister, 99

Ultimate Vocal Voyage (Borch), 241, 247–48
Ultimate Vocal Voyage (Zangger), 242–43
unamplified singing, 21–23
undergraduate education, 267–68
universities, 28, 29, 114, 120, 267–68
University of Miami, 5

upper body anchoring, 180
upper respiratory infection, 62
urination, 53

Valli, Frankie, 179
varicose veins, 57
Vennard, William, 167, 288
venues, *26*
vibrations, 33, 43, 74
vibrato, 19, 23, 136, 138–41, 143, 190, 234–35
vibrator, larynx as, 39–44
videos, teaching, 188–89
visualizations, 61, 201, 205
visual stage image, 145
vitamins, 53, 59
vocal acoustics, 168
The Vocal Athlete (LaBorgne & Rosenberg), 226, 280
vocal balance, 252, 261
vocal color. *See* color
vocal damage, 117, 164–65, 203, 274–76
vocal demands, 27, 63, 175, 236, 277
vocal development, 63
vocal effects processors, 91, 273
vocal empowerment, 166
vocal extremes, 86, 88
vocal fitness programs, 64, 67
vocal folds, 40, *41*, 296; abnormalities of, 52; air pressure and, 141, 143; breath and, 118; damage to, 62; function, 262; inflammation of, 41; lesions of, 58; location of, 41; mucous of, 53–54; pitch and, 41; polyps, 69; pressing, 190; registration and, 257; speech and, 65; structure of, 257; vibrations of, 43, *43*
vocal fry, 24

INDEX

vocal function, 10, 41–42, 231, 288, 289, 295
vocal gesture, 203
vocal habits, 53
vocal harm, 72, 164, 190
vocal health. *See* health
vocal hygiene, 62, 165
vocal identity, 199, 207
vocal injuries. *See* injuries
vocal intensity, 65, 67
vocalises, 63, 64, 67, 129
vocal ligament, 41
vocal limitations, 163
vocal longevity. *See* longevity
vocal maintenance, 176
vocal mastery, 190
vocal modes. *See* four vocal modes
vocal naps, 66
Vocal Power Academy, 146
"Vocal Power Academy" workshops, 8
Vocal Power Method, 8, 134, 137, 140–41, 295
Vocal Power Showcases, 137
Vocal Power Singer Showcases, 146
Vocal Power Trainers, 146
Vocal Power workshops, 148, 149
vocal problems, 140, 164–65, 211, 212, 217, 223, 242
vocal production, 166, 203–4
vocal qualities, 22, 23, 24, 52, 72, 152, 153, 179
vocal science, 162
vocal stretches, 64
vocal tract, 24, 42–48, 115, 119, 176, 177, 201, 208, 231, 257
vocal wellness, 52, 62–66, 68–70
Vocal Workout of the Day (Borch), 242–43, 247
voce faringea, 200–201, 210n1, 295

VoceVista, 201, 205, 239
Vocology, 296
voice: building, 102, 115–16; conservation, 67–68; disorders, 62; dysfunction, 119; flexibility of, 214; function, 119; healing, 102; as instrument, 120, 142; loudness of, 72; medication and, 57–58; medicine, 165, 167–68, 193; production, 6, 45, 63; reflux and, 58–59
voice box. *See* larynx
Voice Foundation Symposium, 126, 151, 165, 181, 183, 193, 208, 220, 289
voice performance majors, 267–68
Voiceprint, 157
Voice Research Society, 184
voice science, 9, 23, 113, 116–17, 125, 161, 165, 208, 213, 245; expansion of, 171; Riggs and, 259
voice teachers. *See* teachers
Voiceworks Method, 7, 185, 195, 296
volume, 73, 272–73
volume control, 191
vowels, 44, 46, 48–49, 93, 127, 207; acoustic properties of, 231; closed, 233; configurations of, 261; formant/harmonic ratios and, 47; glottis and, 271; open, 232–33; purity of, 161, 254; quality of, 254; resonance and, 226, 232–33
vulnerability, 147

Ward, David, 5
warm-ups, 64, 99, 108, 119, 192, 245
water, 54
wellness, 52–56, 60–66, 68–70
white noise, 121
Wicked, 198

Winehouse, Amy, 66
wireless microphones, 22
Wizard of Oz, 192
women, in middle voice, 231–32
Wonder, Stevie, 246, 255
woofers, 92
workshops, 18, 195, 280, 287
World War II, 146, 267
worship music. *See* church music
written word, 172

Yankovic, "Weird Al," 191
yodel exercises, 235
Young, John Lloyd, 100
YoungArts, 158
youth, 179
YouTube, 101, 149, 200, 225

Zappa, Frank, 191–92
Zipper Effect, 296

ABOUT THE EDITOR AND CONTRIBUTORS

Matthew Hoch is associate professor of voice and coordinator of voice studies at Auburn University. Prior to coming to Auburn in 2012, he spent six years as assistant professor of voice at Shorter College, where he taught applied voice and vocal literature and served as coordinator of voice studies. Dr. Hoch's students have gone on to successful careers in both classical and music theater genres and have won awards from the Metropolitan Opera National Council (MONC), National Association of Teachers of Singing (NATS), Music Teachers National Association (MTNA), Kennedy Center American College Theatre Festival (KC-ACTF), the Vann Vocal Institute, and others. Dr. Hoch is the author of three books, including *A Dictionary for the Modern Singer* (2014), *Welcome to Church Music & The Hymnal 1982* (2015), and *Voice Secrets: 100 Performance Strategies for the Advanced Singer* (2016). His articles have appeared in the *Journal of Singing, Journal of Voice, Voice and Speech Review, Opera Journal, Choral Journal, Chorister,* and *Journal of the Association of Anglican Musicians*. From 2008 to 2016, he served as editor-in-chief of *VOICEPrints: The Journal of the NYSTA*. Dr. Hoch has presented his research at many national and international conferences, including the International Congress of Voice Teachers (ICVT), Pan-European Voice Conference (PEVOC), Pan-American Vocology Association (PAVA), National Association of Teachers of

Singing (NATS), Music Teachers National Association (MTNA), Voice and Speech Trainers Association (VASTA), National Opera Association (NOA), College Music Society (CMS), Hawaii International Conference on Arts and Humanities (HICAH), Society for American Music (SAM), National Association for Music Education (NAfME), Southeastern Theatre Conference (SETC), Acoustical Society of America (ASA), International Horn Symposium (IHS), Hymn Society of the United States and Canada, Voice Foundation Symposium in Philadelphia, and the International Symposium on Singing and Song in St. John's, Newfoundland and Labrador. He holds the BM from Ithaca College, MM from the Hartt School, DMA from the New England Conservatory, and the Certificate in Vocology from the National Center for Voice and Speech. As a recipient of the 2007 NATS Voice Pedagogy Award, he completed all three levels of Somatic Voicework at Shenandoah University under the tutelage of Jeannette LoVetri. He is the 2016 winner of the Van L. Lawrence Fellowship, awarded jointly by the Voice Foundation and NATS.

* * *

Matthew Edwards is associate professor of voice and voice pedagogy at Shenandoah Conservatory and artistic director of the CCM Voice Pedagogy Institute. His current and former students have performed on and off Broadway as well as on national and international tours and major motion picture soundtracks and have appeared on Billboard music charts. Edwards is the author of *So You Want to Sing Rock 'n' Roll* and has contributed chapters to *Manual of Singing Voice Rehabilitation, The Vocal Athlete, Get the Callback,* and *A Dictionary for the Modern Singer.* He has authored articles for the *Journal of Singing, Journal of Voice, American Music Teacher, VOICEPrints,* and *Southern Theatre.* Edwards regularly presents workshops on functional training for the CCM singer at conferences and universities throughout the United States. He is the 2017 winner of the Van L. Lawrence Fellowship, awarded jointly by the Voice Foundation and NATS.

Wendy LeBorgne is a voice pathologist, speaker, author, and master class clinician. She actively presents nationally and internationally on the professional voice and is the clinical director of two successful private practice voice centers: the ProVoice Center in Cincinnati and BBIVAR in Dayton. Dr. LeBorgne holds an adjunct professorship at University of Cincinnati College-Conservatory of Music as a voice consultant, where she also teaches voice pedagogy and wellness courses. She completed a BFA in musical theater from Shenandoah Conservatory and her graduate and doctoral degrees from the University of Cincinnati. Original peer-reviewed research has been published in multiple journals, and she is a contributing author to several voice textbooks. Most recently, she coauthored *The Vocal Athlete* textbook and workbook with Marci Rosenberg. Her patients and private students currently can be found on radio, television, film, cruise ships, Broadway, Off-Broadway, national tours, commercial music tours, and opera stages around the world.

Scott McCoy is a noted author, singer, conductor, and pianist with extensive performance experience in concert and opera. He is professor of voice and pedagogy, director of the Swank Voice Laboratory, and director of the interdisciplinary program in singing health at Ohio State University. His voice science and pedagogy textbook, *Your Voice: An Inside View*, is used extensively by colleges and universities throughout the United States and abroad. McCoy is the associate editor of the *Journal of Singing* for voice pedagogy and is a past president of the National Association of Teachers of Singing (NATS). He also served NATS as vice president for workshops, program chair for the 2006 and 2008 national conferences, chair of the voice science advisory committee, and a master teacher for the intern program. Deeply committed to teacher education, McCoy is a founding faculty member in the NYSTA Professional Development Program (PDP), teaching classes in voice anatomy, physiology, acoustics, and voice analysis. He is a member of the distinguished American Academy of Teachers of Singing (AATS).

Darren Wicks is a vocalist, jazz pianist, and choral conductor with a passion for working with singers and music educators. His career spans twenty years and includes work as a high school music teacher, work with community music groups, studio teaching, conducting school and community choirs, amateur music theater groups, university teaching, and teacher education. Fascinated by comparative pedagogies, Dr.

Wicks has studied and is certified in several approaches to singing and music education. He has also been a board member for professional associations in Australia. His doctoral work investigated vocal teaching and teacher effectiveness, leading him to consult with hundreds of voice teachers and grapple with concepts that make for best practice in voice pedagogy. Over the course of many visits to the United States, Dr. Wicks has studied with contemporary voice educators and with R&B artists in New York, Nashville, and Los Angeles, developing his understanding of how to translate contemporary singing styles to Australian culture. He uses these skills to direct the 120-voice Melbourne Singers of Gospel and is passionate about the value and importance of community singing.

Printed in Great Britain
by Amazon